Excel 2022

From Basic to Advanced

The Most Exhaustive Guide to Become a Pro in Less Than 7 Days and Master All the Functions and Formulas. Includes Practical Examples and Step-by-Step Instructions

George Halperin

TABLE OF CONTENTS

CHAPTER 1 : FEATURES OF MICROSOFT EXCEL 8
    Features Of A Microsoft Excel 8
CHAPTER 2: BASICS OF THE MICROSOFT EXCEL 12
    The Basics – Insert, Autofill, Filters, Sort, Duplicates, Paste Special, Format Painter 12
    Inserting Rows Or Columns 12
CHAPTER 3: MS EXCEL FORMULAS 18
    What Is Excel Formulas? 18
    Basic Terms In Excel 18
    Difference Between Functions And Formulas In Excel 18
    Basic Excel Formulas 19
        2. IF 20
        3. Percentage 20
        4. Subtraction 21
        5. Multiplication 21
        6. Division 21
        7. DATE 21
        8. Array 22
        9. COUNT 22
        10. AVERAGE 22
        11. SUMIF 22
        12. TRIM 23
        13. LEFT, MID, And RIGHT 23
        14. VLOOKUP 24
        15. RANDOMIZE 24
    What Are Array Formulas? 25
        Completing An Array Formula In Excel 25
        Why Are Array Formulas Used? 25
        Array Formulas Offer The Following Advantages: 25
        Syntax Of An Array Formula 26
        Entering And Changing Array Formulae 26
        Creating An Array Formula 26

- Creating Single Cell Array Formula 27
- Creating Multi-Cell Array Formula 27
- Using Array Constant To Enter Values In Column 29
  - Using Array Constant To Enter Values In The Row 30
  - Using Named Ranges In Excel Formulas 31
- Working With The Name Box 32
  - How To Add Linking Formulas To Excel 33
  - What Is Circular Reference In Excel? Everything You Need To Know 33
- What Is Circular Reference In Excel? 34
  - Examples Of Circular Reference In Excel 34
  - Indirect Circular Reference 35
  - Finding Circular Reference In Excel 37
  - Manual Method 38
  - Automatic Method 38
  - How To Enable/Disable Circular Reference In Excel 39
- How To Copy And Paste Formulas In Excel 41
  - How To Copy A Formula From One Cell To Another In Excel 41
  - Copy Formula From One Cell To Multiple Cells 44
  - Copy Formula To An Entire Column Or Row 45
  - Copy a Formula To A Range Without Copying Formatting 46
  - Copy An Excel Formula With Only Number Formatting 47
  - Copy A Formula To Non-Adjacent/Non-Contiguous Cells 48
  - Copying Formulas Without Changing Cell References In Excel 48
  - Copy Formula With Absolute Cell Reference Using Copy-Paste Method 48
  - Copy Formulas With Absolute Or Mixed Cell References 50
  - Copy Paste Excel Formulas Without Changing References Using Notepad 51
  - Copy The Exact Formulas Using Excel's Find And Replace 53
  - Manual Calculation 56
  - Why Does My Calculation Change To Manual? 57
- CHAPTER 4: MS EXCEL LOGICAL FUNCTIONS 58
  - Excel AND Function 58
  - Excel OR function 59
  - Excel IF Function 61
  - Excel MAX Function 63

Excel MIN Function 64

Excel EVEN Function 65

Excel ODD Function 67

Excel IFS Function 68

Excel NOT Function 70

CHAPTER 5 : MS EXCEL LOOKUP AND TEXT'S FUNCTIONS 72

What Is The HLOOKUP Function? 72

Important Points To Keep In Mind About HLOOKUP 75

Excel LOOKUP Function 76

Formula (Array) LOOKUP Function 77

Example Of LOOKUP Function To Find The Latest Price 78

LOOKUP(Lookup_Value, Array) // Array Form 78

LOOKUP Function Array Form Example 79

Excel CONCATENATE Function 79

What Is "Concatenate" In Excel? 80

Excel Len Function 81

Excel LEFT Function 82

Excel PROPER Function 83

Excel RIGHT Function 85

Excel TEXTJOIN Function 86

Excel TRIM Function 88

Excel UPPER function 89

Excel LOWER Function 90

Excel MID Function 91

CHAPTER 6: MS EXCEL COUNTING FUNCTIONS 93

Excel COUNT Function 93

Various Count Functions In Excel 94

CHAPTER 7: MS EXCEL DATE AND TIME 95

What Is The DATE Function? 95

Important Points About The DATE Function 96

Excel DATE Function 98

Excel DATE Formula Examples 98

1. Excel DAYS360 Function 99

2. Excel DATEDIF Function 100

- DATEDIF Difference In Days 102
- DATEDIF Difference In Months 103
- DATEDIF Difference In Years 103
- 3. Excel EOMONTH Function 104
- 4. Excel DATEVALUE Function 105
- 5. Excel TODAY Function 107
- 6. Excel DAY Function 108
- 7. Excel EDATE Function 109
- 8. Excel DATE Function 111
- 9. Excel WORKDAY Function 113
- Time Functions 117

CHAPTER 8: STATISTICAL FUNCTIONS 123
- Commonly Used Statistical Functions 123
- Example Of Statistical Function 124
- Intermediate Statistical Function 126
- Round 132

CHAPTER 9: MS EXCEL FINANCIAL FUNCTIONS 140
- What Are Financial Functions In Excel 140
- 1. PV Function In Excel 140
- The PV Function Uses The Following Arguments: 141
  - Calculate PV of Investment Based On Its Future Value 142
  - Difference Between NPV And PV Formula In Excel 144
  - Critical Differences Between NPV And PV: 145
- 2. NPV Functions 145
- What Net Present Value Can Tell You 147
- 3. FV Functions 149
  - What Is The Excel FV Function? 149
  - Basic Future Value Formula In Excel 150
  - FV Formula For Periodic Payments 151
  - FV Formula For A Lump-Sum Investment 152
- 4. The PMT Functions 155
- Building Statistic Functions 161
- 5. XNPV: Financial Function In Excel 165
- 6. PMT: Financial Function In Excel 166

7. PPMT: Financial Function In Excel 167

8. Internal Rate Of Return (IRR): Financial Function In Excel 168

9. Modified Internal Rate Of Return (MIRR): Financial Function In Excel 169

10. XIRR: Financial Function In Excel 170

11. NPER: Financial Function In Excel 171

12. RATE: Financial Function In Excel 172

13. EFFECT: Financial Function In Excel 173

14. NOMINAL: Financial Function In Excel 173

15. SLN: Financial Function In Excel 174

CHAPTER 10: EXCEL CHARTING BASICS 175

Explanation Of Charts 175

Types Of Graphs In Excel 179

How To Make A Chart In Excel 181

How To Make A Graph In Excel 202

How To Create A Table In Excel 203

CHAPTER 11: PIVOT TABLE IN MS EXCEL 206

What Is A Pivot Table? 206

What Are Pivot Tables Used For? 206

How To Create A Pivot Table 208

An Introduction To Pivot Table In Excel 213

Practical Examples Of A Pivot Table 222

    1. Pivot Table Count With Percentage 222

    2. Pivot Table Count Blanks 226

    3. Pivot Table Conditional Formatting 228

    4. Pivot Table Calculated Field Example 231

    5. Pivot Table Basic Sum 234

    6. Pivot Table Latest Values 236

    7. Pivot Table Count By Year 238

    9. Pivot Table Filter By Weekday 243

CHAPTER 12: MACROS AND VBA 246

What Is An Excel Macro? 246

Example Of Recording A Macro In Excel 248

How To Work With Recorded Macros In Excel 250

    Macro Name 252

- How To Run A Recorded Macro 253
- How To Save Macros In Excel 254
- Excel Macros: What Is And What Isn't Recorded 255
- Record A Macro For Selection Rather Than Specific Cells.. 259
- Adding Loops To VBA 261
- Adding Logic To VBA 262
- Excel Macro Basics 264
- VBA Editor 265

CHAPTER 13: TIPS AND SHORTCUT FOR MS EXCEL 268
- Microsoft Excel Shortcut keys 268
- Ways To Improve Your Excel Skills... 271

CHAPTER 1 : FEATURES OF MICROSOFT EXCEL

Microsoft Excel

Microsoft Excel is an electronic spreadsheet. The worksheet, also known as a spreadsheet, can be used to store data. Who can use it to divide your data into rows and columns? Who can also use it to perform mathematical calculations quickly? It can show data in the form of line graphs, histograms, charts, and a minimal three-dimensional graphical display.

Benefits of Excel

- The most effective method of storing data.
- You can do calculations.
- All of the data analysis tools.
- Charts make it simple to visualize data.
- Reports are simple to print.
- There are so many free templates to choose from.
- You can automate by coding.
- Data transformation and cleaning

Context & Applications

- Entering and storing data Excel is an excellent tool for data entry and storage at its most basic level.
- Excel is an excellent tool for data entry and storage at its most basic level.
- Collection and Verification of Business Data
- Administrative and managerial duties
- Accounting and budgeting
- Data Analysis
- Reporting + Visualizations
- Forecasting.

Features Of A Microsoft Excel

1. File

When you open a new file in Excel, the first tab you will see is File. Look carefully - you may miss it because it is a different colour than the other tabs (depending on what colour scheme your desktop is set on). The File tab has just what you would think: options related to the entire File, such as save, print, share, and open.

2. Home

The Home tab has the most commonly used features, especially related to modifying text. In the Home tab, you can select your font, size, colour, attributes (bold, italics, underline), and alignment (left, centre, right). You can also select a style, a predetermined text made to fit certain document parts, such as headings, subtitles, and text.

3. Insert

Under the Insert tab, there are several choices. There are many types of visual aids and highlights you can add to a file to help summarize and present information in an Excel document. In the Insert ribbon tab, you can find options for graphics, charts, hyperlinks, page breaks, headers, footers, text boxes, and reference information, such as date and time, comments, page numbers, and bookmarks.

5. Page Layout

The Page Layout ribbon is a vital tab to determine how your document looks. This tab has the options to modify margins, page orientation, paper size, columns, indents, spacing, page breaks, and the arranging of any parts of the document, such as text and graphics or tables.

8. Review

Here, you can find the track changes options, commenting tools, language and translation tools, and what you might expect to see in a review section: spell check, thesaurus, word count, etc.

9. Formulas

The Formulas menu is where you find all the number-crunching options. Excel comes with many formulas, including financial, logical, text, date & time, lookup & reference, and math & trigonometry.

10. Data

The Data menu also contains many essential functions in Excel, including imports and connections with databases. On the Data menu, you also access the sort, filter, remove duplicates, data validation, consolidation, group, ungroup, and subtotal functions.

11. Review

Earlier in this book, we mentioned Excel's ability to collaborate on spreadsheets. The Review menu is where many of those tasks take place. You can make comments in cells for your colleagues, check to spell, track changes, and restrict permission using items in the Review menu.

12. View

On the View menu, you customize the way spreadsheets appear on your screen. Options include displaying gridlines between cells, toggling the formula bar and headings, and more. This menu also gives you options to view and record macros; macros let you register common steps you perform so you don't have to repeat the same things repeatedly!

13. Quick Access Toolbar

This is where who can place all the essential tools. When you start Excel for the first time, it has only three icons (Save, Undo, Redo). But you can add any feature of Excel to Quick Access Toolbar to easily access it from anywhere (hence the name).

14. Ribbon

Ribbon is like an expanded menu. It depicts all the features of Excel in easy to understand form. Since Excel has 1000s of parts, they are grouped into several ribbons. The most critical ribbons are – Home, Insert, Formulas, Page Layout & Data.

15. Formula Bar

This is where any calculations or formulas you write will appear. You will understand the relevance of it once you start building procedures.

16. Spreadsheet Grid

This is where all your numbers, data, charts & drawings will go. Each Excel file can contain several sheets. But the spreadsheet grid shows a few rows & columns of the active spreadsheet. You can use the scroll bars to the left or at the bottom to see more rows or columns. If you want to access other sheets, click on the sheet name (or use the shortcut CTRL+Page Up or CTRL+Page Down).

17. Status Bar

This tells us what is going on with Excel at any time. You can tell if Excel is busy calculating a formula, creating a pivot report or recording a macro by just looking at the status bar. The status bar also shows quick summaries of selected cells (count, sum, average, minimum or maximum values). You can change this by right-clicking on it and choosing which recaps to show.

18. A Worksheet Or Sheet

Is a single page in a file created with an electronic spreadsheet program such as Microsoft Excel or Google Sheets.

19. A Workbook

Is the name given to an Excel file and contains one or more worksheets. When you open an electronic spreadsheet program, it loads an empty workbook file consisting of one or more blank worksheets for you to use.

20. Spreadsheet

A spreadsheet is a computer program that can capture, display and manipulate data arranged in rows and columns. Spreadsheets are one of the most popular tools available with personal computers.

21. Sorting

Sorting lists is a typical spreadsheet task that allows you to reorder your data quickly. The most common type of sorting is alphabetical ordering, which you can do in ascending or descending order.

22. Grouping

Grouping is a useful Excel feature that controls how the information is displayed. It would help if you sorted before you can group.

23. Formula Auditing

Formula auditing in Excel allows you to display the relationship between formulas and cells. The example below helps you master Formula Auditing quickly and easily.

24. Find And Replace In Excel

If we want to search anything in our workbook like a specific number or text string, we can use the Find and Replace features in Excel. We have the option of locating the search item for reference or replacing it with anything else. We can include various wildcards in our search terms, such as asterisks, tides, question marks, and numbers. We can search by rows and columns, search within values or comments, and search with a worksheet or entire workbooks.

If we work with a large amount of data in Excel, finding specific information can be challenging and time-consuming. We may use the Find feature to search our workbook quickly, and we can also use the Replace option to change the text.

When working with large Excel spreadsheets, it's critical to locate the information we need at any given time quickly. Scanning hundreds of rows and columns is not the best way to proceed, so let's take a deeper look at what Excel's Find and Replace feature offers.

25. Formula Bar

Formula Bar in Excel is a section where we can see values and formulas stored. The Formula generally is already seen below the menu bar. But if it is not there, we can activate this from the View menu option under the Show section. Who can also start it from the Excel Option's Advanced tab? Apart from showing the values and Formula of any cell, Formula Bar also tells which cell we have kept the cursor and the Insert Function option denoted by fx.

The content of the current cell or where the selection is pointed will be visible in the formula bar. Visibility includes:

- Current cell selection.
- The Formula is applied in the active cell.
- The range of cells selected in the excel.

26. Password Protection: Security vs. Protection

Before discussing Excel's password-protection feature, let's clarify what we mean by security. Although the terms security and protection are bantered about interchangeably, feature-wise in Excel, they aren't the same thing. Security lets you choose who gets in and, underdoing so, who doesn't; protection limits users who are already in. Security is about access; protection is about maintaining integrity.

Encrypt an Excel file with a password so that it requires a password to open it. To password protect an Excel file, execute the following steps.

- Open an Excel file.
- On the File tab, click Save As.
- Click Browse.
- Click on the Tools button and click General Options.
- In the Password to open box, enter a password and click OK.
- Reenter the password and click OK.
- **Note:** This feature also encrypts your Excel file. If you lose or forget the password, it cannot be recovered.
- Enter a file name and click Save.
- Click Save

27. How To Insert Headers And Footers In Microsoft Excel

You can add additional information to your Excel worksheets that stays consistent throughout the workbook with headers and footers. It can be a page number, an image, or custom text you want to appear on all pages.

How To Add Headers And Footers In Microsoft Excel

Follow the below steps to add headers and footers in Microsoft Excel:

- Open Microsoft Excel.
- Go to the Insert tab and click on the Header & Footer icon in the Text group.
- Who will add the header margin divided into the left, middle, and right sections?
- In the Design tab, you can enter custom information, or select presets such as Page Number, Number of Pages, Current Date, etc.
- Adding Preset Page Number in Left Section of Header and Custom Text in the Middle Section of Microsoft Excel Worksheet
- To let the changes take effect, click anywhere on the Excel sheet.
- Go to Insert > Header & Footer > Go to Footer.
- Adding Footer in Microsoft Excel File in the Design Tab
- Fill out the three sections of the footer margin using the custom data or any available presets.
- For changes to take effect, click anywhere on the worksheet.

The steps above will add a header and footer to the Excel sheet. The title and footer are only displayed when viewing the page layout. To return to the original view, go to view> Normal. You can switch between these two views at any time.

28. Cell

A cell in Excel is a rectangular-shaped box on the spreadsheet and the basic unit of Excel. Cells are the intersection of columns (labelled as alphabets) and rows (labelled as numbers). Cells can store values in numbers, text, date format, the combination of numbers and readers, etc. Cells can support various data types ranging from numeric, alphanumeric, string and formulas. The individuality of a cell is defined by the cell number and the letter of the alphabet at the point of intersection.

CHAPTER 2: BASICS OF THE MICROSOFT EXCEL

Sometimes, Excel seems too good to be true. Need to combine the information in multiple cells? Excel can do it. Need to copy formatting across an array of cells? Excel can do that, too.

The Basics – Insert, Autofill, Filters, Sort, Duplicates, Paste Special, Format Painter

Before spending hours and hours counting cells or copying and pasting data, look for a quick fix in Excel; you'll likely find one. In working more efficiently and avoiding tedious, manual work, let's start this Excel deep dive with the basics. Once you have these functions down, you'll be ready to tackle the advanced Excel lessons.

Learn Now:

- Insert Row / Column
- Autofill
- Filters
- Sort
- Remove Duplicates
- Paste Special
- Text to Columns
- Format Painter

Inserting Rows Or Columns

As you play around with your data, you might constantly need to add more rows and columns. Sometimes, you may even need to add hundreds of rows. Doing this one-by-one would be super tedious. Luckily, there's always an easier way.

To add multiple rows or columns in a spreadsheet, highlight the same number of pre-existing rows or columns that you want to add. Then, right-click and select "Insert."

In the example below, I want to add three rows. By highlighting three rows and then clicking insert, I can add three blank rows into my spreadsheet quickly and easily.

	A	B	C	D
1	First Name	Last Name	Email	House
2	Harry	Potter	hpotter@hogwarts.edu	Gryffindor
3	Hermione	Granger	hgranger@hogwarts.edu	Gryffindor
4	Ron	Weasley	rweasley@hogwarts.edu	Gryffindor
5	Draco	Malfoy	dmalfoy@hogwarts.edu	Slytherin
6	Cho	Chang	cchang@hogwarts.edu	Ravenclaw
7	Luna	Lovegood	llovegood@hogwarts.edu	Ravenclaw
8	Nymphadora	Tonks	ntonks@hogwarts.edu	Hufflepuff
9	Hannah	Abbott	habbott@hogwarts.edu	Hufflepuff
10				
11				
12				
13				
14				

Autofill

If you have any basic Excel knowledge, it's likely you already know this quick trick. But to cover our bases, allow me to show you the glory of Autofill. This lets you quickly fill adjacent cells with several data types, including values, series, and formulas.

There are multiple ways to deploy this feature, but the fill handle is among the easiest. Select the cells you want to be the source, locate the fill handle in the lower-right corner of the cell, and either drag the fill handle to cover the cells you want to fill or just double click.

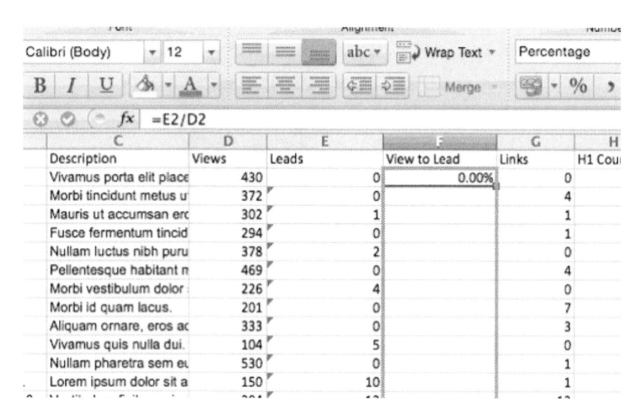

Filters

When looking at massive data sets (as marketers often do), you don't usually need to look at every row simultaneously. Sometimes, you only want to look at data that fit specific criteria. That's where filters come in.

Filters allow you to pare down your data to only look at specific rows at one time. In Excel, who can add a filter to each column in your data. You can then choose which cells you want to view at once.

Let's take a look at the example below. Add a filter by clicking the Data tab and selecting "Filter." Click the arrow next to the column headers, and you'll be able to choose whether you want your data to be organized in ascending or descending order and which rows you want to show.

In my Harry Potter example, let's say I only want to see the students in Gryffindor. By selecting the Gryffindor filter, the other rows disappear.

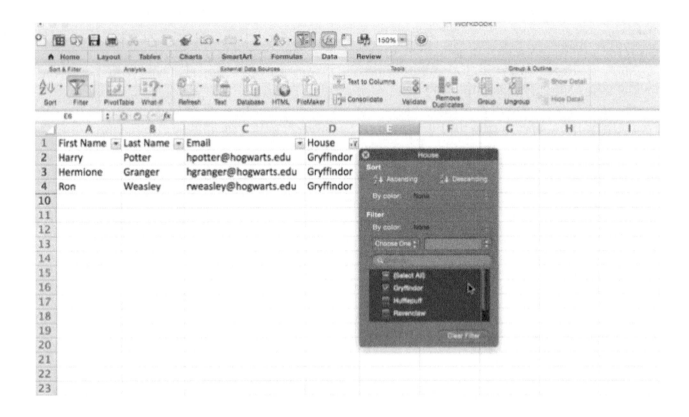

Pro Tip: Copy and paste the values in the spreadsheet when a filter is on to do additional analysis in another spreadsheet.

Sort

Sometimes you may have a list of data that has no organization whatsoever. Maybe you exported a list of your marketing contacts or blog posts. Whatever the case may be, Excel's sort feature will help you alphabetize any list.

Click on the data in the column you want to sort. Then click on the "Data" tab in your toolbar and look for the "Sort" option on the left. If the "A" is on top of the "Z," you can just click on that button once. If the "Z" is on top of the "A," click on the button twice. When the "A" is on top of the "Z," your list will be sorted in alphabetical order. However, when the "Z" is on top of the "A," your list will be sorted in reverse alphabetical order.

Remove Duplicates

Larger datasets tend to have duplicate content. You may have a list of multiple contacts in a company and only want to see the number of companies you have. In situations like this, removing duplicates comes in handy.

To remove your duplicates, highlight the row or column you want to release copies of. Then, go to the Data tab, and select "Remove Duplicates" (under Tools). A pop-up will appear to confirm which data you want to work with. Select "Remove Duplicates," and you're good to go.

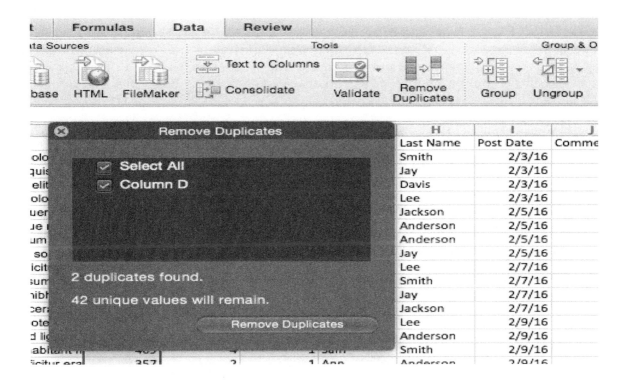

You can also use this feature to remove an entire row based on a duplicate column value. So if you have three rows with Harry Potter information and only need to see one, you can select the whole dataset and then remove duplicates based on email. Your resulting list will have unique names without any copies.

Paste Special

Often, you'll want to transform the items in a row of data into a column (or vice versa). It would take a lot of time to copy and paste each header. You may easily fall into one of the most extensive, most unfortunate Excel traps of human error.

Instead, let Excel do the work for you. Go ahead and highlight the column or row you want to transpose. Right-click and select "Copy." Next, select the cells in your spreadsheet where you want your first row or column to begin. Right-click on the cell, and then select "Paste Special." When the module appears, choose the option to transpose.

Paste Special is one function I find myself returning to time and time again. You can also choose between copying formulas, values, formats, or even column widths in the module. This is especially helpful in copying the results of your pivot table (we'll get there...) into a chart you can format and graph.

Text To Columns

What if you want to split information in one cell into two different cells? For example, maybe you want to pull out someone's company name through their email address. Or perhaps you want to separate someone's full name into a first and last name for your email marketing templates.

Thanks to Excel, both are possible:

1. Highlight the column that you want to split up.

2. Go to the Data tab and select "Text to Columns." A module will appear with additional information.

3. You need to choose either "Delimited" or "Fixed Width."

"Delimited" means you want to break up the column based on characters such as commas, spaces, or tabs.

"Fixed Width" means you want to select the exact location in all the columns where the split occurs.

In the example case below, let's select "Delimited" to separate the full name into first name and last name.

Then, it's time to choose the delimiters. This could be a tab, semicolon, comma, space, etc. ("Something else" could be the "@" sign used in an email address, for example.) In our example, let's choose the space. Excel will then show you a preview of what your new columns will look like.

When you're happy with the preview, press "Next." This page will allow you to select Advanced Formats if you choose to. When you're done, click "Finish."

Format Painter

As you've probably noticed, Excel has many features to make crunching numbers and analyzing your data quick and easy. But if you ever spent some time formatting a sheet to your liking, you know it can get a bit tedious.

Don't waste time repeating the same formatting commands over and over again. Use the format painter to easily copy the formatting from one area of the worksheet to another. Choose the cell you'd like to replicate, then select the format painter option (paintbrush icon) from the top toolbar.

CHAPTER 3: MS EXCEL FORMULAS

What Is Excel Formulas?

Excel formulas help you identify relationships between values in the cells of your spreadsheet, perform mathematical calculations using those values, and return the resulting value in the cell of your choice. Formulas you can automatically perform include sum, subtraction, percentage, division, average, and event dates/times.

One such feature that allows Excel to stand out is - Excel formulas. In this article, we'll be discussing the various Microsoft Excel functions and formulas. These formulas and functions enable you to perform calculations and data analysis faster. Here, we will look into the top 25 Excel formulas that one must know while working on Excel. The topics that we will be covering in this ebook are as follows:

- What is Excel Formula?
- Excel Formulas and Functions

In Microsoft Excel, a formula is an expression that operates on values in a range of cells. These formulas return a result, even when it is an error. Excel formulas enable you to perform calculations such as addition, subtraction, multiplication, and division. In addition to these, you can find out averages and calculate percentages in excel for a range of cells, manipulate date and time values, and do a lot more.

There is another term that is very familiar to Excel formulas, and that is "function". The two words, "formulas" and "functions" are sometimes interchangeable. They are closely related, but yet different. A formula begins with an equal sign. Meanwhile, functions are used to perform complex calculations that cannot be done manually. Functions in excel have names that reflect their intended use.

Excel formulas and functions help you perform your tasks efficiently, and it's time-saving. Let's proceed and learn the different types of functions available in Excel and use relevant formulas as and when required.

Basic Terms In Excel

There are two basic ways to perform calculations in Excel: Formulas and Functions.

1. Formulas

In Excel, a formula is an expression that operates on values in a range of cells or a cell. For example, =A1+A2+A3, which finds the sum of the content of values from cell A1 to cell A3.

2. Functions

Functions are predefined formulas in Excel. They eliminate laborious manual entry of formulas while giving them human-friendly names. For example: =SUM(A1:A3). The function sums all the values from A1 to A3.

Difference Between Functions And Formulas In Excel

The difference between a formula and a function is that a formula is defined as the statement used for the calculation. These formulas could be complex or straightforward and always stars with equal to operator.

While function is defined as the code designed for the calculations and is used inside the formula.

Examples Of A Formula

When users type an equals sign in a cell, they start to create a formula.

Examples of formulas include:

=4+3

=A3+C9

=B7+B8-(4*2)+1 [see screenshot below]

Examples Of A Function

A function begins to be implemented when a user types an equals sign followed by a predefined set of letters (or clicks on the Fx button in the formula bar).

=SUM(A3:A27)

=AVERAGE(F4:F8) [see screenshot below]

=NPV(0.12,A5:G5)

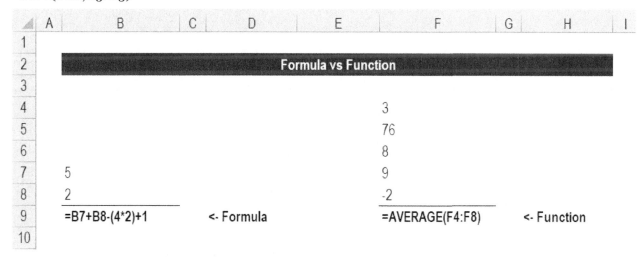

Basic Excel Formulas

- SUM
- IF
- Percentage
- Subtraction
- Multiplication
- Division
- DATE
- Array
- COUNT
- AVERAGE
- SUMIF
- TRIM
- LEFT, MID, and RIGHT
- VLOOKUP
- RANDOMIZE

1. SUM

All Excel formulas begin with the equals sign, =, followed by a specific text tag denoting the formula you'd like Excel to perform. The SUM formula in Excel is one of the most basic formulas you can enter into a spreadsheet, allowing you to find the sum (or total) of two or more values. To perform the SUM formula, enter the values you'd like to add together using the format, =SUM(value 1, value 2, etc.). The values you enter into the SUM formula can either be actual numbers or equal to the number in a specific cell of your spreadsheet.

To find the SUM of 30 and 80, for example, type the following formula into a cell of your spreadsheet: =SUM(30, 80). Press "Enter," and the cell will produce the total of both numbers: 110.

To find the SUM of the values in cells B2 and B11, for example, type the following formula into a cell of your spreadsheet: =SUM(B2, B11). Press "Enter," and the cell will produce the total of the numbers currently filled in cells B2 and B11. If there are no numbers in either cell, the formula will return 0.

Keep in mind you can also find the total value of a list of numbers in Excel. To find, the SUM of the values in cells B2 through B11, type the following formula into a cell of your spreadsheet: =SUM(B2:B11). Note the colon between both cells, rather than a comma.

2. IF

The IF formula in Excel is denoted =IF(logical_test, value_if_true, value_if_false). This allows you to enter a text value into the cell "if" something else in your spreadsheet is true or false. For example, =IF(D2="Gryffindor", "10", "0") would award 10 points to cell D2 if that cell contained the word "Gryffindor."

There are times when we want to know how many times a value appears in our spreadsheets. But there are also those times when we want to find the cells that contain those values and input specific data next to them.

We'll go back to Sprung's example for this one. Suppose we want to award 10 points to everyone who belongs in the Gryffindor house, instead of manually typing in 10's next to each Gryffindor student's name. In that case, we'll use the IF-THEN formula to say: If the student is in Gryffindor, then he or she should get ten points.

- **The Formula:** IF(logical_test, value_if_true, value_if_false)
- **Logical_Test:** The logical test is the "IF" part of the statement. In this case, the logic is D2="Gryffindor." Make sure your Logical_Test value is in quotation marks.
- **Value_If_True:** If the value is actual, that is, if the student lives in Gryffindor, this value is the one that we want to be displayed. In this case, we want it to be the number 10, to indicate that the student was awarded the 10 points. Note: Only use quotation marks if you want the result to be text instead of a number.
- **Value_If_False:** If the value is false and the student does not live in Gryffindor, we want the cell to show "0," for 0 points.

3. Percentage

To perform the percentage formula in Excel, enter the cells you're finding a percentage for in the format, =A1/B1. To convert the resulting decimal value to a percentage, highlight the cell, click the Home tab, and select "Percentage" from the numbers dropdown.

There isn't an Excel "formula" for percentages per se, but Excel makes it easy to convert the value of any cell into a percentage so you're not stuck calculating and reentering the numbers yourself.

The basic setting to convert a cell's value into a percentage is under Excel's Home tab. Select this tab, highlight the cell(s) you'd like to convert to a percentage, and click into the drop-down menu next to Conditional Formatting (this menu button might say "General" at first). Then, select "Percentage" from the list of options that appears. This will convert the value of each cell you've highlighted into a percentage.

Keep in mind if you're using other formulas, such as the division formula (denoted =A1/B1), to return new values, your values might show up as decimals by default. Simply highlight your cells before or after you perform this formula, and set these cells' format to "Percentage" from the Home tab.

4. Subtraction

To perform the subtraction formula in Excel, enter the cells you're subtracting in the format, =SUM(A1, -B1). This will subtract a cell using the SUM formula by adding a negative sign before the cell you're subtracting. For example, if A1 was ten and B1 was 6, =SUM(A1, -B1) would perform 10 + -6, returning a value of 4.

Like percentages, subtracting doesn't have its formula in Excel either, but that doesn't mean it can't be done. You can subtract any values (or those values inside cells) in two different ways.

- **Using The =SUM Formula:** To subtract multiple values from one another, enter the cells you'd like to subtract in the format =SUM(A1, -B1), with a negative sign (denoted with a hyphen) before the cell whose value you're subtracting. Press enter to return the difference between both cells included in the parentheses. See how this looks in the screenshot above.
- **Using The Format, =A1-B1:** To subtract multiple values from one another, simply type an equals sign followed by your first value or cell, a hyphen, and the value or cell you're subtracting. Press Enter to return the difference between both values.

5. Multiplication

To perform the multiplication formula in Excel, enter the cells you're multiplying in the format, =A1*B1. This formula uses an asterisk to multiply cell A1 by cell B1. For example, if A1 was ten and B1 was 6, =A1*B1 would return a value of 60.

You might think multiplying values in Excel has its formula or uses the "x" character to denote multiplication between multiple values. It's as easy as an asterisk -- *.

To multiply two or more values in an Excel spreadsheet, highlight an empty cell. Then, enter the values or cells you want to multiply together in the format, =A1*B1*C1 ... etc. The asterisk will effectively multiply each value included in the formula.

Press Enter to return your desired product.

6. Division

To perform the division formula in Excel, enter the cells you're dividing in the format, =A1/B1. This formula uses a forward slash, "/," to divide cell A1 by cell B1. For example, if A1 was five and B1 was 10, =A1/B1 would return a decimal value of 0.5.

Division in Excel is one of the simplest functions you can perform. To do so, highlight an empty cell, enter an equals sign, "=," and follow it up with the two (or more) values you'd like to divide with a forward slash, "/," in between. The result should be in the following format: =B2/A2. Hit Enter and your desired quotient should appear in the cell you initially highlighted.

7. DATE

The Excel DATE formula is denoted =DATE(year, month, day). This formula will return a date that corresponds to the values entered in the parentheses -- even values referred from other cells. For example, if A1 was 2018, B1 was 7, and C1 was 11, =DATE(A1, B1, C1) would return 7/11/2018.

Creating dates in the cells of an Excel spreadsheet can be a fickle task now and then. Luckily, there's a handy formula to make formatting your dates easy. There are two ways to use this formula:

- **Create Dates From A Series Of Cell Values:** To do this, highlight an empty cell, enter "=DATE," and in parentheses, enter the cells whose values create your desired date, starting with the year, then the month number, then the day. The final format should look like this: =DATE(year, month, day).
- **Automatically Set Today's Date:** To do this, highlight an empty cell and enter the following string of text: =DATE(YEAR(TODAY()), MONTH(TODAY()), DAY(TODAY())). Pressing enter will return the current date you're working in your Excel spreadsheet.

In either usage of Excel's date formula, your returned date should be in the form of "mm/dd/yy", unless your Excel program is formatted differently.

8. Array

Array formula in Excel surrounds a simple formula in brace characters using the format, {=(Start Value 1:End Value 1)*(Start Value 2:End Value 2)}. By pressing ctrl+shift+center, this will calculate and return value from multiple ranges, rather than just individual cells added to or multiplied by one another.

Calculating the sum, product, or quotient of individual cells is easy just use the =SUM formula and enter the cells, values, or range of cells you want to perform that arithmetic on. But what about multiple ranges? How do you find the combined value of a large group of cells?

Numerical arrays are a useful way to perform more than one formula at the same time in a single cell so you can see one final sum, difference, product, or quotient. If you're looking to find total sales revenue from several sold units, for example, the array formula in Excel is perfect for you. Here's how you'd do it:

- To start using the array formula, type "=SUM," and in parentheses, enter the first of two (or three, or four) ranges of cells you'd like to multiply together. Here's what your progress might look like: =SUM(C2:C5
- Next, add an asterisk after the last cell of the first range you included in your formula. This stands for multiplication. Following this asterisk, enter your second range of cells. You'll be multiplying this second range of cells by the first. Your progress in this formula should now look like this: =SUM(C2:C5*D2:D5)
- Ready to press Enter? Not so fast ... Because this formula is so complicated, Excel reserves a different keyboard command for arrays. Once you've closed the parentheses on your array formula, press Ctrl+Shift+Enter. This will recognize your formula as an array, wrapping your formula in brace characters and successfully returning your product of both ranges combined.

In revenue calculations, this can cut down on your time and effort significantly.

9. COUNT

The COUNT formula in Excel is denoted =COUNT(Start Cell: End Cell). This formula will return a value that is equal to the number of entries found within your desired range of cells. For example, if there are eight cells with entered values between A1 and A10, =COUNT(A1:A10) will return a value of 8.

The COUNT formula in Excel is particularly useful for large spreadsheets, wherein you want to see how many cells contain actual entries. Don't be fooled: This formula won't do any math on the values of the cells themselves. This formula is simply to find out how many cells in a selected range are occupied with something.

10. AVERAGE

To perform, the average formula in Excel, enter the values, cells, or range of cells of which you're calculating the average in the format, =AVERAGE(number1, number2, etc.) or =AVERAGE(Start Value: End Value). This will calculate the average of all the values or range of cells included in the parentheses.

Finding the average of a range of cells in Excel keeps you from having to find individual sums and then performing a separate division equation on your total. Using =AVERAGE as your initial text entry, you can let Excel do all the work for you.

For reference, the average of a group of numbers is equal to the sum of those numbers, divided by the number of items in that group.

11. SUMIF

The SUMIF formula in Excel is denoted =SUMIF(range, criteria, [sum range]). This will return the sum of the values within the desired range of cells that all meet one criterion. For example,

=SUMIF(C3:C12,">70,000") would return the sum of values between cells C3 and C12 from only the cells that are greater than 70,000.

Let's say you want to determine the profit you generated from a list of leads who are associated with specific area codes or calculate the sum of certain employees' salaries but only if they fall above a particular amount. Doing that manually sounds a bit time-consuming, to say the least.

With, the SUMIF function, it doesn't have to be

you can easily add up the sum of cells that meet certain criteria.

- **The Formula:** =SUMIF(range, criteria, [sum_range])
- **Range:** The range that is being tested using your criteria.
- **Criteria:** The criteria that determine which cells in Criteria_range1 will be added together
- **[Sum_Range]:** An optional range of cells you're going to add up in addition to the first Range entered. This field may be omitted.

12. TRIM

The TRIM formula in Excel is denoted =TRIM(text). This formula will remove any spaces entered before and after the text is entered in the cell. For example, if A2 includes the name "Steve Peterson" with unwanted spaces before the first name, =TRIM(A2) would return "Steve Peterson" with no spaces in a new cell.

Email and file sharing are wonderful tools in today's workplace. That is until one of your colleagues sends you a worksheet with some funky spacing. Not only can those rogue spaces make it difficult to search for data, but they also affect the results when you try to add up columns of numbers.

Rather than painstakingly removing and adding spaces as needed, you can clean up any irregular spacing using the TRIM function, which is used to remove extra spaces from data (except for single areas between words).

The formula: =TRIM(text).

Text: The text or cell from which you want to remove spaces.

Here's an example of how we used the TRIM function to remove extra spaces before a list of names. To do so, we entered =TRIM("A2") into the Formula Bar, and replicated this for each name below it in a new column next to the column with unwanted spaces.

13. LEFT, MID, And RIGHT

Let's say you have a line of text within a cell that you want to break down into a few different segments. Rather than manually retyping each piece of the code into its respective column, users can leverage a series of string functions to deconstruct the sequence as needed: LEFT, MID, or RIGHT.

LEFT

- **Purpose:** Used to extract the first X numbers or characters in a cell.
- **The Formula:** =LEFT(text, number_of_characters)
- **Text:** The string that you wish to extract from.
- **Number_Of_Characters:** The number of characters that you wish to extract starting from the left-most character.

MID

- **Purpose:** Used to extract characters or numbers in the middle based on position.
- **The Formula:** =MID(text, start_position, number_of_characters)
- **Text:** The string that you wish to extract from.
- **Start_Position:** The position in the string that you want to begin extracting from. For example, the first position in the string is 1.

- **Number_Of_Characters:** The number of characters that you wish to extract.

RIGHT

- **Purpose:** Used to extract the last X numbers or characters in a cell.
- **The Formula:** =RIGHT(text, number_of_characters)
- **Text:** The string that you wish to extract from.
- **Number_Of_Characters:** The number of characters that you want to extract starting from the right-most character.

14. VLOOKUP

This one is an oldie, but a goodie and it's a bit more in-depth than some of the other formulas we've listed here. But it's especially helpful for that times when you have two sets of data on two different spreadsheets and want to combine them into a single spreadsheet.

My colleague, Rachel Sprung whose "How to Use Excel" tutorial is a must-read for anyone who wants to learn, uses a list of names, email addresses, and companies as an example. If you have a list of people's names next to their email addresses in one spreadsheet, and a list of those same people's email addresses next to their company names in the other, but you want the names, email addresses, and company names of those people to appear in one place, that's where VLOOKUP comes in.

Note: When using this formula, you must be certain that at least one column appears identically in both spreadsheets. Scour your data sets to make sure the column of data you're using to combine your information is the same, including no extra spaces.

- **The Formula:** VLOOKUP(lookup value, table array, column number, [range lookup])
- **Lookup Value:** The identical value you have in both spreadsheets. Choose the first value in your first spreadsheet. In Sprung's example that follows, this means the first email address on the list, or cell 2 (C2).
- **Table Array:** The range of columns on Sheet 2 you're going to pull your data from, including the column of data identical to your lookup value (in our example, email addresses) in Sheet 1 as well as the column of data you're trying to copy to Sheet 1. In our example, this is "Sheet2!A: B." "A" means Column A in Sheet 2, which is the column in Sheet 2 where the data identical to our lookup value (email) in Sheet 1 is listed. The "B" means Column B, which contains the information that's only available in Sheet 2 that you want to translate to Sheet 1.
- **Column Number:** The table array tells Excel where (which column) the new data you want to copy to Sheet 1 is located. In our example, this would be the "House" column, the second one in our table array, making it column number 2.
- **Range Lookup:** Use FALSE to ensure you pull in only exact value matches.

15. RANDOMIZE

There's a great book that likens Excel's RANDOMIZE formula to shuffling a deck of cards. The entire deck is a column, and each card, 52 in a deck, is a row. "To shuffle the deck," writes Steve McDonnell, "you can compute a new column of data, populate each cell in the column with a random number, and sort the workbook based on the random number field."

In marketing, you might use this feature when you want to assign a random number to a list of contacts, like if you wanted to experiment with a new email campaign and had to use blind criteria to select who would receive it. By assigning numbers to said contacts, you could apply the rule, "Any contact with a figure of six or above will be added to the new campaign."

The Formula: RAND()

Start with a single column of contacts. Then, in the column adjacent to it, type "RAND()", without the quotation marks, starting with the top contact's row.

For The Example Below: RANDBETWEEN(Bottom, Top)

RANDBETWEEN allows you to dictate the range of numbers that you want to be assigned. In the case of this example, I wanted to use one through 10.

Bottom: The lowest number in the range.

Top: The highest number in the range,

How To Create Excel Array Formulas

To become a skilful and accomplished Excel user, a person should have sufficient knowledge of using Excel Array formulas to perform calculations and functions that cannot be performed using non-array procedures. They are applied to a range of cells and are helpful by increasing consistency and reducing the creation of similar formulae having the same functionality.

What Are Array Formulas?

An array formula is used to execute multiple calculations on one or more of the cells in an array. You can think of an array as a collection of cells with similar values stored in them, whether a row of values, a column of values, or even a combination of rows and columns of values. Who can use array formulas to either return a single result, as in the case of Array Formulas giving a single outcome or multiple results, as in the case of Array Formulas showing multiple results?

For example, In a society, if the total working hours need to be computed for employees working for other months separately, who would use an array formula giving multiple results; however, if the total working hours need to be calculated for employees working for a year, in totality, who would use an array formula giving single result.

An array formula that includes multiple cells and produces multiple results is called a multi-cell formula. An array formula in a single cell, producing a single result, is called a single-cell formula.

Completing An Array Formula In Excel

Array formulas are also often referred to as CSE (Ctrl+Shift+Enter) formulas. Instead of just pressing Enter to produce the result, you need to press Ctrl+Shift+Enter to complete the formula and produce the result.

Why Are Array Formulas Used?

Who can use Excel to perform various complex and sophisticated mathematical operations and calculations by using simple formulas? While who can apply some of the formulas to single cells, array formulas in Excel offer the advantage of producing results applied to a range of cells. For example: In an organization of employees, they can use array formulas to calculate the total salary of each employee for a year, that are provided monthly (Multi-Cell Array Formula) and the total compensation of all the employees by using the SUM function (Single-Cell Array Formula).

Thus, who can use array Formulas to perform a variety of diverse and complex tasks such as:

- Count the number of values contained in a range of cells.
- Sum or count numbers that meet certain conditional formatting conditions, such as the lowest values in a range of numbers that fall between an upper and lower boundary.
- Calculate the sum of a particular value in a range of values.

Array Formulas Offer The Following Advantages:

1. Array formulas provide consistency, precision and accuracy in the formulas and values computed, being applied to a range of cells.

2. Array formulas reduce wastage of time in non-productive operations by applying formulas directly to a range of cells and need not be required to be used separately.

3. Array formulas ensure non-redundancy and provide safety to their users, as a component of a multi-cell array formula cannot be replaced by any other value, and the entire cell array formula needs to be

selected for modification or permanent deletion. Also, as an added precautionary measure, you have to press CSE simultaneously for the Change of formula.

4. Array formulas make File sizes smaller by using a single formula and not various similar intermediate formulas.

5. Array formulas reduce the chances of erroneous results when formulas are misapplied.

For example, when the sum of the working hours for each quarter of months has to be computed, who can apply a single formula of sum to the array (multi-cell array formula) rather than using four different array formulas.

Syntax Of An Array Formula

The syntax of an Excel formula is very general and constructed upon various built-in functions. The array formula begins with an equal (=) sign like other formulae. The critical difference between a general arithmetic formula and an array arithmetic formula is that when using an array formula, you press Ctrl+Shift+Enter to produce the result of an entered formula. In contrast, Enter is used to create an impact in the former case. When this is done, Excel automatically surrounds your array formula with braces. Manually typing the braces would convert it into a text string, as in the case of other computer languages such as C, and simply won't work and serve the function.

Array functions provide an efficient and effective way to build a complex formula and perform various complex calculations.

For Example: To compute the sum of working hours of different employees and award the best employee with the most number of working hours is done as follows:

{=D3:D12+E3:E12+F3:F12+G3:G12}

which is the same as

=SUM(D3:G3) applied to H3, =SUM(D4:G4) applied to H4, ..., =SUM(D12:G12) applied to H12.

This is a multi-cell array formula.

Entering And Changing Array Formulae

An array formula always begins with an equal sign.

Once the array formula is typed and applied to a range of cells, whether a single cell or multi-cell, its functionality can be applied only when Ctrl+Shift+Enter is simultaneously entered to produce the result, this is used to recognize it as an array formula and store it in its memory by applying braces automatically to the formulae. Typing braces would make Excel treat it as a text string that won't serve the requisite function.

While working with multi-cell formulae, always apply the result by selecting the 'range' of cells on which the array formulae need to be used.

The individual contents of a particular cell in an array formula cannot be changed or modified. If an attempt is made in doing so, Excel displays the message that you cannot change part of an array, as when an array formula is entered, Excel treats it as data that are related to each other and need to be changed collectively.

Citing the above point, who cannot delete the individual cell, and who must delete the entire array by selecting collection as the whole and pressing delete. To delete an array formula, like the whole formula (for example, =D3:D12+E3:E12+F3:F12+G3:G12), press Delete, and then press Ctrl+Shift+Enter.

Creating An Array Formula

Creating an array formula, either single cell or multi-cell, as followed above, follows a standard syntax, the detailed procedure for which is discussed below:

Creating Single Cell Array Formula

This type of array formula simplifies a worksheet by applying an array formula using a range of cells to produce a single result, rather than operating different intermediate formulae on various degrees of cells and further using them to create the single result. The latter approach is erroneous and tedious.

The sequential procedure to create a single cell array formula is:

1. You need to click on a cell where you want to enter the array formula.

2. Begin the array formula with the equal sign, follow the standard formula syntax, and use mathematical operators or built-in functions in the Excel formula.

For example:

To calculate the total working hours of all the employees collectively and produce a result in cell H13, the array formula used is

=SUM(D3:D12,E3:E12,F3:F12,G3:G12)

Press Ctrl+Shift+Enter to produce the desired result. This is done so that Excel automatically inserts braces within the formula and recognizes it as an Array Formula.

Note: Manually typing braces around a formula will not convert it into an array formula but would consider it as a text string.

Also, who could have performed the following function of calculating total working hours by using a multi-cell array formula applied to a range of cells from H3:H12 and displaying the sum in H13.

Creating Multi-Cell Array Formula

This type of array formula simplifies a worksheet by applying an array formula using a range of cells to produce multiple results, rather than operating different intermediate formulae on various ranges of cells and further using them to create the other results. The latter approach is erroneous and tedious.

Note: In a multi-cell array formula calculating multiple results, the array formula needs to be entered in the range of cells with the same number of rows and columns as applied in the array formula.

The sequential procedure to create a single cell array formula is:

- You need to click on the range of cells you want to enter the array formula.
- Begin the array formula with the equal sign, follow the standard formula syntax, and use mathematical operators or built-in functions in the Excel formula.

For Example:

To calculate the working hours of each employee within the year and produce a result in the range of cells from H3:H12, the array formula used is:

{=D3:D12+E3:E12+F3:F12+G3:G12}

Press Ctrl+Shift+Enter to produce the desired result. This is done so that Excel automatically inserts braces within the formula and recognizes it as an Array Formula.

Editing An Array Formula

As discussed above, the elements or values of an array formula cannot be modified individually and can only be limited collectively. Excel would display the dialogue box, saying who cannot change parts of an array.

Editing A Single Cell Array Formula

The following steps need to be followed sequentially to edit the single-cell array formula:

- Select the cell in which the single-cell array formula is applied.
- Press key F2 on the keyboard.
- Make the requisite changes.
- Press Ctrl+Shift+Enter on the keyboard.
- The formula is edited.

Editing A Multi-Cell Array Formula

The following steps need to be followed sequentially to edit the single-cell array formula:

- Select the range of cells in which the multi-cell array formula is applied.
- Press key F2 on the keyboard.
- Make the requisite changes.
- Press Ctrl+Shift+Enter on the keyboard.
- The formula is edited.

Moving An Array Formula

who cannot move the individual cells containing the array formula, but all can be moved collectively as an array. The cell references contained in the formula will automatically change.

The following steps need to be followed sequentially to move an array formula:

- Select the range of cells that need to be moved.
- Press Ctrl+X on the keyboard.
- Select the new location of cells.
- Press Ctrl+V on the keyboard to locate them to the new desired position.

Deleting An Array Formula

Individual cells involved in an array formula cannot be deleted as a part of an array cannot be modified, manipulated or deleted. However, we can delete the entire formula and write the new formula to produce the desired result.

When you delete an array formula, the result of the formula is deleted as well. If the value of the array formula needs to be retained, then who can remove only the array formula.

Deleting An Array Formula Completely (Not Retaining Result Of Array Formula)

The following steps need to be followed sequentially to delete the array formula completely:

- Select the cell or range of cells that contain the mathematical array formula.
- Press Delete on the keyboard.
- The desired function of complete deletion is accomplished.

Removing An Array Formula (Keeping Result Of Array Formula)

The following steps need to be followed sequentially to draw the array formula while retaining the results of the array formula:

- Select the cell or range of cells containing the formula that needs to be removed.
- On the Home tab, under Editing Section, click on Find & Select option, and then click on Go To.
- Click Current array.
- On the Home tab, in the Clipboard group, click Copy.
- On the Home tab, in the Clipboard group, click the arrow below Paste, and then click Paste Values.
- Select the range of cells and press delete.

Using Array Constants

Array constants are values added inside braces, such that it makes it easier to deal with related values together by naming an array constant and processing them together. They collectively use constants as well as a range of values. While using an array formula, type an opening brace, enter the desired values you want, and finally, type a closing brace. For example: =PRODUCT(A1:E1*{1,2,3,4,5})

Note: The braces in array constants are typed manually. The rest of the array formula is entered as desired, and Ctrl+Shift+Enter is pressed to produce the desired result for the array constant.

Using Array Constant To Enter Values In Column

Let us solve the following using an example:

If we need to enter five values, namely, 10, 20, 30, 40 and 50, in a single column A sequentially, the following steps need to be adopted:

- Select the cells where the values need to be entered.
- Enter an equal sign and the desired constant values that need to be contained in cells. If the value is a string, the text is in doubly inverted commas (").
- Separate the values of the constants with semicolons and not commas.
- Press Ctrl+Shift+Enter on the keyboard such that the values in a column are contained.

For example: ={10;20;30;40;50}

This is also referred to as a one-dimensional vertical constant array.

Using Array Constant To Enter Values In The Row

Let us solve the following using an example:

If we need to enter five values, namely, 10, 20, 30, 40 and 50, in a single row 1 sequentially, the following steps need to be adopted:

- Select the cells where the values need to be entered.
- Enter an equal sign and the desired constant values that need to be contained in cells. If the value is a string, the text is in doubly inverted commas ("). Separate the values of the constants with commas now and not semicolons.
- Press Ctrl+Shift+Enter on the keyboard such that the values in the row are contained.

For example: ={10;20;30;40;50}

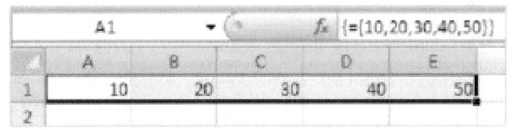

This is also referred to as a one-dimensional horizontal constant array.

Using Array Constant To Enter Values In Rows And Columns

Let us solve the following using an example:

If we need to enter twenty-five values, namely, 10, 20, 30, 40,50.....240,250 sequentially, in multiple rows and columns, constituting five rows and columns, the following steps need to be followed:

- Select the cells where the values need to be entered.
- Enter an equal sign and the desired constant values that need to be contained in cells. If the value is a string, the text is in doubly inverted commas (").
- Separate the values of the constants that need to be contained in rows with commas and semicolons, wherein the importance of the constants needs to be included in columns.
- Press Ctrl+Shift+Enter on the keyboard such that the values in the row are contained.

For Example:

={10,20,30,40,50;60,70,80,90,100;110,120,130,140,150;160,170,180,190,200;210,220,230,240,250}

This is also called a two-dimensional constant array because it constitutes rows and columns.

Points To Remember
- Equal to sign(=) needs to be added at the beginning of each Excel Array Formula.
- Who cannot manually put in braces while dealing with Array Formula? They can only be placed manually while dealing with array constants.
- You can use numbers and texts in entering array constants. However, while dealing with array constants containing text, enter it in double-quotes (").

Using Named Ranges In Excel Formulas

A named range in Excel is nothing more than a cell or range of cells that has been given a friendly, descriptive name. Naming your contents allows you to use easily recognizable names in your formulas instead of cell addresses.

For instance, say that you have line-item sales in cells A1:A25 and a per cent tax in cell B1. You could calculate a total sale amount with tax using this formula:

=SUM(A1:A25)*(1+B1)

Now imagine that you gave your ranges descriptive names, calling cells A1:25 Sale_Items, and calling cell B1 Tax_Percent. You could then calculate the total sale amount with tax by using this formula:

=SUM(Sales_Items)*(1+Tax_Percent)

Immediately, you can see how much easier it is to understand what is going on in the formula. The formula is easier to read and explain to others who aren't familiar with the workbook.

Another benefit to naming these ranges is that creating new formulas with these named ranges becomes easier because you can simply use the easily remembered descriptive name instead of trying to remember that line-item sales live in cells A1:A25.

Creating A Named Range

Follow these steps to create a named range:

Select the cell or range of cells you want to name.

Choose Define Name from the Formulas tab. This activates the New Name dialogue box.

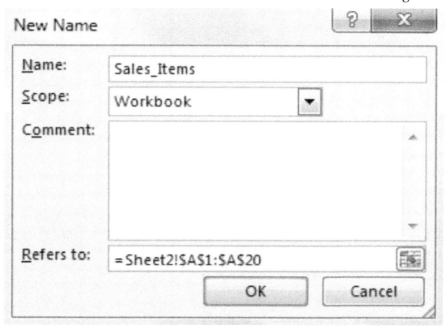

Enter a friendly, descriptive name for your range in the Name input box.

Select whether you want your named range to be available for use throughout the workbook or just on a specific sheet in the Scope drop-down box.

Press the OK button to create your named range.

Keep these rules and best practices in mind when choosing a name for your range:

- You cannot use spaces in range names. Use an underscore to emulate a space instead (Sales_Items).
- Range names must begin with a letter or an underscore.
- Range names cannot be the same as cell addresses. For instance, you cannot name your range Q1 because Excel already has a cell Q1.
- You can use any single letter as a range name except for R and C. These are reserved in Excel for the R1C1 reference style.
- You cannot use operator symbols (+, −, *, /, <, >, &) in range names. The only symbols valid in range names are the period (.), question mark (?), underscore (_), and backslash () symbols, as long as they are not used as the first character of the name.
- Avoid using names that Excel uses internally, for example, Print_Area. Although Excel allows this name, using it can cause name conflict errors in the workbook. Other names to avoid are Auto_Activate, Auto_Close, Auto_Deactivate, Auto_Open, Consolidate_Area, Criteria, Data_Form, Database, Extract, FilterDatabase, Print_Titles, Recorder, and Sheet_Title.
- The maximum length for a range name is 255 characters. That being said, you should avoid very long-range names in general. Remember that the purpose of a range name is to provide a meaningful, easy-to-remember name that you can quickly type into a formula.

Working With The Name Box

The Name Box, found to the left of the Formula Bar, offers a couple of handy features for working with named ranges. You can click the drop-down selector in the Name Box to see all the named ranges in your workbook. Clicking any of the named ranges in the list automatically selects that range.

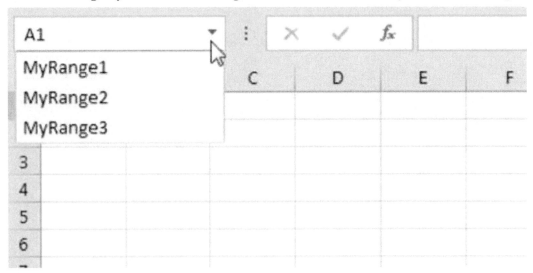

The Name Box also serves as a faster way to create a named range. To create a named range with the Name Box:

1. Select the cell or range you want to name.

2. Enter a valid name directly into the Name Box.

3. Press the Enter key to create the name.

Tip: The Name Box is resizable. If you have a name that is too long for the Name Box, simply move your mouse cursor over the right edge of the Name Box until it turns into a horizontal arrow. When your cursor becomes a horizontal arrow, click and drag to widen the Name Box.

How To Add Linking Formulas To Excel

Linking formulas transfer a constant or another formula to a new place in the same worksheet, same workbook, or even a different workbook without copying it to its new location. When you create a linking formula, it brings forward the constant or original formula to a new location so that the result in the linking formula remains dynamically tied to the original.

Suppose you change the original constant or any of the cells referred to in the original formula. In that case, the result in the cell containing the linking formula is updated simultaneously as the cell containing the foremost constant or formula.

You can create a linking formula in one of two ways:

Select the cell where you want the linking formula, type = (equal sign), and then click the cell with the constant (text or number) or the formula you want to bring forward to that cell. Complete the cell entry by clicking the Enter button on the Formula bar or pressing the Enter key.

Select the cell with the constant or formula you want to bring to a new location, and then click the Copy button in the Clipboard group on the Ribbon's Home tab or press Ctrl+C. Then click the cell where the linking formula is to appear before you choose the Paste Link option from the Paste button's drop-down menu.

When you use the first simple formula method to create a link, Excel uses a relative cell reference to refer to the cell containing the original value or formula (as in =A10 when referring to an entry in cell A10). However, when using the second copy-and-paste link method, Excel uses an absolute cell reference to refer to the original cell (as in =$A$10 when referring to an entry in cell A10).

When you create a linking formula to a cell on a different sheet of the same workbook, Excel inserts the worksheet name (followed by an exclamation point) in front of the cell address. So, if you copy and paste a link to a formula in cell A10 on a different worksheet called Income 15, Excel inserts the following linking formula:

= 'Income 15'!$A$10

When you create a linking formula to a cell in a different workbook, Excel inserts the workbook filename enclosed in square brackets before the worksheet's name, which precedes the cell address. So, if you bring forward the formula in cell A10 on a worksheet called Cost Analysis in the Projected Income 16 workbook, Excel inserts this linking formula:

=' [Projected Income 16. xls]Cost Analysis'!$A$10

If you ever need to sever a link between the cell containing the original value or formula and the cell to which it's been brought forward, you can do so by editing the linking formula. Press F2, immediately recalculate the formula by pressing F9 and click the Enter button on the Formula bar or press Enter.

This replaces the linking formula with the currently calculated result. Because you've converted the dynamic formula into a constant, changes to the original cell no longer affect the one who initially brought it forward.

What Is Circular Reference In Excel? Everything You Need To Know

A circular reference is an error in Excel that occurs when a formula in a cell tries to calculate itself.

There are certain times when you try to enter a formula in a cell, and it returns with an error. It tells you something about the circular reference that you haven't heard before. But don't worry. Others face the same issue sometimes as well.

This typically occurs when you force an Excel formula to calculate the same cell where the formula is being executed. As a result, you see an error message, which states the existence of circular references.

Circular references are troublesome in Excel and can affect your workflow sometimes. In this book, you'll learn all about circular references in Excel.

What Is Circular Reference In Excel?

In Excel, a circular reference occurs when a formula repeatedly refers to the same cell. As a result, this creates an endless loop between multiple cells. This will slow down your spreadsheet's processing speed, and it may continue unless you stop it.

Here's a succinct definition from Microsoft for Circular Reference in Excel: "When an Excel formula refers back to its cell, directly or indirectly, it creates a circular reference."

There Are Two Types Of Circular References In Excel:

- Direct circular reference
- Indirect circular reference

The circular reference faced most widely by users is the direct circular reference. This can be a result of a clerical error. Let's explain circular references in more detail.

Examples Of Circular Reference In Excel

We discussed above that there are two types of circular references in Excel Direct and Indirect. Let's see an example of both cases.

Direct Circular Reference

A direct circular reference is simple to understand. It occurs when the formula of a cell refers to its cell directly. To illustrate this scenario, we'll take an example.

In the spreadsheet, we have two values in the cells, A1 and A2. If we type the formula =A1+A2+A3 in the A3 cell, A3 refers to itself directly. Logically, this is not possible.

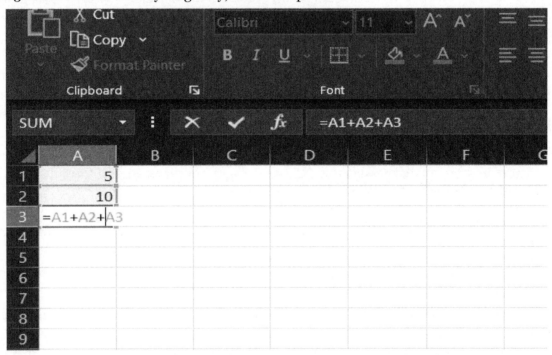

Once you press Enter, you'll see the Circular reference error pop up. If you click OK, Excel returns with the value 0.

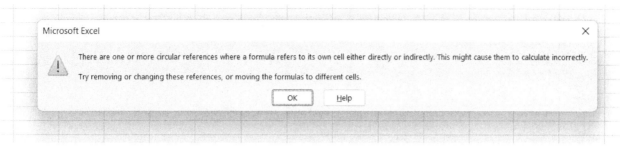

If you take a closer look, you will see that the A1 cell has the value 5, added to the A2 cell with the value 10. The result should be 15 in the A3 cell.

However, when you add the A3 cell to the answer, it keeps adding itself repeatedly and goes to infinity with no definite value. As a result, the A3 cell interprets the result as 0.

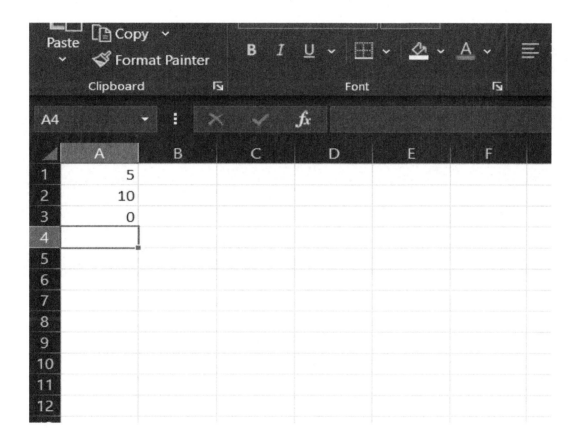

Indirect Circular Reference

This circular reference is similar to the direct circular reference. The only difference is that we do it indirectly instead of directly referring to its cell. Let's illustrate this with a scenario.

Let's take cell D2 with the value 5. And another cell, F4, with value =D2*2. Once you hit Enter, you'll see the result 10.

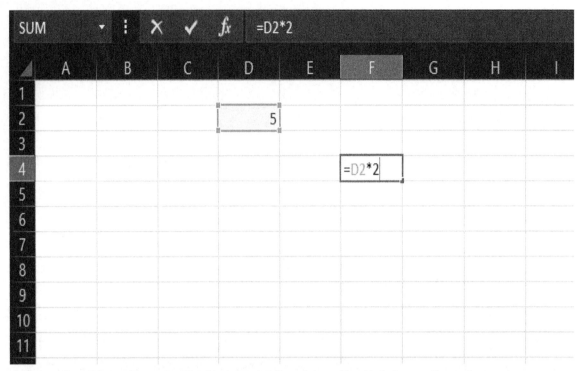

Now, let's take another cell, B4, with a value =F4*2. This will result in a value of 20.

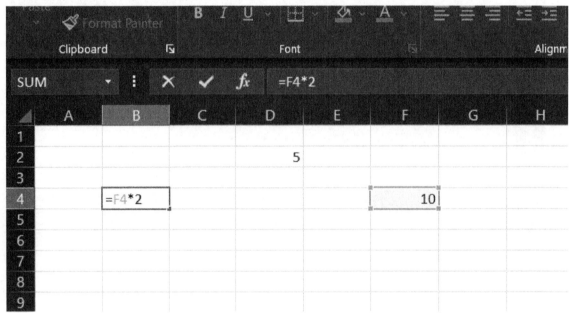

For the final step, let's just go to the first cell, which is D2. If we edit the value in the cell to =B4*2, it'll create a loop between these three cells.

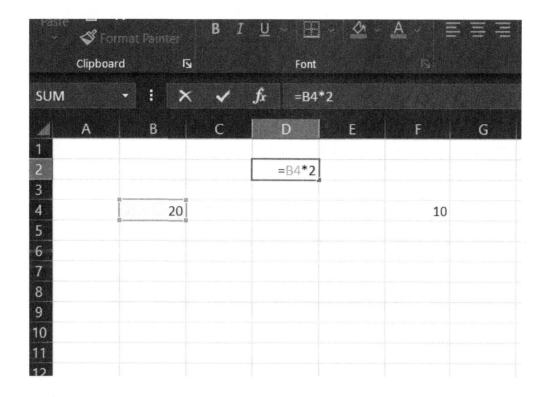

As a result, you'll see the circular reference error pop up. If you press Enter, the result will be 0, as usual.

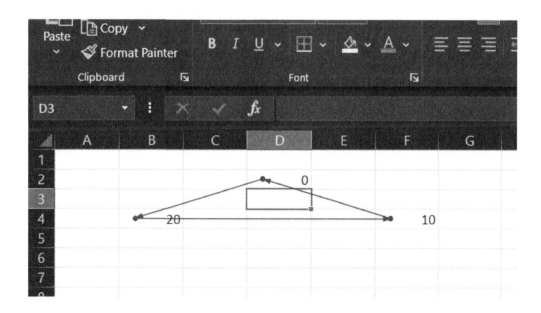

Finding Circular Reference In Excel

You can find the circular reference in Excel using manually or automatically. We'll explain both the processes here. While the manual method is challenging to process, you can go with the automatic method if you have a lot of cells to consider.

Let's look at an indirect circular reference example from the previous models.

Manual Method

To manually find the circular reference cell, follow the steps below:

- Open the spreadsheet where you want to find the circular reference.
- Head over to the Formulas tab in the ribbon menu.
- Click on the Show Formulas option. This will show all the formulas mentioned in their respective cells.

- Find the cell that's causing the circular reference in the spreadsheet.
- Correct the cell that's causing the error.

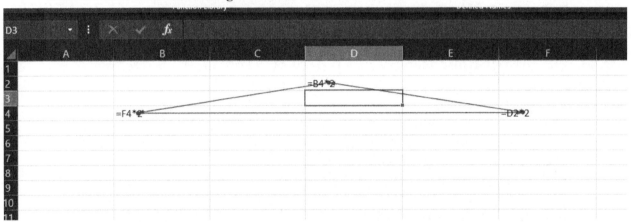

Now it's done. Even though the manual process is a little tedious, it works best when you have fewer cells to check.

Automatic Method

To automatically find the circular reference cell, follow the steps below:

- Open the spreadsheet where you want to find the circular reference.
- Head over to the Formulas tab in the ribbon menu.
- Click on the down arrow next to the Error Checking option.
- From the drop-down, select the Circular References option, and then you'll see the list of cells affected by the circular reference error.

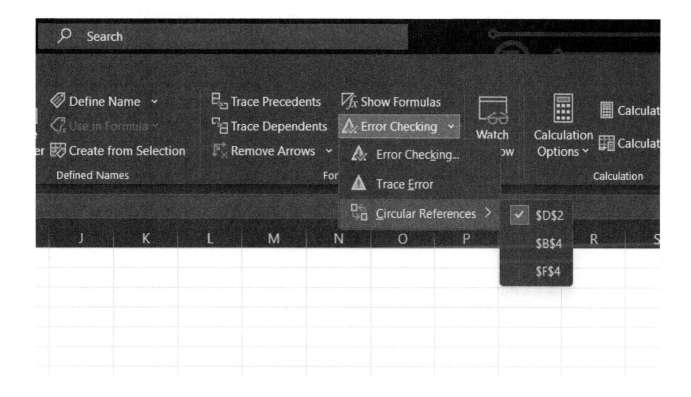

- After you know the cell, go ahead and correct it.

If you want to find more cells with circular references, keep repeating the steps above, and you'll be able to find them sooner. You can also look at the left-side bottom of the spreadsheet, which shows the cells with circular references.

How To Enable/Disable Circular Reference In Excel

By default, iterative calculations are turned off in Excel, resulting in frequent circular references pop-ups. If you want circular references in your spreadsheet, follow the steps below to enable iterative calculations.

- Click on the File option.
- Select the Options menu, and a dialogue box will open.
- Click on the Formula tab.

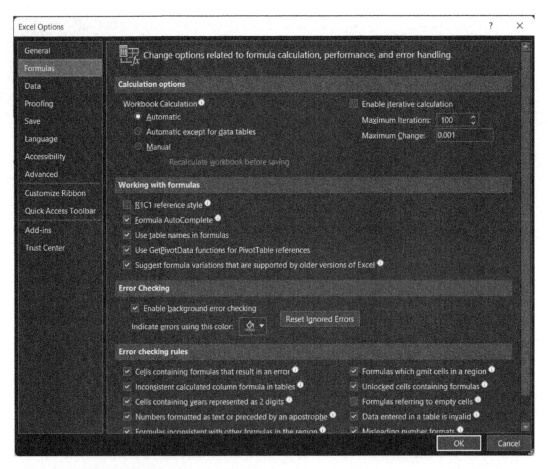

- Check the Enable Iterative Calculation option.
- Click OK, and it will be done.

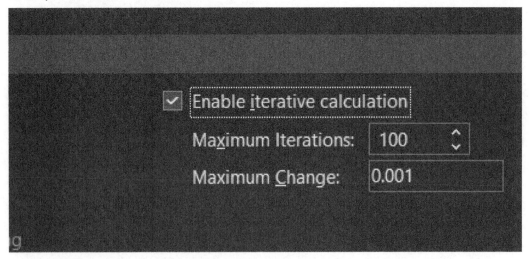

If you are on an older version of Excel, and couldn't find these options, follow these steps:

- Click the Office button.
- Click on Excel options in the options.
- Click the Formula tab.
- Check the Iterative Calculations option.
- Click OK, and you'll be good to go.

When you turn on Iterative Calculations, who'll present you with two options, Maximum Iterations and Maximum Change options.

Maximum Iterations: It calculates how many times the formula can recalculate.

Maximum Change is used for top Change between the calculation results.

The default settings for Maximum Iterations are 100, while the Maximum Change is set to 0.001. You can change them as per your liking.

Try To Avoid Circular References

The circular reference error is caused by looping cells in a formula. There might be times when circular references are not obvious; it's best to use Excel's automated functions.

How To Copy A Formula In Excel

Learn how to copy formulas to multiple cells, down a column, non-adjacent cells, and copy formulas with absolute or mixed cell references.

Copying formulas is one of the most common and easiest tasks in a typical spreadsheet that relies mainly on procedures. Rather than typing the same formula repeatedly in Excel, you can just easily copy and paste a formula from one cell to multiple cells.

After writing a formula in Excel, you can use the Copy and paste commands to multiple cells, multiple non-adjacent cells, or entire columns. If you don't do it right, you'll have that awful # REF and DIV0 errors.

How To Copy And Paste Formulas In Excel

Microsoft Excel provides various ways to copy formulas with relative cell references, absolute cell references, or cross-references.

- Copy formula from one cell to another
- Copy formula one cell to multiple cells
- Copying formula to the entire column
- Copying formula without formatting
- Copy formulas to non-adjacent cells
- Copy formulas without changing cell references

How To Copy A Formula From One Cell To Another In Excel

Sometimes you may want to copy a formula from one cell to another in excel to avoid retyping the entire procedure and save some time.

Let's say we have this table:

	A	B	C
1	20	5	612
2	10	6	12
3	25	98	452
4	0	23	963
5	95	12	3
6	32	96	6

There are a few methods to copy formulas from one cell to another.

First, select the cell with the formula and right-click, and in the context menu, select 'Copy' to copy the formula. Or you can use the 'Copy' option in the 'Clipboard' section of the 'Home' tab.

But you also copy formulas by simply pressing the keyboard shortcut Ctrl + C. This is a more efficient and time-saving method.

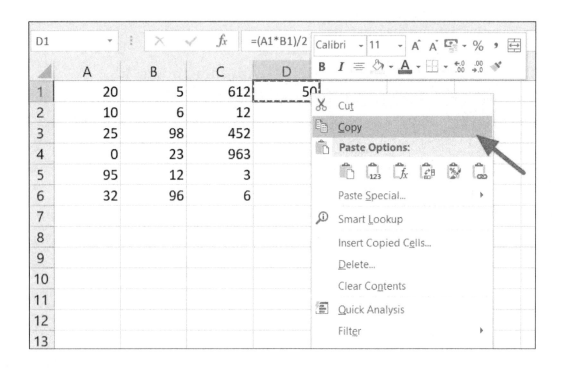

Then we go to the cell we want to paste and press the shortcut Ctrl + V to paste the formula. Or right-click on the partition you want to paste and click the options under 'Paste Options': either simple 'Paste (P)' option or paste as 'Formula (F)' option.

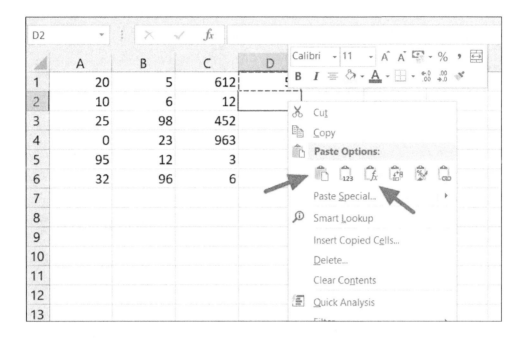

Alternatively, click on 'Paste Special' below the six paste icons to open the 'Paste Special' dialogue box. Here, you have several options, including the six paste options from the context menu. Select 'All' or 'Formulas' under the Paste section and click 'OK'.

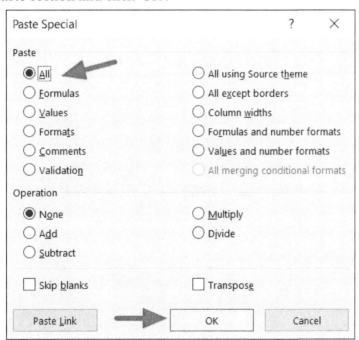

The cell with pasted formula should have the same formulas (as the one in a copied cell) but with different cell references. The cell address is self-adjusted by the excel to match the row number of the pasted cell.

	A	B	C	D	E	F	G
1	20	5	612	50			
2	10	6	12	30			
3	25	98	452				
4	0	23	963				
5	95	12	3				
6	32	96	6				
7	30	20					
8	29	36					

D2: =(A2*B2)/2

Copy Formula From One Cell To Multiple Cells

The same paste operation works just the same if we select multiple cells or a range of cells.

Select the cell with the formula and press Ctrl + C to copy the formula. Then, select all the cells where you want to paste the formula and press Ctrl + V to paste the procedure or use one of the above paste methods to paste the system (like we did for the single cell).

	A	B	C	D	E	F	G
1	20	5	612	50			
2	10	6	12	30	36		
3	25	98	452	1225	22148		
4	0	23	963	0	11074.5		
5	95	12	3	570	18		
6	32	96	6	1536	288		
7	30	20					
8	29	36					

D2: =(A2*B2)/2

Copy Formula To An Entire Column Or Row

You can quickly copy a formula to an entire column or a row in Excel.

To Copy A Formula To A Column Or A Row:
- Enter a formula in a cell.
- Select the formula cell (D1), and hover your cursor over a small green square at the lower right corner of the cell. As you approach, the cursor will change to a black plus sign (+) called the Fill Handle.
- Click and hold that fill handle, and drag it in any direction you want (column or row) over the cells to copy the formula.

	A	B	C	D
1	20	5	612	50
2	10	6	12	
3	25	98	452	
4	0	23	963	
5	95	12	3	
6	32	96	6	
7	30	20		
8	29	36		

D1: =(A1*B1)/2

When you copy a formula to a range of cells, cell references will automatically adjust based on the relative location of rows and columns. The procedure will perform calculations based on the values in those cell references (See below).

	A	B	C	D
1	20	5	612	50
2	10	6	12	30
3	25	98	452	1225
4	0	23	963	0
5	95	12	3	570
6	32	96	6	1536
7	30	20		300
8	29	36		522

D1: =(A1*B1)/2

In the above example, when the formula in D1 (=A1*B1)/2) is copied to cell D2, the relative reference changes bases on its location (=A2*B2)/2) and so on.

In the same way, you can drag the formula into adjacent cells to the left, to the right, or upwards.

Another way to copy the formula to an entire column is by double-clicking the fill handle instead of dragging it. When you double-click the fill handle, it immediately applies the procedure as far as any data is to the adjacent cell.

Copy a Formula To A Range Without Copying Formatting

When you copy a formula to a range of cells with the fill handle, it also copies the source cell's formatting, such as font colour or background colour, currency, percentage, time, etc. (as shown below).

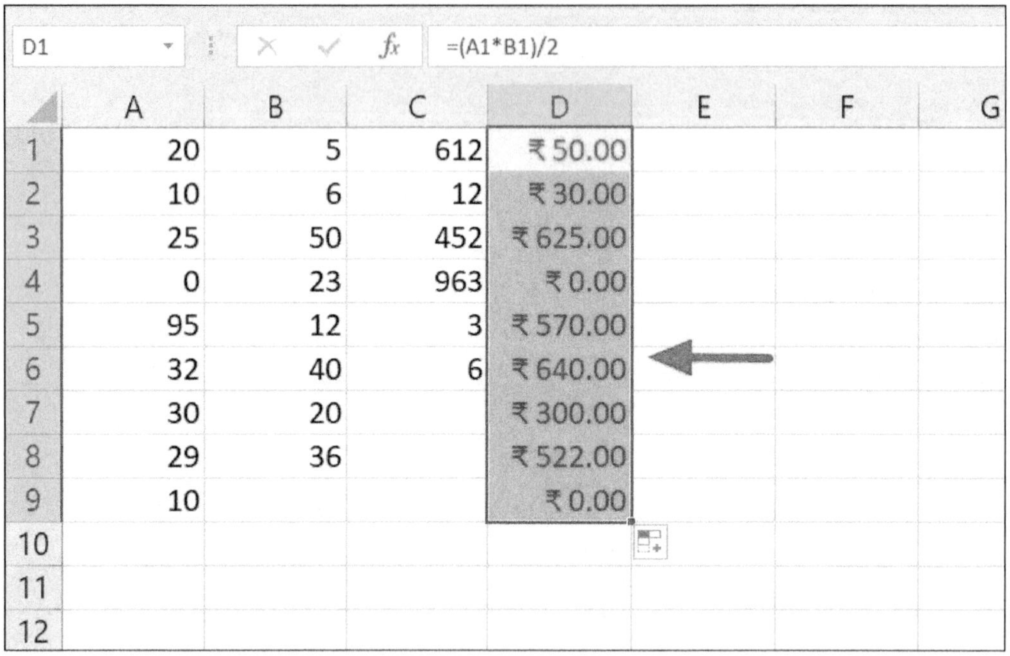

	A	B	C	D	E	F	G
1	20	5	612	₹50.00			
2	10	6	12	₹30.00			
3	25	50	452	₹625.00			
4	0	23	963	₹0.00			
5	95	12	3	₹570.00			
6	32	40	6	₹640.00			
7	30	20		₹300.00			
8	29	36		₹522.00			
9	10			₹0.00			
10							
11							
12							

D1: =(A1*B1)/2

To prevent copying the cell formatting, drag the fill handle and click the 'Auto Fill Options' at the lower right-hand corner of the last cell. Then, in the drop-down menu, select 'Fill Without Formatting.

A	B	C	D	E	F	G
20	5	612	₹50.00			
10	6	12	₹30.00			
25	50	452	₹625.00			
0	23	963	₹0.00			
95	12	3	₹570.00			
32	40	6	₹640.00			
30	20		₹300.00			
29	36		₹522.00			
10			₹0.00			

- ● Copy Cells
- ○ Fill Formatting Only
- ○ Fill Without Formatting
- ○ Flash Fill

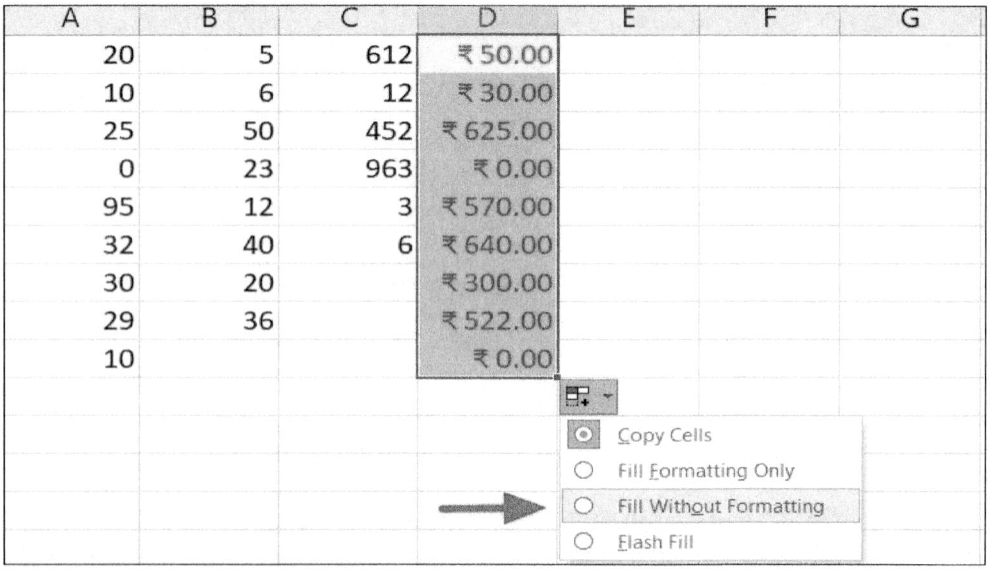

The result:

	A	B	C	D
1	20	5	612	₹ 50.00
2	10	6	12	30
3	25	50	452	625
4	0	23	963	0
5	95	12	3	570
6	32	40	6	640
7	30	20		300
8	29	36		522
9	10			0

Copy An Excel Formula With Only Number Formatting

If you want to copy the formula with only the procedure and the formatting such as percentage format, decimal points, etc.

Copy the formula and select all the cells to which you want to copy the formula. On the 'Home' tab, click the arrow below the 'Paste' button on the ribbon. Then, click the 'Formulas & Number Formatting' icon (the icon with % fx) from the drop-down to paste only the formula and the number formatting.

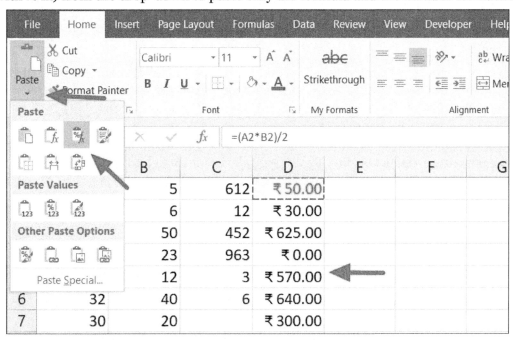

This option only copies formula and number formatting but ignores all other cell formattings like background colour, font colour, etc.

Copy A Formula To Non-Adjacent/Non-Contiguous Cells

If you want to copy a formula to non-adjacent cells or non-adjacent ranges, you can do that with the help of the Ctrl key.

Select the cell with the formula and press Ctrl + C to copy it. Then, select non-adjacent cells/ranges while pressing and holding the Ctrl key. Then, press Ctrl + V to paste the formula and hit Enter to complete.

	A	B	C	D	E	F	G
1	20	5	612	50	1530		
2	10	6	12		36		
3	25	50	452	625		141250	
4	0	23	963		11074.5		
5	95	12	3	570			
6	32	96	6		288		
7	30	20					
8	29	36		522			
9							
10							
11							
12							

F3: =(C3*D3)/2

Copying Formulas Without Changing Cell References In Excel

When a formula is copied to another cell, Excel automatically changes the cell references to match its new location. These cell references use the relative size of a cell address. Hence they are called relative cell references (without $). For example, if you have the formula '=A1*B1' in cell C1, and you copy this formula to cell C2, the procedure will change to '=A2*B2'. All the methods we discussed above use relative references.

When you copy a formula with relative cell references, it automatically changes references so that the procedure refers to the corresponding rows and columns. If you use absolute references in a recipe, the same formula gets copied without changing the cell references.

Putting a dollar sign ($) in front of the column letter and row number of a cell (For example, $A$1) turns the cell into an absolute cell. No matter where you copy the formula containing the definitive cell reference, the procedure will never. But if you have relative or mixed cell references in a recipe, use any of the following methods to copy without changing cell references.

Copy Formula With Absolute Cell Reference Using Copy-Paste Method

Occasionally, you may need to copy/apply the exact formula down the column without changing the cell references. If you want to copy or move a straightforward formula with absolute reference, then do this:

First, select the cell with the formula you want to copy. Then, click on the formula bar, select the formula using the mouse, and press Ctrl + C to copy it. Suppose you want to move the formula; press Ctrl + X to cut it. Next, hit the Esc key to leave the formula bar.

	A	B	C	D	E	F	G
1	20	5	612	50			
2	10	6	12				
3	25	50	452				
4	0	23	963				
5	95	12	3				
6	32	96	6				
7	30	20					
8							
9	=SUM(A1:A7)						
10							

Formula bar: DOLLAR =SUM(A1:A7)

Alternatively, select the cell with the formula and hit the F2 key or double-click the cell. This will put the selected cell into edit mode. Then, select the formula in the cell and hit Ctrl + C to copy the formula in the cell as text.

Then, select the destination cell and press Ctrl + V to paste the formula.

	A	B	C	D	E	F	G
1	20	5	612	50			
2	10	6	12				
3	25	50	452				
4	0	23	963				
5	95	12	3				
6	32	96	6				
7	30	20					
8	29	36					
9	212			212			
10					(Ctrl) ▼		

Formula bar: D9 =SUM(A1:A7)

The exact formula gets copied into the destination cell without any cell reference changes.

Copy Formulas With Absolute Or Mixed Cell References

If you'd like to move or copy exact formulas without changing cell references, you should change cell relative references to absolute references. For example, adding the ($) sign to relative cell reference (B1) makes it a complete reference ($B$1), so it remains static no matter where the formula is copied or moved.

But sometimes, you may need to use mixed cell references ($B1 or B$1) by adding a dollar ($) sign in front of the column letter or the row number to lock either a row or a column in place.

Let us explain with an example. Suppose you have this table that calculates the monthly savings by subtracting rent (B9) from earnings (in column B) every month.

In the example below, the formula uses an absolute cell reference ($B$9) to lock the rent amount to cell B9 and a relative cell reference to cell B2 because it needs to be adjusted for each row to match each month. B9 is made absolute cell reference ($B$9) because you want to subtract the same rent amount from each month's earnings.

	A	B	C
1	Month	Earnings	Balance
2	Jan	₹ 7,000.00	₹ 5,000.00
3	Feb	₹ 5,500.00	₹ 3,500.00
4	Mar	₹ 7,500.00	₹ 5,500.00
5	Apr	₹ 9,000.00	₹ 7,000.00
6	May	₹ 3,966.00	₹ 1,966.00
7	Jun	₹ 6,800.00	₹ 4,800.00
8			
9	Rent :	₹ 2,000.00	

C2 fx =B2-$B$9

Let's say you want to move the balances from column C to column E. If you copy the formula (by the usual copy/paste method) from cell C2, (=B2-$B$9) will change to =D2-$B$9 when pasted in cell E2, making your calculations all wrong!

Change the relative cell reference (B2) to a mixed cell reference ($B2) by adding the '$' sign in front of the column letter of the formula entered in cell C2.

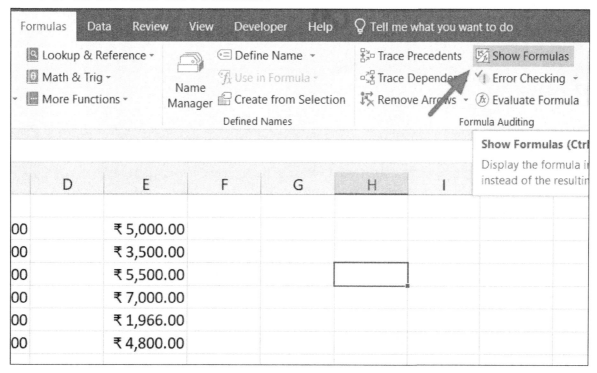

And now, if you copy or move the formula from cell C2 to E2, or any other cell, and apply the formula down the column, the column reference will remain the same while who will adjust the row number for each cell.

Copy Paste Excel Formulas Without Changing References Using Notepad

You can see every formula in your Excel spreadsheet using the Show Formula options. To do that, go to the 'Formulas' tab and select 'Show Formulas'.

Alternatively, you can enter the formula view mode by pressing the Ctrl + ` shortcut, displaying every formula in your worksheet. You can find the grave accent key (`) at the top left corner of your keyboard on the row with the number keys (below the ESC key and before the number 1 key).

B	C	D
Earnings	**Balance**	
7000	=B2-B9	=C2+1500+B9
5500	=B3-B10	
7500	=B4-B11	
9000	=B5-B12	=IF(C6>5000, "Low","High")
3966	=B6-B9	=IF(C6<4000, "Low","OK")
6800	=B7-B14	
2000		

Select all the cells with the formulas you want to copy and press Ctrl + C to copy them or Ctrl + X to cut them. Then open the notepad and press Ctrl + V to paste the formulas into the notepad.

```
*Untitled - Notepad
File  Edit  Format  View  Help
=B2-B9    =C2+1500+B9
=B3-B10
=B4-B11
=B5-B12   =IF(C6>5000, "Low","High")
=B6-B9    =IF(C6<4000, "Low","OK")
=B7-B14
|
```

Next, select the formula and Copy (Ctrl + C) it from the notepad, and paste it(Ctrl + V) in the cell where you want the exact formula copied. You can copy and paste them one by one or all at once.

After pasting the formulas, turn off the formula view mode by pressing Ctrl + ` or again go to 'Formulas' –> 'Show formulas'.

Copy The Exact Formulas Using Excel's Find And Replace

If you want to copy a range of Exact formulas, you can also use Excel's Find and Replace tool.

Select all the cells that have the formulas that you want to copy. Then go to the 'Home' tab, click 'Find & Select' on the Editing group, select the 'Replace' option, Or simply press Ctrl + H to open the Find & Replace dialogue box.

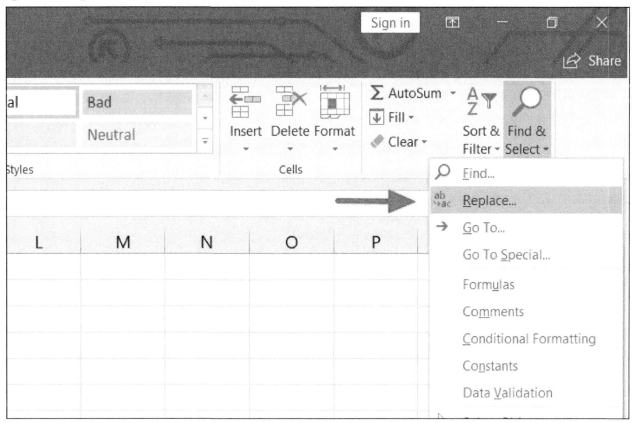

In the Find and Replace dialogue box, enter the equal sign (=) in the 'Find what' field. In the 'Replace with' domain, enter a symbol or character not already part of your formulas, like #, etc. Then, click the 'Replace All' button.

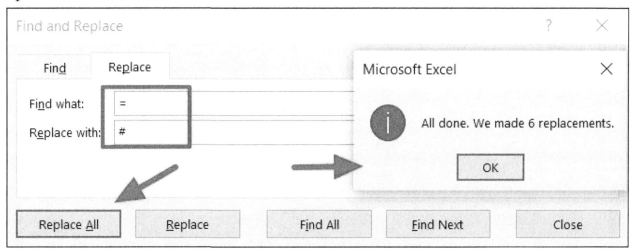

You'll get a prompt message box saying 'We made six replacements' (because we selected six cells with formulas). Then click 'OK' and 'Close' to close both dialogues. This replaces all equal to (=) signs with the hash (#) signs and turns formulas into text strings. Now the cell references of the formulas won't be changed when copied.

	A	B	C	D	E
1	Month	Earnings	Balance		
2	Jan	₹ 7,000.00	#IF(B2-B9>5000, "Low","High")		
3	Feb	₹ 5,500.00	#B3-B10		
4	Mar	₹ 7,500.00	#B4-B11		
5	Apr	₹ 9,000.00	#B5-B12		
6	May	₹ 3,966.00	#IF(B6-B9<5000, "Low","High")		
7	Jun	₹ 6,800.00	#B7-B14		
8					
9	Rent :	₹ 2,000.00			
10					
11					
12					
13					

You can select these cells, press Ctrl + C to copy them, and paste them into destination cells with Ctrl + V.

C	D	E
Balance		
#IF(B2-B9>5000, "Low","High")		#IF(B2-B9>5000, "Low","High")
#B3-B10		#B3-B10
#B4-B11		#B4-B11
#B5-B12		#B5-B12
#IF(B6-B9<5000, "Low","High")		#IF(B6-B9<5000, "Low","High")
#B7-B14		#B7-B14

Finally, you need to change the (#) signs back to (=) characters. Select both ranges (original and copied range) and press Ctrl + H to open the Find & Replace dialogue box. This time, type the hash (#) sign in the 'Find what' field, equal to the (=) sign in the 'Replace with' field and click the 'Replace All' button. Click 'Close' to close the dialogue.

Now, the text strings are converted back to the formulas, and you will get this result: Done!

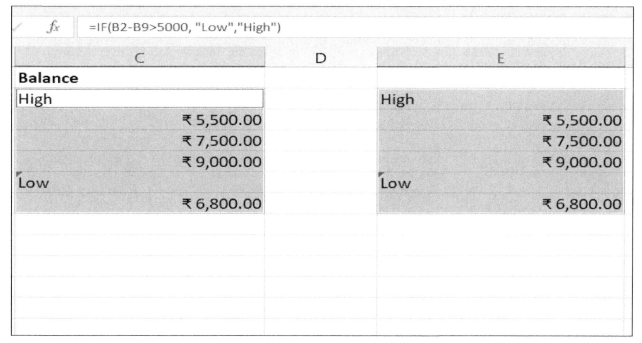

Calculation

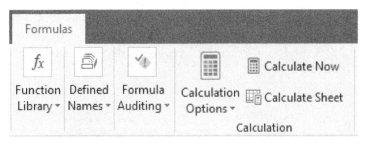

A workbook can be updated (or calculated) when opened or closed.

You can also typically interrupt the calculation process by pressing Escape several times.

- **(F9) - Smart Calculation:** Calculates All the worksheets in All the open workbooks (only cells containing formulas that have changed since who will update the last calculation). [Application.Calculate]
- **-(Shift + F9):** Smart Calculation. Calculates the Active / Selected worksheets in the Active workbook (only cells containing formulas that have changed since who will update the last calculation). [Sheets(1).Calculate]
- **(Ctrl + Alt + F9):** Full Calculation. Calculates All the worksheets in All the open workbooks. (all cells containing formulas). [Application.CalculateFull]
- **(Ctrl + Alt + Shift + F9):** Full Recalculation. Calculates All the worksheets in All the open workbooks (all cells containing formulas and rebuilding the dependency tree and calculation chain). [Application.CalculateFullRebuild]

There is currently no way to quickly perform a complete calculation of all the cells in just the active workbook.

(Ctrl + Shift + F9): This is not a default shortcut key, but some third party add-ins use this for performing a full calculation of all the cells in just the active workbook.

Options > Formulas Tab

The File> Options - Formulas Tab contains all the options for controlling formula calculation.

Automatic Calculation

- The default setting is Automatic. This means that Excel will automatically recalculate all the necessary cells in a workbook when a value is changed.
- This type of calculation is the default and is what some people call a minimum recalculation.
- This means that the data and formulas in your workbook are constantly up-to-date.
- When the workbook is pretty simple, recalculation takes a fraction of a second since the majority of the cells will be unaffected.
- When you have a complicated workbook containing a lot of formulas, Excel will determine which cells to recalculate and in what order.
- It is important to remember that Excel can only track 65,536 dependencies to unique references.
- If Excel finds more than 65,536 dependencies, the whole workbook is calculated, and the word "Calculate" may remain in the status bar - check.

Manual Calculation

- This lets you select or clear the Recalculate Before Save check box.
- The "Recalculate Workbook Before Save" check box controls if the formulas are recalculated before the workbook is closed.
- This is often a good idea, as it prevents a user from opening the workbook to display data that is not up-to-date.
- The manual calculation is a good idea when you have large workbooks as you want to control when a recalculation occurs.

- If your workbook contains any uncalculated formulas in the active workbook when working on Manual calculation, the word "Calculate" will be displayed in the status bar.
-

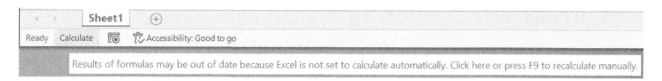

Why Does My Calculation Change To Manual?

Your calculation setting (and your iteration setting) is an Application Setting rather than a workbook set.

However, it is saved into your workbooks despite an application setting.

The calculation settings are taken from the first workbook you open (in that session) and then ignored in subsequent workbooks.

Depending on the order in which you open your workbooks, your settings may change.

For example, let's say that all of your workbooks have been saved with calculation settings of Automatic.

This works fine for you until, by chance, the first workbook you open in your session happens to be a workbook created by someone else (who, by mistake, has saved it with the manual calculation).

In this scenario, your calculation settings will be manual, and when you open up your workbooks, the calculation will still be manual.

CHAPTER 4: MS EXCEL LOGICAL FUNCTIONS

Excel AND Function

The Excel AND function is a logical function used to require more than one condition simultaneously. AND returns either TRUE or FALSE. To test if a number in A1 is more significant than zero and less than 10, use =AND(A1>0, A1<10). The AND function can be used as the logical test inside the IF function to avoid extra nested IFs and combined with the OR function.

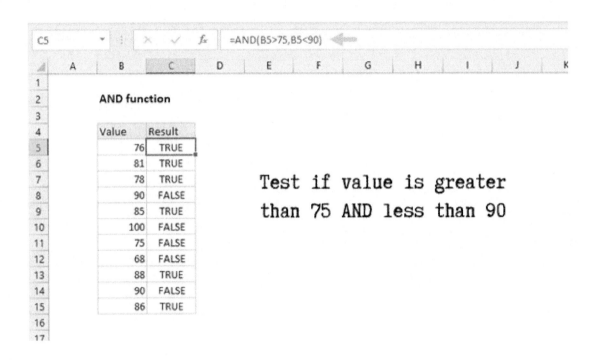

Purpose: Test multiple conditions with AND

Return Value: TRUE if all arguments evaluate TRUE; FALSE if 1

Syntax: =AND (logical1, [logical2], ...)

Arguments

- logical1: The first condition or logical value to evaluate.
- logical2: [optional] The second condition or logical value to evaluate.

Usage Notes

The AND function is used to check more than one logical condition simultaneously, up to 255 requirements, supplied as arguments. Each argument (logical1, logical2, etc.) must be an expression that returns TRUE or FALSE or a value that can evaluate as TRUE or FALSE. The arguments provided to the AND function can be constants, cell references, arrays, or logical expressions.

The purpose of the AND function is to evaluate more than one logical test simultaneously and return TRUE only if all results are TRUE. For example, if A1 contains the number 50, then:

=AND(A1>0,A1>10,A1<100) // returns TRUE

=AND(A1>0,A1>10,A1<30) // returns FALSE

The AND function will evaluate all values supplied and return TRUE only if all values consider TRUE. If any value evaluates to FALSE, the AND function will return FALSE. Note: Excel will evaluate any number except zero (0) as TRUE.

Both the AND function and the OR function will aggregate results to a single value. This means who can't use them in array operations that need to deliver an array of results. To work around this limitation, you can use Boolean logic. For more information, see Array formulas with AND and OR logic.

Examples

To test if the value in A1 is greater than 0 and less than 5, you can use AND like this:

=AND(A1>0,A1<5)

You can embed the AND function inside the IF function. Using the above example, you can supply AND as the logical_test for the IF function like so:

=IF(AND(A1>0,A1<5), "Approved", "Denied")

This formula will return "Approved" only if the value in A1 is greater than 0 and less than 5.

You can combine the AND function with the OR function. The formula below returns TRUE when A1 > 100 and B1 is "complete" or "pending":

=AND(A1>100,OR(B1="complete",B1="pending"))

Notes

- The AND function is not case-sensitive.
- The AND function does not support wildcards.
- Text values or empty cells supplied as arguments are ignored.
- The AND function will return #VALUE if no logical values are found or created during evaluation.

Excel OR function

The Excel OR function returns TRUE if any given argument evaluates to TRUE and returns FALSE if all supplied arguments evaluate to FALSE. For example, to test A1 for either "x" or "y", use =OR(A1="x",A1="y"). The OR function can be used as the logical test inside the IF function to avoid nested IFs and combined with the AND function.

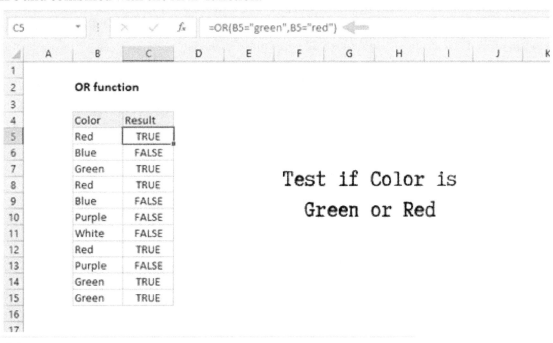

Purpose: Test multiple conditions with OR

Return Value: TRUE if any arguments evaluate TRUE; FALSE if not.

Syntax: =OR (logical1, [logical2], ...)

Arguments

- logical1: The first condition or logical value to evaluate.
- logical2: [optional] The second condition or logical value to evaluate.

Usage Notes

The OR function returns TRUE if any given arguments evaluate TRUE and return FALSE only if all supplied arguments evaluate FALSE. The OR function can be used as the logical test inside the IF function to avoid nested IFs and combined with the AND function.

The OR function checks more than one logical condition simultaneously, up to 255 requirements, supplied as arguments. Each argument (logical1, logical2, etc.) must be an expression that returns TRUE or FALSE or a value that can evaluate as TRUE or FALSE. The ideas provided to the OR function can be constants, cell references, arrays, or logical expressions.

The purpose of the OR function is to evaluate more than one logical test simultaneously and return TRUE if any result is TRUE. For example, if A1 contains the number 50, then:

=AND(A1>0,A1>75,A1>100) // returns TRUE

=AND(A1<0,A1=25,A1>100) // returns FALSE

The OR function will evaluate all values supplied and return TRUE if any value evaluates to TRUE. If all logic evaluates to FALSE, the OR function will return FALSE. Note: Excel will evaluate any number except zero (0) as TRUE.

Both the AND function and the OR function will aggregate results to a single value. This means who can't use them in array operations that need to deliver an array of results. To work around this limitation, you can use Boolean logic. For more information, see Array formulas with AND and OR logic.

Examples

For example, to test if the value in A1 OR the value in B1 is greater than 75, use the following formula:

=OR(A1>75,B1>75)

OR can be used to extend the functionality of functions like the IF function. Using the above example, you can supply OR as the logical_test for an IF function like so:

=IF(OR(A1>75,B1>75), "Pass", "Fail")

This formula will return "Pass" if the value in A1 is more excellent than 75 OR the value in B1 is greater than 75.

Array Form

If you enter OR as an array formula, you can test all values in a range against a condition. For example, this array formula will return TRUE if any cell in A1:A100 is greater than 15:

=OR(A1:A100>15

Note: this is an array formula and must be entered with control + shift + enter, except Excel 365.

Notes

- Each logical condition must evaluate TRUE or FALSE or be arrays or references containing logical values.
- Text values or empty cells supplied as arguments are ignored.
- The OR function will return #VALUE if no logical values are found.

Excel IF Function

The IF function runs a logical test and returns one value for a TRUE result and another for a FALSE result. For example, to "pass" scores above 70: =IF(A1>70,"Pass","Fail"). More than one condition can be tested by nesting IF functions. To extend the logical test, who can combine the IF function with logical functions like AND and OR?

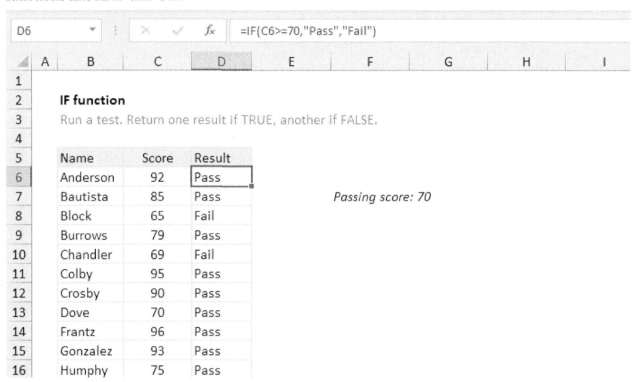

Purpose: Test for a specific condition

Return Value: The values you supply for TRUE or FALSE

Syntax: =IF (logical_test, [value_if_true], [value_if_false])

Arguments

- **logical_test:** A value or logical expression that can be evaluated as TRUE or FALSE.
- **value_if_true:** [optional] The value to return when logical_test evaluates to TRUE.
- **value_if_false:** [optional] The value to return when logical_test evaluates to FALSE.

Usage Notes

The IF function runs a logical test and reacts differently depending on whether the result is TRUE or FALSE. The first argument, logical_test, is an expression that returns either TRUE or FALSE. Both value_if_true and value_if_false are optional, but who must provide at least one of them. The result from IF can be a value, a cell reference, or even another formula.

We want to assign either "Pass" or "Fail" based on a test score in the example shown above. A passing score is 70 or higher. The formula in D6, copied down, is:

=IF(C6>=70,"Pass","Fail")

Translation: If the value in C6 is greater than or equal to 70, return "Pass ."Otherwise, return "Fail."

Who can reverse the logical flow of this formula? The formula below returns the same result:

=IF(C6<70,"Fail","Pass")

Translation: If the value in C6 is less than 70, return "Fail ."Otherwise, return "Pass."

Both formulas above, when copied down, will return correct results.

Another Formula

The IF function can return another formula as a result. For example, the formula below will return A1*5% when A1 is less than 100 and A1*7% when A1 is greater than or equal to 100:

=IF(A1<100,A1*5%,A1*7%)

Nested IF Statements

The IF function can be "nested ."A "nested IF" refers to a formula where at least one IF function is nested inside another to test for more conditions and return more possible results. Each IF statement needs to be carefully "nested" inside another to correct the logic.

For example, who can use the following formula to assign a grade rather than a pass / fail result:

=IF(C6<70,"F",IF(C6<75,"D",IF(C6<85,"C",IF(C6<95,"B","A"))))

Up to 64 IF functions can be nested. However, you should generally consider other functions, like VLOOKUP or HLOOKUP, for more complex scenarios because they can handle more conditions much more streamlined fashion.

Logical Operators

When you are constructing a test with IF, you can use any of the following logical operators:

Comparison Operator Meaning Example

= equal to A1=D1

> greater than A1>D1

>= greater than or equal to A1>=D1

< less than A1

<= less than or equal to A1<=D1

<> not equal to A1<>D1

The IF function doesn't support wildcards, but you can combine IF with COUNTIF to get basic wildcard functionality.

Notes

- To count things conditionally, use the COUNTIF or the COUNTIFS functions.
- To sum things conditionally, use the SUMIF or the SUMIFS functions.
- If any of the arguments to IF are supplied as arrays, the IF function will evaluate every array element.

Excel MAX Function

The Excel MAX function returns the most significant numeric value in the data provided. MAX ignores empty cells, the logic TRUE and FALSE, and text values.

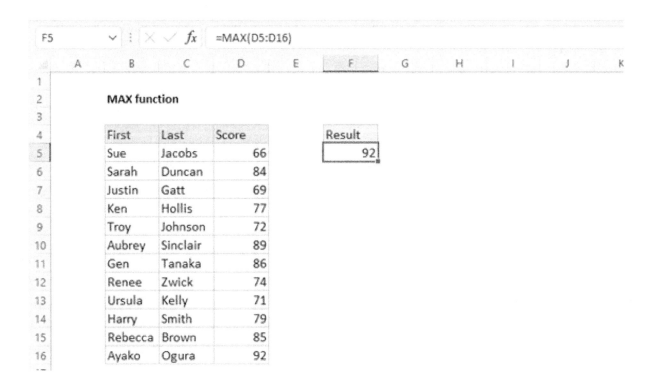

Purpose: Get the largest value

Return Value: The largest value in supplied data

Syntax: =MAX (number1, [number2], ...)

Arguments

- Number1: Number, reference to a numeric value, or range that contains numeric values.
- Number2: [optional] number, reference to a numeric value, or range that contains numeric values.

Usage Notes

The MAX function returns the most significant numeric value in the data provided. Who can use the MAX function to produce the essential value from any numeric data type? For example, MAX can return the slowest time in a race, the latest data, the most significant percentage, the highest temperature, or the top sales number.

The MAX function takes multiple arguments in the form number1, number2, number3, etc., up to 255. Arguments can be a hardcoded constant, a cell reference, or a range in any combination. MAX ignores empty cells, text values, and the logical values TRUE and FALSE.

Examples

The MAX function returns the most significant numeric value in supplied data:

=MAX(12,17,25,11,23) // returns 25

The MAX function can accept values as separate argu9ments or in ranges or arrays:

=MAX(5,10)

=MAX(A1,A2,A3)

=MAX(A1:A10)

=MAX(A1:A10,C1:C10)

MAX ignores logical values and numbers entered as text unless they are provided as arguments:

=MAX(-1,TRUE) // returns 1

=MAX(-1,TRUE,"3") // returns 3

To return the maximum value with criteria, use the MAXIFS function. Use the LARGE part to retrieve the nth most significant value in a data set. To determine the rank of a number in a data group, use the RANK function.

Notes

- Arguments can be provided as numbers, names, arrays, or references.
- MAX accepts up to 255 arguments. If arguments contain no numbers, MAX returns 0.
- MAX ignores empty cells, text values, and TRUE and FALSE in references.
- MAX will evaluate numbers as text, and logical values supplied directly as arguments.
- To include logical values in a reference, see the MAXA function.

Excel MIN Function

The Excel MIN function returns the smallest numeric value in the data provided. The MIN function ignores empty cells, the logical values TRUE and FALSE, and text values.

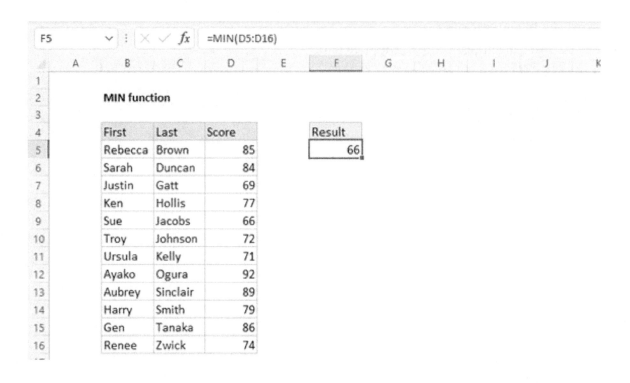

64 | Page

Purpose: Get the smallest value.

Return Value: The smallest value in supplied data

Syntax: =MIN (number1, [number2], ...)

Arguments

- Number 1: Number, reference to a numeric value, or range that contains numeric values.
- Number 2: [optional] number, reference to a numeric value, or range that contains numeric values.

Usage Notes

The MIN function returns the smallest numeric value in the data provided. Who can use the MIN function to return the smallest value from any numeric data type? For example, MIN can return the fastest time in a race, the earliest date, the smallest percentage, the lowest temperature, or the bottom sales number.

The MIN function takes multiple arguments in the form number1, number2, number3, etc., up to 255. Arguments can be a hardcoded constant, a cell reference, or a range in any combination. MIN ignores empty cells, text values, and the logical values TRUE and FALSE.

Examples

The MIN function returns the smallest numeric value in supplied data:

=MIN(12,17,25,11,23) // returns 11

The MIN function can accept values as separate arguments or in ranges or arrays:

=MIN(5,10)

=MIN(A1,A2,A3)

=MIN(A1:A10)

=MIN(A1:A10,C1:C10)

MIN ignores logical values and numbers entered as text unless they are provided as arguments:

=MIN(5,TRUE) // returns 1

=MIN(7,5,"3") // returns 3

To return the minimum value with criteria, use the MINIFS function. Use the SMALL function to retrieve the nth smallest value in a data set. To determine the rank of a number in a data collection, use the RANK function.

Notes

- Arguments can be provided as numbers, names, arrays, or references.
- MIN accepts up to 255 arguments. If arguments contain no numbers, MIN returns 0.
- MIN ignores empty cells, text values, and TRUE and FALSE in references.
- MIN will evaluate numbers as text, and logical values supplied directly as arguments.

Excel EVEN Function

The Excel EVEN function rounds numbers up to the next even integer. The EVEN function always rounds numbers away from zero, so positive numbers become more significant and negative numbers minor (i.e., more negative).

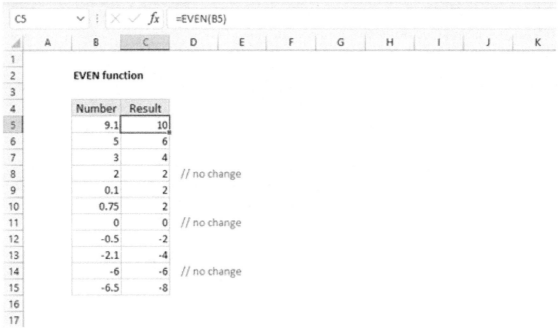

Purpose: Round a number up to the next even integer

Return Value: An even integer

Syntax: =EVEN (number)

Arguments

- Number: The number to round up to an even integer.

Usage Notes

The EVEN function rounds numbers up to the next even integer. EVEN always rounds numbers away from zero, so positive numbers become more extensive and harmful numbers minor (i.e., more negative).

EVEN takes just one argument, a number, which should be a numeric value. With positive numbers, EVEN rounds number up to the next even integer. With negative values, EVEN rounds number down away from zero to the following negative integer. The number is unchanged with zero (0) and numbers that are already even integers.

Examples

The EVEN function rounds positive numbers up to the next even integer:

=EVEN(1) // returns 2

=EVEN(3.1) // returns 4

Negative numbers are rounded away from zero to the next even integer:

=EVEN(-1) // returns -2

=EVEN(-3.1) // returns -4

Zero and numbers that are already even integers are unaffected:

=EVEN(2) // returns 2

=EVEN(0) // returns 0

=EVEN(-2) // returns -2

To round numbers up to the next odd integer, see the ODD function.

Excel ODD Function

The Excel ODD function returns the next odd integer after rounding a given number up. The ODD function always rounds numbers away from zero, so positive numbers become more extensive and harmful ones smaller (i.e., more negative).

Number	Result	
9.1	11	
5	5	// no change
5.5	7	
2	3	
1	1	// no change
0.75	1	
0	1	
-0.5	-1	
-2.1	-3	
-5	-5	// no change
-6.5	-7	

Purpose: Round a number up to the next odd integer

Return Value: A rounded number.

Syntax: =ODD (number)

Arguments
- **Number:** The number to round up to an odd integer.

Usage Notes

The ODD function rounds numbers up to the next odd integer. ODD always rounds numbers away from zero, so positive numbers become more extensive and harmful ones smaller (i.e., more negative).

ODD takes just one argument, a number, which should be a numeric value. With positive numbers, ODD rounds number up to the next odd integer. ODD rounds number down from zero to the next weird negative integer with negative values. With one (1) and numbers already odd integers, the number is unchanged.

Examples

The ODD function rounds positive numbers up to the next odd integer:
- =ODD(2) // returns 3
- =ODD(5.1) // returns 7

Negative numbers are rounded away from zero to the next odd integer:
- =ODD(-2) // returns -3
- =ODD(-5.1) // returns -7

The number 1 and numbers that are already odd integers are unaffected:
- =ODD(3) // returns 3
- =ODD(1) // returns 1
- =ODD(-3) // returns -3

To round numbers up to the next even integer, see the EVEN function.

Excel IFS Function

The Excel IFS function can run multiple tests and return a value corresponding to the first TRUE result. Use the IFS function to evaluate numerous conditions without numerous nested IF statements. IFS allows shorter, easier-to-read formulas.

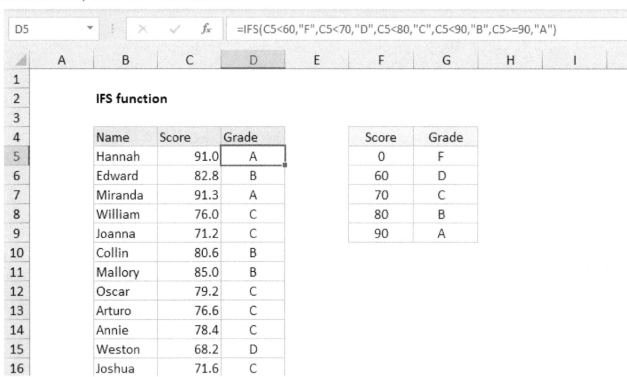

Purpose: Test multiple conditions, return first true

Return Value: Value corresponding with first TRUE result

Syntax: =IFS (test1, value1, [test2, value2], ...)

Arguments
- **Test 1:** First logical test.
- **Value 1:** Result when test1 is TRUE.
- **Test 2, Value 2:** [optional] Second test/value pair.

Usage Notes

The IFs function evaluates multiple expressions and returns a result corresponding to the first TRUE result. You can use the IFS function when you want a self-contained formula to test numerous conditions simultaneously without nesting multiple IF statements. Formulas based on IFS are shorter and easier to read and write.

Conditions are provided to the IFS function as test/value pairs, and IFS can handle up to 127 needs. Each test represents a logical test that returns TRUE or FALSE, and the value that follows will be returned when the test returns TRUE. If more than one condition returns TRUE, the value corresponding to the first TRUE result is returned. For this reason, it is essential to consider the order in which conditions appear.

Structure

who can visualize an IFS formula with three tests like this:

=IFS(

test1,value1 // pair 1

test2,value2 // pair 2

test3,value3 // pair 3

)

A value is returned by IFS only when the previous test returns TRUE, and the first test to produce TRUE "wins ."You can add line breaks to an IFS formula for better readability, as shown above.

Note: The IFS function does not provide an argument for a default value. See Example 3 below for a workaround.

Example 1 - Grades, Lowest To Highest

In the example shown below, the IFS function assigns a grade based on a score. The formula in E5, copied down, is:

=IFS(C5<60,"F",C5<70,"D",C5<80,"C",C5<90,"B",C5>=90,"A")

Notice the conditions are entered "in order" to test lower scores first. The grade associated with the first test to return TRUE is returned.

Example 2 - Rating, Highest To Lowest

In a simple rating system, a score of 3 or greater is "Good," a score between 2 and 3 is "Average," and anything below 2 is "Poor ."To assign these values with IFS, three conditions are used:

=IFS(A1>=3,"Good",A1>=2,"Average",A1<2,"Poor")

Notice in this case and conditions are arranged to test higher values first.

Example 3 - Default Value

The IFS function does not have a built-in default value when all conditions are FALSE. However, to provide a default value, you can enter TRUE as a final test, followed by a value to use as a default.

In the example below, a status code of 100 is "OK," a code of 200 is "Warning," and a code of 300 is "Error ."Any other code value is invalid, so TRUE is provided as the final test, and "Invalid" is supplied as a "default" value.

=IFS(A1=100,"OK",A1=200,"Warning",A1=300,"Error",TRUE,"Invalid")

When the value in A1 is 100, 200, or 300, IFS will return the messages shown above. When A1 contains any other value (including when A1 is empty), IFS will return "Invalid ."IFS will return #N/A without this final condition when a code is not recognized.

Note: IFS is a new function available in Excel 365 and Excel 2019.

Excel NOT Function

The Excel NOT function returns the opposite of a given logical or Boolean value. When given TRUE, NOT returns FALSE. When given FALSE, NOT returns TRUE. Use the NOT function to reverse a logical value.

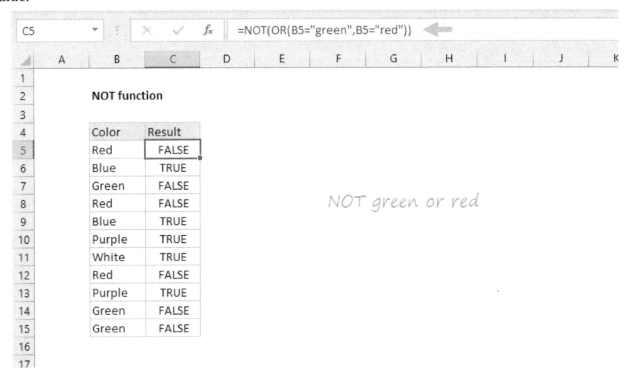

Purpose: Reverse arguments or results

Return Value: A reversed logical value

Syntax: =NOT (logical)

Arguments

- **Logical:** A value or rational expression that can be evaluated as TRUE or FALSE.

Usage Notes

The NOT function returns the opposite of a given logical or Boolean value. Use the NOT function to reverse a Boolean value or the result of a logical expression.

When given FALSE, NOT returns TRUE.

When given TRUE, NOT returns FALSE.

Example 1 - Not Green Or Red

In the example shown, the formula in C5, copied down, is:

=NOT(OR(B5="green",B5="red"))

The literal translation of this formula is "NOT green or red ."At each row, the formula returns TRUE if the color in column B is not green or red and FALSE if the color is green or red.

Example 2 - Not blank

An everyday use case for the NOT function is to reverse the behavior of another function. For example, If cell A1 is blank (empty), the ISBLANK function will return TRUE:

=ISBLANK(A1) // TRUE if A1 is empty

To reverse this behavior, wrap the NOT function around the ISBLANK function:

=NOT(ISBLANK(A1)) // TRUE if A1 is NOT empty

By adding NOT, the output from ISBLANK is reversed. This formula will return TRUE when A1 is not empty and FALSE when A1 is empty. You might use this kind of test only to run a calculation if there is a value in A1:

=IF(NOT(ISBLANK(A1)),B1/A1,"")

Translation: if A1 is not blank, divide B1 by A1; otherwise, return an empty string ("). This is an example of nesting one function inside another.

CHAPTER 5 : MS EXCEL LOOKUP AND TEXT'S FUNCTIONS

What Is The HLOOKUP Function?

HLOOKUP stands for Horizontal Lookup and can be used to retrieve information from a table by searching a row for the matching data and outputting from the corresponding column. While VLOOKUP searches for the value in a column, HLOOKUP searches for the value in a row.

Definition HLOOKUP Function

An HLOOKUP function in Excel exists of 4 components:
- The value you want to look up;
- The range in which you want to find the value and the return value;
- The number of the row within your defined range that contains the return value;
- 0 or FALSE for an exact match with the value you are looking for; 1 or TRUE for an approximate match.

Syntax: HLOOKUP([value], [range], [row number], [false or true])

How To Use HLOOKUP In Excel

HLOOKUP in Excel stands for 'Horizontal Lookup.' It is a function that makes Excel search for a specific value in a row (the so-called 'table array') in order to return a value from a different row in the same column.

Formula

=HLOOKUP(value to look up, table area, row number)

How To Use The HLOOKUP Function In Excel?

Let us consider the example below. The marks for four subjects for five students are as follows:

A	B	C	D	E	F
Student name	A	B	C	D	E
Accounts	75	65	70	60	59
Economics	65	72	78	89	67
Management	70	68	90	72	58
Mathematics	80	90	75	65	87

Now, if our objective is to fetch the marks of student D in Management, we can use HLOOKUP as follows:

A	B	C	D	E	F	G	H
Student roll no	A	B	C	D	E		
Accounts	75	65	70	60	59		
Economics	65	72	78	89	67		
Management	70	68	90	72	58		
Mathematics	80	90	75	65	87		

Fetch Marks of D in Management =Hlookup(
HLOOKUP(**lookup_value**, table_array, row_index_num, [range_lookup])

HLOOKUP function in Excel comes with the following arguments:

HLOOKUP(lookup_value, table_array, row_index_num, [range_lookup])

As you can see in the screenshot above, we need to give the lookup_value first. Here, it would be student D as we need to find his marks in Management. Now, remember that lookup_value can be a cell reference or a text string, or it can be a numerical value as well. In our example, it would be the student's name as shown below:

A	B	C	D	E	F	G	H
Student name	A	B	C	D	E		
Accounts	75	65	70	60	59		
Economics	65	72	78	89	67		
Management	70	68	90	72	58		
Mathematics	80	90	75	65	87		

Fetch Marks of D in Management =hlookup("D"
HLOOKUP(**lookup_value**, table_array, row_index_num, [range_lookup])

The next step would be to give the table array. A table array is nothing but rows of data in which who would search the lookup value. A table array can be a normal range, a named range, or even an Excel table. Here we will give row A1:F5 as the reference.

	A	B	C	D	E	F
	Student name	A	B	C	D	E
	Accounts	75	65	70	60	59
	Economics	65	72	78	89	67
	Management	70	68	90	72	58
	Mathematics	80	90	75	65	87

Fetch Marks of D in Management `=hlookup("D",A1:F5`

HLOOKUP(lookup_value, **table_array**, row_index_num, [range_lookup])

Next, we would define 'row_index_num,' the row number in the table_array from where who would return the value. In this case, it would be 4, as we are fetching the value from the fourth row of the given table.

Student name	A	B	C	D	E
Accounts	75	65	70	60	59
Economics	65	72	78	89	67
Management	70	68	90	72	58
Mathematics	80	90	75	65	87

Fetch Marks of D in Management `=HLOOKUP("D",A1:F5,4`

HLOOKUP(lookup_value, table_array, **row_index_num**, [range_lookup])

Suppose, if we require marks in economics, we will put row_index_num as 3.

The next is range_lookup. It makes HLOOKUP search for exact or approximate values. As we are looking out for an actual value, it would be False.

Student name	A	B	C	D	E
Accounts	75	65	70	60	59
Economics	65	72	78	89	67
Management	70	68	90	72	58
Mathematics	80	90	75	65	87

Fetch Marks of D in Management `=HLOOKUP("D",A1:F5,4,)`

HLOOKUP(lookup_value, table_array, row_index_num, [range_lookup])
- TRUE - Approximate match   Approximate match - the values in the first row of table_array must be sorted in ascending order
- FALSE - Exact match

The result would be 72.

	A	B	C	D	E	F	G
1	Student name	A	B	C	D	E	
2	Accounts	75	65	70	60	59	
3	Economics	65	72	78	89	67	
4	Management	70	68	90	72	58	
5	Mathematics	80	90	75	65	87	
6							
7							
8	Fetch Marks of D in Management	72					
9							

B8 fx =HLOOKUP("D",A1:F5,4,FALSE)

Here, HLOOKUP searches for a particular value in the table and returns an exact or approximate value.

Important Points To Keep In Mind About HLOOKUP

- It is a case-insensitive lookup. It will consider, for example, "TIM" and "tim" as the same.
- The 'Lookup_value' should be the topmost row of the 'table_array' when using HLOOKUP. If we need to look somewhere else, we must use another Excel formula.
- HLOOKUP supports wildcard characters such as '*' or '?' in the 'lookup_value' argument (only if 'lookup_value' is text).

Let's understand this using an example.

Suppose we are given the names of students and marks below:

Student name	Amy	Brain	Cathy	Donald	Ela
Accounts	75	65	70	60	59
Economics	65	72	78	89	67
Management	70	68	90	72	58
Mathematics	80	90	75	65	87

If we need to use the Horizontal Lookup formula to find the Math marks of a student whose name starts with a 'D,' the formula will be:

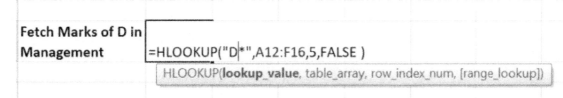

The wild character used is '*.'

4. #N/A error – It would be returned by HLOOKUP if 'range_lookup' is FALSE and the HLOOKUP function cannot find the 'lookup_value' in the given range. We can embed the function in IFERROR and display our message, for example, =IFERROR(HLOOKUP(A4, A1:I2, 2, FALSE), "No value found").

5. If the 'row_index_num' < 1, HLOOKUP would return #VALUE! error. If 'row_index_num'> several columns in 'table_array,' it would give the #REF! Error.

6. Remember HLOOKUP function in Excel can return only one value. This would be the first value n that matches the lookup value. What if there are a few identical records in the table? It is advisable to remove them or create a Pivot table and group them in that scenario. which can then use the array formula on the Pivot table to extract all duplicate values present in the lookup range.

Excel LOOKUP Function

The Excel LOOKUP function performs an approximate match lookup in a one-column or one-row range and returns the corresponding value from another one-column or one-row range. LOOKUP's default behavior makes it helpful in solving specific problems in Excel.

What Is A LOOKUP Function?

Lookup functions in Excel mean referencing a cell to match values in another row or column against the cell, retrieving the corresponding results from the respective rows and columns.

Uses Of LOOKUP Functions

Some benefits of LOOKUP functions are:

- You can find the exact or appropriate match by using the lookup function.
- Users can search for data vertically (columns) and horizontally (rows).
- It is simpler to use and does not require selecting the entire table.

Formula (Vector)

There are two forms of Lookup: Vector and Array.

The vector form of the LOOKUP function will search one row or one column of data for a specified value and then get the data from the same position in another row or column.

The formula for the function is as follows:

=LOOKUP(lookup_value, lookup_vector, [result_vector])

It Uses The Following Arguments:

Lookup_Value (Required Function): This is the value we will search for. It can be a logical value of TRUE or FALSE, a reference to a cell, number, or text.

Lookup_Vector (Required Function): This is the one-dimensional data we wish to search. Remember, we need to sort it in ascending order.

Result_Vector: An optional one-dimensional list of data from which we want to return a value. If supplied, the [result_vector] must be the same length as the lookup_vector. If the [result_vector] is omitted, the result is returned from the lookup_vector.

The array form of LOOKUP looks in the first row or column of an array for the specified value and returns a value from the same position in the last row or column. We need to use this form of LOOKUP when the values we want to match are in the first row or column of the array.

Formula (Array) LOOKUP Function

= LOOKUP(lookup_value, array)

The Arguments Are As Follows:
- **Lookup_Value (Required Argument):** We are searching for this value.
- **Array (Required Argument):** A range of cells that contains text, numbers, or logical values that we want to compare with the lookup_value.

Usage Notes

Use the LOOKUP function to look up a value in a one-column or one-row range and retrieve a value from the same position in another one-column or one-row field. The lookup function has two forms, vector, and array. Most of this article describes the vector form, but the last example below illustrates the array form.

LOOKUP has default behaviors that make it worthwhile when solving specific problems. For example, LOOKUP can retrieve an approximate-matched value instead of a position and find the last value in a row or column. LOOKUP assumes that values in lookup_vector are sorted in ascending order and always perform an approximate match. When LOOKUP can't find a match, it will match the next smallest value.

Example 1 - Basic Usage

In the example shown above, the formula in cell F5 returns the value of the match found in column B. Note that result_vector is not provided:

=LOOKUP(F4,B5:B9) // returns match in level

The formula in cell F6 returns the corresponding Tier value from column C. Notice in this case, both lookup_vector and result_vector are provided:

=LOOKUP(F4,B5:B9,C5:C9) // returns corresponding tier

LOOKUP automatically performs an approximate match in both formulas, and lookup_vector must be sorted in ascending order.

Example 2 - Last Non-Empty Cell

that can use LOOKUP to get the value of the previous filled (non-empty) cell in a column. In the screen below, the formula in F6 is:

=LOOKUP(2,1/(B:B<>""),B:B)

Get value of last non-empty cell with LOOKUP

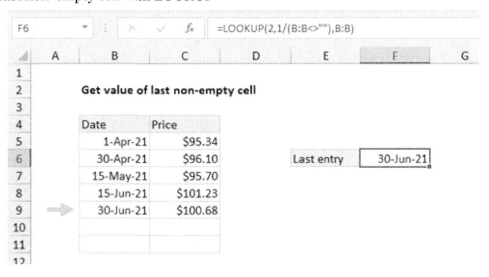

Note the use of a complete column reference. This is not an intuitive formula, but it works well. The key to understanding this formula is recognizing that the lookup_value of 2 is deliberately more significant than any values in the lookup_vector. Detailed explanation here.

Example 3 - Latest Price

Like the above example, who can use the lookup function to look up the latest price in data sorted in ascending order by date? In the screen below, the formula in G5 is:

=LOOKUP(2,1/(item=F5),price)

where the item (B5:B12) and price (D5:D12) are named ranges.

Example Of LOOKUP Function To Find The Latest Price

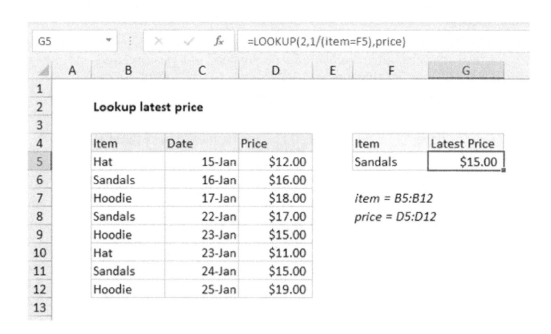

When lookup_value is more significant than all values in lookup_array, the default behavior is to "fall back" to the previous value. This formula exploits this behavior by creating an array that contains only 1s and errors, then deliberately looking for the value 2, which who will never find.

Example 4 - Array Form

The LOOKUP function has an array form as well. In the array configuration, LOOKUP takes just two arguments: the lookup_value and a single two-dimensional array:

LOOKUP(Lookup_Value, Array) // Array Form

LOOKUP evaluates the array and automatically changes behavior based on the array dimensions in the array form. If the variety is more comprehensive than tall, LOOKUP looks for the lookup value in the first row of the array (like HLOOKUP). If the array is more elevated than wide (or square), LOOKUP looks for the lookup value in the first column (like VLOOKUP). In either case, LOOKUP returns a value at the same position from the last row or column in the array. The example below shows how the array form works. The formula in F5 is configured to use a vertical array, and the formula in F6 is configured to use a horizontal array:

- =LOOKUP(E5,B5:C9) // vertical array
- =LOOKUP(E6,C11:G12) // horizontal array

LOOKUP Function Array Form Example

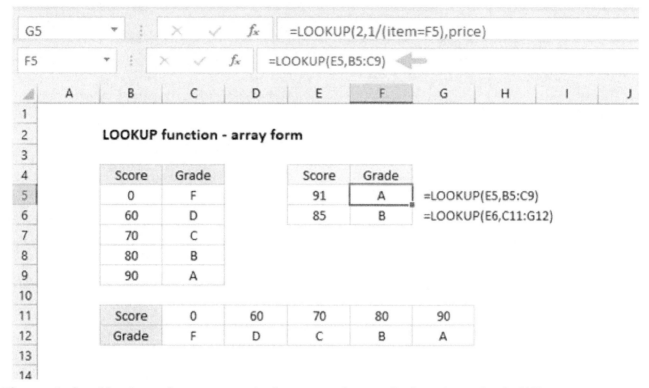

The vertical and horizontal arrays contain the same values; only the orientation is different.

Note: Microsoft discourages using the array form and suggests VLOOKUP and HLOOKUP as better options.

Excel CONCATENATE Function

The Excel CONCATENATE function concatenates (joins) up to 30 values together and returns the result as text.

Notes

- LOOKUP assumes that *lookup_vector* is sorted in ascending order.
- When *lookup_value* can't be found, LOOKUP will match the next smallest value.
- When *lookup_value* is greater than all values in *lookup_vector*, LOOKUP matches the last value.
- When *lookup_value* is less than the first value in *lookup_vector*, LOOKUP returns #N/A.
- *Result_vector* must be the same size as *lookup_vector*.
- LOOKUP is not case-sensitive

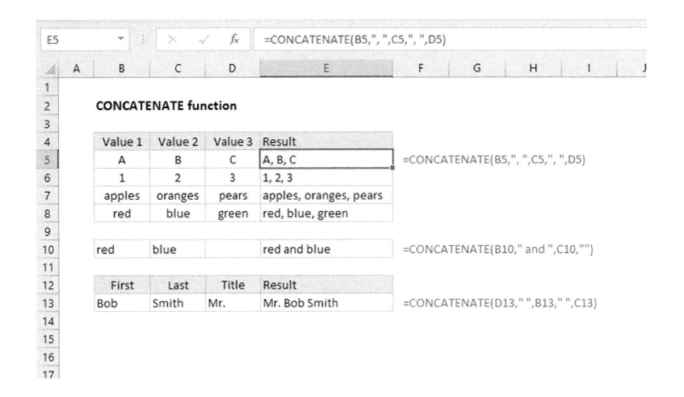

What Is "Concatenate" In Excel?

In essence, there are two ways to combine data in Excel spreadsheets:

- Merge cells
- Concatenate cells' values

When you merge cells, you "physically" merge two or more cells into a single cell. As a result, you have one larger compartment that is displayed across multiple rows and columns in your worksheet.

When you concatenate cells in Excel, you combine only the contents of those cells. In other words, concatenation in Excel is joining two or more values together. This method is often used to connect a few pieces of text that reside in different cells (technically, these are called text strings or simply strings) or insert a formula-calculated value in the middle of some text.

Syntax: =CONCATENATE (text1, text2, [text3], ...)

Arguments

- Text 1: The first text value to join together.
- Text 2: The second text value to join together.
- Text 3: [optional] The third text value to join together.

Usage Notes

The CONCATENATE function concatenates (joins) up to 30 values together and returns the result as text. In Excel 2019 and later, the CONCAT function and TEXTJOIN function are better, more flexible alternatives.

The CONCATENATE function accepts multiple arguments called text1, text2, text3, etc., up to 30 total. Values may be supplied as cell references and hard-coded text strings. Only the first argument is required, and values are concatenated in the order they appear. For example, to concatenate the value of A1 and B1, separated by a space, you can use CONCATENATE like this:

=CONCATENATE(A1," ",B1)

The result of this formula is the same as using the concatenation operator (&) manually like this:

=A1&" "&B1 // manual concatenation

The ampersand character (&) is an alternative to CONCATENATE. The result is the same, but the ampersand is more flexible and creates formulas that are shorter and (arguably) easier to read.

Number Formatting

Number formatting will be lost when concatenating numeric values like dates, times, percentages, etc. For example, with the date 1-Jul-2021 in cell A1, the date reverts to a serial number during concatenation:

=CONCATENATE("Date: ",A1) // returns "Date: 44378"

To apply formatting during concatenation use the TEXT function :

=CONCATENATE("The date is ",TEXT(A1,"mmmm d")) // "Date: July 1"

The CONCATENATE function will not handle ranges:

=CONCATENATE(A1:D1) // does not work

To concatenate values in ranges, see the CONCAT function. To concatenate many values with a standard delimiter, see the TEXTJOIN function. TEXTJOIN can do everything CONCAT can do but accept a delimiter and ignore empty values.

Excel Len Function

The Excel LEN function returns the length of a given text string as the number of characters. LEN will also count characters in numbers, but number formatting is not included.

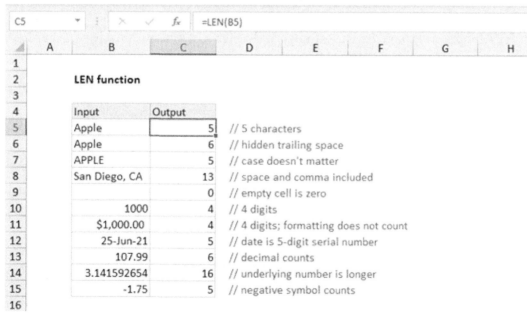

Purpose: Get the length of text.
Return Value: Number of characters
Syntax: =LEN (text)

Arguments
- **Text:** The text for which to calculate length.

Usage Notes

The LEN function returns the number of characters in a given text string. LEN takes just one argument, text. LEN counts the number of characters in the text, including space and punctuation, and returns a number. If text is an empty string ("") or text is a reference to an open-cell, LEN returns zero. LEN will also count characters in numbers, but number formatting is not included.

Examples

LEN returns the count of characters in a text string:

=LEN("apple") // returns 5

Space characters are included in the count:

=LEN("apple ") // returns 6

LEN also works with numeric values, but number formatting is not included:

=LEN(1000) // returns 4

=LEN($1,000) // returns 4

The LEN function often appears in other formulas that manipulate text somehow. For example, it can be used with the RIGHT and FIND functions to extract text to the right of a given character:

=RIGHT(A1,LEN(A1)-FIND(char,A1)) // get text to right of char

FIND returns the character's position, subtracted from the length, calculated with LEN. RIGHT returns the text to the right of that position.

Excel LEFT Function

The Excel LEFT function extracts a given number of characters from the left side of a supplied text string. For example, LEFT("apple",3) returns "app".

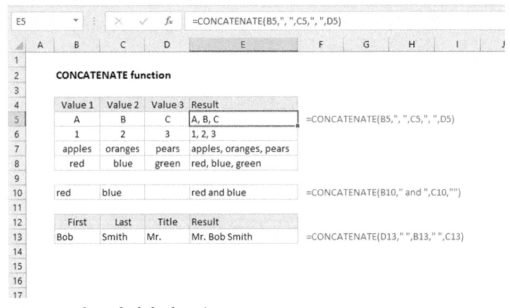

Purpose: Extract text from the left of a string

Return Value: One or more characters.

Syntax: =LEFT (text, [num_chars])

Arguments

- **Text:** The text from which to extract characters.
- **Num_Chars:** [optional] The number of characters to extract, starting on the left side of the text. Default = 1.

Usage Notes

The LEFT function extracts a given number of characters from the left side of a supplied text string. The second argument, called num_chars, controls the number of characters to pull. If num_chars is not provided, it defaults to 1. If num_chars is greater than the number of characters available, LEFT returns the entire text string.

Examples

To extract the first three characters of "January":

=LEFT("January",3) // returns "Jan"

If the optional argument num_chars is not provided, it defaults to 1:

=LEFT("ABC") // returns "A"

If num_chars exceeds the string length, LEFT returns the entire string:

=LEFT("apple",100) // returns "apple"

When LEFT is used on a numeric value, the result is the text:

=LEFT(1000,3) // returns "100" as text

The LEFT function is often combined with LEN and FIND to extract text in more complex formulas. For example, to split text at a specific character, use LEFT with the FIND function like this:

=LEFT(text,FIND(char,text)-1) // returns text to left of char

FIND returns the character's position, and LEFT returns all text to the left of that position. Full explanation here.

Excel PROPER Function

The Excel PROPER function capitalizes each word in a given text string. Numbers, punctuation, and spaces are not affected.

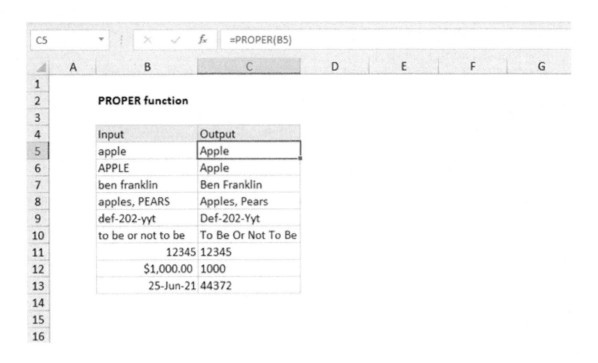

Purpose: Capitalize the first letter in each word

Return Value: Text in good case.

Syntax: =PROPER (text)

Arguments

- **Text:** The text that should convert to the proper point.

Usage Notes

The PROPER function capitalizes each word in a given text string. The PROPER function takes just one argument, text, which can be a text value or cell reference. PROPER first lowercase any uppercase letters, then capitalize each word in the provided text string. Numbers, punctuation, and spaces are not affected. PROPER will convert numbers to text with number formatting removed.

Examples

=PROPER("apple") // returns "Apple"

=PROPER("APPLE") // returns "Apple"

Numbers or punctuation characters inside a text string are unaffected:

=PROPER("XYY-020-kwp") // returns "Xyy-020-Kwp"

If a numeric value is given to PROPER, number formatting is removed. For example, if cell A1 contains the date June 26, 2021, date formatting will be lost, and PROPER will return a date serial number as text:

=PROPER(A1) // returns "44373"

Excel RIGHT Function

The Excel RIGHT function extracts a given number of characters from the right side of a supplied text string. For example, RIGHT("apple",3) returns "ple".

	A	B	C	D
			C5 =RIGHT(B5)	
2		RIGHT function		
4		Input	Output	Formula
5		ABC	C	=RIGHT(B5)
6		ABC	BC	=RIGHT(B6,2)
7		ABC	ABC	=RIGHT(B7,3)
8		Portland, OR	OR	=RIGHT(B8,2)
9		San Francisco, CA	CA	=RIGHT(B9,2)
10		google.com	com	=RIGHT(B10,3)
11		exceljet.net	net	=RIGHT(B11,3)
12		+1 303-512-4271	303-512-4271	=RIGHT(B12,12)
13		February 2001	2001	=RIGHT(B13,4)
14		2000 x 3000	3000	=RIGHT(B14,4)

Purpose: Extract text from the right of a string

Return Value: One or more characters.

Syntax: =RIGHT (text, [num_chars])

Arguments

- **Text:** The text from which to extract characters on the right.
- **Num_Chars:** [optional] The number of characters to extract, starting on the right. Optional, default = 1.

Usage Notes

The RIGHT function extracts a given number of characters from the right side of a supplied text string. The second argument, called num_chars, specifies the number of characters to pull. If num_chars is not provided, it defaults to 1. RIGHT returns the entire text string if num_chars is greater than the number of characters available.

Examples

In the example below, we extract the state code "OR" (Oregon) from the string "Portland, OR"

=RIGHT("Portland, OR",2) // returns "OR"

If the optional argument num_chars is not provided, it defaults to 1:

=RIGHT("ABC") // returns "C"

If num_chars exceeds the string length, LEFT returns the entire string:

=RIGHT("apple",100) // returns "apple"

When LEFT is used on a numeric value, the result is the text:

=RIGHT(1200,3) // returns "200" as text

The RIGHT function is often combined with LEN and FIND to extract text in more complex formulas. For example, to extract text in cell A1 to the right of a specific character (char), use RIGHT with the FIND and LEN functions like this:

=RIGHT(A1,LEN(A1)-FIND(char,A1)) // text to right char

FIND returns the character's position, and RIGHT returns the text to the right of that position.

Excel TEXTJOIN Function

The Excel TEXTJOIN function concatenates multiple values together with or without a delimiter. TEXTJOIN can concatenate values provided as cell references, ranges, or constants and can optionally ignore empty cells.

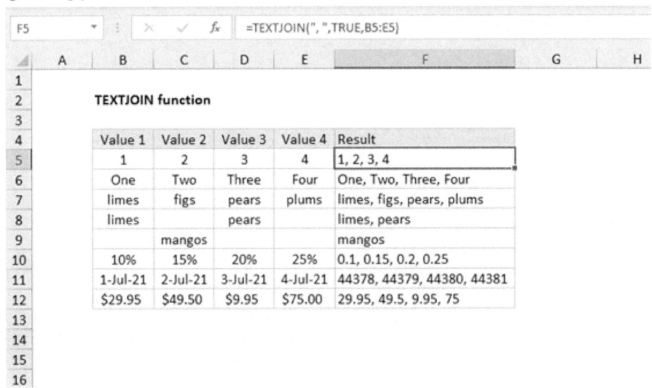

Purpose: Join text values with a delimiter

Return Value: Concatenated text

Syntax: =TEXTJOIN (delimiter, ignore_empty, text1, [text2], ...)

Arguments

- **Delimiter:** Separator between each text.
- **Ignore_Empty:** Whether to ignore empty cells or not.
- **Text 1:** First text value or range.
- **Text 2:** [optional] Second text value or range.

Usage Notes

The TEXTJOIN function concatenates multiple values together with or without a delimiter. TEXTJOIN can concatenate values provided as cell references, ranges, or constants and optionally ignore empty cells.

The TEXTJOIN function takes three required arguments: delimiter, ignore_empty, and text1. The delimiter is the text to use between values that are concatenated together and should be enclosed in double-quotes ("), for example, a space ("") or a comma with a space (, "). To use no delimiter, supply an empty string (").

Ignore_empty is a Boolean (TRUE/FALSE) value that controls whether empty values should be ignored or added to the result. This is often set to TRUE to avoid delimiters with no content in the development from TEXTJOIN. Text1 is the first value to join together. This can be a cell reference, a range, or a hard-coded text value. Subsequent optional arguments, text2, text3, text4, etc., can be provided up to 252 values.

Values are concatenated in the order they appear. With "Hello" in A1 and "World" in A2, the following formula returns "Hello World":

=TEXTJOIN(" ",TRUE,A1,A2) // returns "Hello World"

Changing the delimiter to a comma (", ") and reversing A1 and A2, we get "World, Hello":

=TEXTJOIN(", ",TRUE,A2,A1) // returns "World, Hello"

Concatenating a range

To join cells in the range A1:A3 with a comma and space, you can use TEXTJOIN like this:

=TEXTJOIN(", ",TRUE,A1:A3)

TEXTJOIN Basic Example

The second argument, ignore_empty, controls behavior for empty cells and text values. If set TRUE, empty values are skipped so that the delimiter is not repeated in the final result. If set to FALSE, TEXTJOIN will include open values in the output.

Name With Title

In the example below, TEXTJOIN is set up to concatenate names. Notice the cell reference for the title is provided first, followed by a range for First, Middle, and Last. Ignore empty is set to 1 (TRUE) to avoid adding extra space to names without Middle or Title values. The formula in F3 is:

=TEXTJOIN(" ",1,E3,B3:D3)

TEXTJOIN example with names

Number Formatting

When concatenating numbers, number formatting is lost. For example, with the date 1-Jul-2021 in cell A1, and 2-Jul-2021 in A2, the dates revert to serial numbers:

=TEXTJOIN("-",1,A1,A2) // returns "44378-44379"

Use the TEXT function to apply formatting during concatenation:

=TEXTJOIN("-",1,TEXT(A1,"mmm d"),TEXT(A2,"mmm d")) // "Jul 1-Jul 2"

The formula above returns the text "Jul 1-Jul 2".

Adjust the number formatting as desired.

TEXTJOIN Versus CONCAT

TEXTJOIN and CONCAT are newer functions in Excel that replace the older CONCATENATE function. Like the CONCAT function, TEXTJOIN will accept a range of cells to concatenate. The main difference is that TEXTJOIN also agrees with a delimiter when joining values together.

Excel TRIM Function

The Excel TRIM function strips extra spaces from text, leaving only a single space between words and no space characters at the start or end of the text.

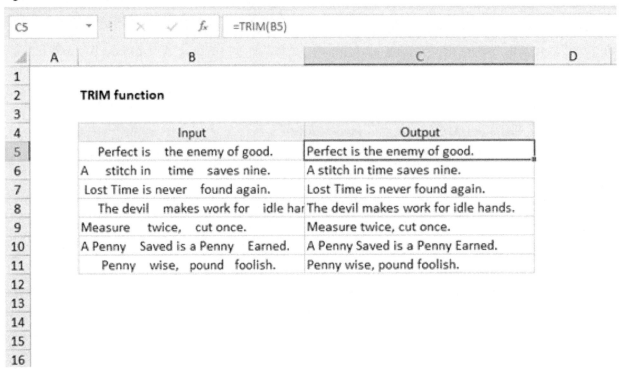

Purpose: Remove extra spaces from the text

Return Value: Text with extra spaces removed.

Syntax: =TRIM (text)

Arguments

- **Text:** The text from which to remove extra space.

Usage Notes

The TRIM function strips extra spaces from text, leaving only a single space between words and removing any leading or trailing space. For example:

=TRIM(" A stitch

in time. ") // returns "A stitch in time."

who can use the TRIM function together with the CLEAN function to remove extra space and strip out other non-printing characters:

=TRIM(CLEAN(A1)) // trim and clean

TRIM often appears in other more advanced text formulas. For example, the formula below will count the number of words in cell A1:

LEN(TRIM(A1))-LEN(SUBSTITUTE(A1," ",""))+1

Because this formula depends on single spaces to get an accurate word count, TRIM is used to normalize space before the count is calculated.

Excel UPPER function

The Excel UPPER function converts a text string to all uppercase letters. Numbers, punctuation, and spaces are not affected.

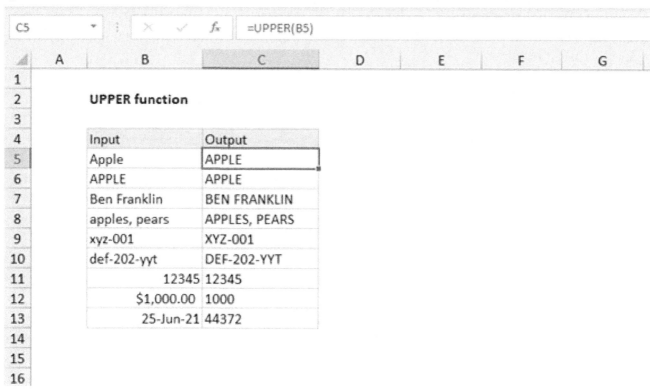

Purpose: Convert text to upper case

Return Value: Uppercase text.

Syntax: =UPPER (text)

Arguments

- **Text:** The text that is to be converted to upper case.

Usage Notes

The UPPER function converts a text string to all uppercase letters. The UPPER function takes just one argument, text, which can be a text value or cell reference. UPPER changes any lowercase characters in the text value to uppercase. Numbers, punctuation, and spaces are not affected. UPPER will convert numbers to text with number formatting removed.

Examples

=UPPER("Apple") // returns "APPLE"

=UPPER("pear") // returns "PEAR"

Numbers or punctuation characters inside a text string are unaffected:

=UPPER("xyy-020-kwp") // returns "XYY-020-KWP"

If a numeric value is given to UPPER, number formatting is removed. For example, if cell A1 contains the date June 26, 2021, date formatting will be lost, and UPPER will return a date serial number as text:

=UPPER(A1) // returns "44373"

If necessary, you can use the TEXT function to work around this limitation. Use TEXT to convert the number to a text value, then pass that value into UPPER:

=UPPER(TEXT(A1,"mmmm d, yyyy")) // returns "JUNE 26, 2021"

Excel LOWER Function

The Excel LOWER function converts a text string to all lowercase letters. Numbers, punctuation, and spaces are not affected.

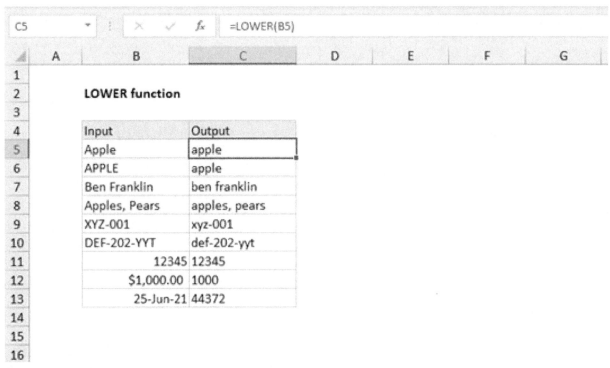

Purpose: Convert text to lower case

Return Value: Text in lower case.

Syntax: =LOWER (text)

Arguments

- **Text:** The text that should convert to reduce the chance.

Usage Notes

The LOWER function converts a text string to all lowercase letters. The LOWER function takes just one argument, text, which can be a text value or cell reference. LOWER changes any uppercase characters in the text value to lowercase. Numbers, punctuation, and spaces are not affected. LOWER will convert numbers to text with number formatting removed.

Examples

=LOWER("Apple") // returns "apple"

=LOWER("APPLE") // returns "apple"

Numbers or punctuation characters inside a text string are unaffected:

=LOWER("XYY-020-KWP") // returns "xyy-020-kwp"

If a numeric value is given to LOWER, number formatting is removed. For example, if cell A1 contains the date June 26, 2021, date formatting will be lost, and LOWER will return a date serial number as text:

=LOWER(A1) // returns "44373"

If necessary, you can use the TEXT function to work around this limitation. Use TEXT to convert the number to a text value, then pass that value into lower:

=LOWER(TEXT(A1,"mmmm d, yyyy")) // returns "June 26, 2021"

Excel MID Function

The Excel MID function extracts a given number of characters from the middle of a supplied text string. For example, =MID("apple",2,3) returns "ppl".

Input	Output	Formula
ABC	A	=MID(B5,1,1)
ABC	B	=MID(B6,2,1)
ABC	C	=MID(B7,3,1)
The cat in the hat	cat	=MID(B8,5,3)
The cat in the hat	hat	=MID(B9,16,3)
Las Vegas, NV 88901	Las Vegas	=MID(B10,1,9)
Las Vegas, NV 88901	NV	=MID(B11,12,2)
Las Vegas, NV 88901	88901	=MID(B12,15,5)
303-512-4271	303	=MID(B13,1,3)
James Brown	James	=MID(B14,1,FIND(" ",B14))
James Brown	Brown	=MID(B15,FIND(" ",B15)+1,30,

Purpose: Extract text from inside a string

Return Value: The characters are extracted.

Syntax: =MID (text, start_num, num_chars)

Arguments

- **Text:** The text to extract from.
- **Start_Num:** The location of the first character to extract.
- **num_Chars:** The number of characters to extract.

Usage Notes

The MID function extracts a given number of characters from the middle of a supplied text string. MID takes three arguments, all of which are required. The first argument, text, is the text string to start with. The second argument, start_num, is the position of the first character to extract. The third argument, num_chars, is the number of characters to pull. MID returns all remaining characters if num_chars is greater than the number of characters available.

Examples

The formula below returns three characters starting at the 5th character:

=MID("The cat in the hat",5,3) // returns "cat"

This formula will extract three characters starting at character 16:

=MID("The cat in the hat",16,3) // returns "hat"

If num_chars is more significant than remaining characters, MID will all remaining characters:

=MID("apple",3,100) // returns "ple"

MID can extract text from numbers, but the result is the text:

=MID(12348,3,4) // returns "348" as text

CHAPTER 6: MS EXCEL COUNTING FUNCTIONS

Excel COUNT Function

The Excel COUNT function returns a count of values that number. Numbers include negative numbers, percentages, dates, times, fractions, and formulas that return numbers. Empty cells and text values are ignored.

Purpose: Count numbers

Return Value: Count of numeric values

Syntax: =COUNT (value1, [value2], ...)

Arguments

- Value 1: An item, cell reference, or range.
- Value 2: [optional] An item, cell reference, or range.

Usage Notes

The COUNT function returns the count of numeric values in the list of supplied arguments. COUNT takes multiple arguments in the form value1, value2, value3, etc. Arguments can be individual hardcoded values, cell references, or ranges up to 255 arguments. All numbers are counted, including negative numbers, percentages, dates, times, fractions, and formulas that return numbers. Empty cells and text values are ignored.

Examples

The COUNT function counts numeric values and ignores text values:

=COUNT(1,2,3) // returns 3

=COUNT(1,"a","b") // returns 1

=COUNT("apple",100,125,150,"orange") // returns 3

Typically, the COUNT function is used on a range. For example, to count numeric values in the range A1:A10:

=COUNT(A1:A100) // count numbers in A1:A10

In the example shown, COUNT is set up to count numbers in the range B5:B15:

=COUNT(B5:B15) // returns 6

COUNT returns six since there are six numeric values in the range B5:B15. Text values and blank cells are ignored. Note that dates and times are numbers, therefore included in the count.

The COUNTA function works like the COUNT function, but COUNTA includes numbers and text in the count.

Functions For Counting

- To count numbers only, use the COUNT function.
- To count numbers and text, use the COUNTA function.
- To count with one condition, use the COUNTIF function.
- To count with multiple conditions, use the COUNTIFS function.
- To count empty cells, use the COUNTBLANK function.

Various Count Functions In Excel

Excel has several counting formulas that provide great flexibility in summarizing data. There are many circumstances where it is helpful to rely on items in Excel. Sometimes you just want to know how many cells have "something" in them, whatever that something is. Other times, you want to know how many cells don't have anything. Still, other times you might want to count only cells that include specific text. Fortunately, Excel has many ways to help you count data. Let's look at a few of the options available to you.

1. **COUNT Function**

The COUNT function returns the number of cells in a range or array that contains numeric values. These values can be integers, decimals, dates, or even numbers enclosed in quotations. It is not counted if a cell contains text, blank space, or any other non-number. This function uses the format COUNT(Value1, Value2,... value [n]), where "n" is limited to a maximum of 255. "Value1" is required, but the other values are optional. Suppose, for example, and you have a spreadsheet that holds importance in cells A2, A3, and A5; COUNT(A2:A5) would return "3."

2. **COUNTA Function**

In contrast to COUNT, COUNTA returns a value for the number of non-empty cells in a given range. The cells can contain data of any type, such as numbers, text, or logical values. The function will also count empty text "and error values, but blank cells won't be counted. The formula for this function is COUNTA(Value1, Value2,...Value[n]), where only "Value1" is required, and "n" can go up to 255 more items. For example, suppose you have three rows of numbers starting in A1 to A3, and each row stops at column D. To count the number of cells containing values, use COUNTA(A1:D1, A2:D2, A3:D3).

3. **COUNTBLANK Function**

If you need to count cells that contain no data, use COUNTBLANK. This function counts the number of empty cells in a range. Its format is COUNTBLANK(range). Cells containing open text values "are counted, but zeros are not. So, if you have a spreadsheet with values in cells A2 to A3 and A5, and cell A4 is left empty, COUNTBLANK(A2:A5) would return "1."

4. **COUNTIF Function**

If you need to count cells only if certain conditions are met, use COUNTIF. This function counts the number of cells in a range that meet a specific situation. The format is COUNTIF(range, criteria). You can use this function, for example, to count the number of clients in cells A2 to A10 whose last name is "Doe" as follows: COUNTIF (A2:A10, Doe). As another example, if the cells have a series of numbers and you want to find values of less than "10," use COUNTIF(A2:A10, "<10").

CHAPTER 7: MS EXCEL DATE AND TIME

Understanding Date And Time

Date Functions

What Is The DATE Function?

The DATE function is an Excel function that combines three different values (year, month, and day) to form a date. When used along with other Excel functions, who can use it to perform various tasks related to dates, including returning specified dates. The function is also proper when dates are input to other functions such as SUMIF or COUNTIF.

The DATE Function in Excel is categorized under Excel Date/Time Functions. It is the main function used to calculate dates in Excel. The DATE function is handy for financial analysts because financial modeling requires specific periods. For example, an analyst can use the DATE function in Excel in their economic model to dynamically link the year, month, and day from different cells into one function.

Key Learning Points

- The DATE function is a date/time function in Excel that combines three separate values to form a date
- The function, when combined with other Excel functions, has various applications in financial modeling
- The function is also proper when dates serve as an input to other functions, including SUMIF and COUNTIF
- The function has three required arguments: Year, Month, and Day
- #NUM! error is caused if the year argument is <0 or >=10000
- #VALUE! error is generated if non-numeric statements are entered

Excel displays dates as serial numbers as a default option. To view the results of this function as dates, you need to change the cell format to 'Date.'

Syntax

The syntax includes the following required arguments:

1. Year: Represents years whose value can range from a single digit (e.g., 2) to four digits (e.g., 1902). Microsoft Excel for Windows uses the 1900 date system as a default. So, if you enter a single digit' 2' in the year field, Excel will assume the year to be 1902. It is better to enter 4-digit years to avoid confusion.

2. Month: Represents months of a year whose value can range from 1 to 12, depending on the month (starting from January). For example, if we enter two as an argument, the function will return the month of February.

We can also enter a negative integer as a month. For example, if we enter DATE (2025,-2,2) as arguments, the function will subtract two months from the first month of 2025.

3. Day: The day of the month whose value can range from 1 to 31, representing the number of days in a month.

Similar to the month, the day can also be negative. For example, if we enter (2024,10,-2) as the day, it will subtract two days from the 1st day of October and show the date as September 28, 2024.

Important Points About The DATE Function

- If the year argument is less than 0 or greater than/equal to 10000, it results in a #NUM! error
- If a non-numeric argument is entered, it leads to a #VALUE! error
- By default, Excel stores dates as sequential numbers, starting from 01-01-1900 (1 for Excel). The cell in which this function is entered must be set to the date format. Who can do this by selecting the Date dropdown in the Number group (part of the Home tab)? You can also change the structure to date using the format cells option.

Example 1:

Using the information given below, combine the year, month, and day to form a date.

	A	B	C	D	E	F
7		Year	Month	Day		
8		2022	2.0	1.0		
9		2024	5.0	2.0		
10		2026	8.0	8.0		
11		2023	6.0	5.0		
12		2021	3.0	7.0		

The dates can be created in a single cell using the DATE function as shown below:

	A	B	C	D	E	F
7		Year	Month	Day	Date	
8		2022	2.0	1.0	01/02/2022	=DATE(B8,C8,D8)
9		2024	5.0	2.0	02/05/2024	=DATE(B9,C9,D9)
10		2026	8.0	8.0	08/08/2026	=DATE(B10,C10,D10)
11		2023	6.0	5.0	05/06/2023	=DATE(B11,C11,D11)
12		2021	3.0	7.0	07/03/2021	=DATE(B12,C12,D12)

Example 2:

We have been asked to add 15 days to each of the DATE function results in the previous example.

To solve the above, we need to add '+15' to the formula.

It is best to reference other cells in formulas instead of hardcoding. This allows you to update all affected formulas quickly rather than each one individually.

	A	B	C	D	E	F
17		Days	15.0			
18						
19		16/02/2022	=E8+$C$17			
20		17/05/2024	=E9+$C$17			
21		23/08/2026	=E10+$C$17			
22		20/06/2023	=E11+$C$17			
23		22/03/2021	=E12+$C$17			

The dates have changed to 15 days after the original arguments were calculated.

We can also add years and months to any of the dates. For example, if we want to calculate the 10th anniversary of each of these dates, we will add 10 to the year argument while leaving the other arguments unchanged.

Example 3:

From the information given above, calculate the number of dates after December 31, 2022.

This is an example of using the DATE function with other functions to get the desired result. Here, we will be using the COUNTIF function, which only counts cells that meet a specified condition.

As a first step, we assemble this date using the DATE function. This step allows us to easily change the days, which the function can update automatically.

A	B	C	D	E	F
28	Year	Month	Day	Date	
29	2022	12	31	31/12/2022	=DATE(B29,C29,D29)

Next, we use the COUNTIF function by selecting the date range and have asked it to count dates more significant than the date in cell E29.

A	B	C	D	E	F
28	Year	Month	Day	Date	
29	2022	12	31	31/12/2022	=DATE(B29,C29,D29)
30					
31		3.0	=COUNTIF(B19:B23,">"&E29)		

There are three dates in the range after this date.

The Main Function To Calculate Dates In Excel:

DATE Function

Get Current Date And Time:

TODAY: Returns today's date

NOW: Returns the current date and time

Convert Dates To/From The Text:

DATEVALUE: Converts a date in the text format to date format

TEXT: Converts a date to a text value

Retrieve Dates In Excel:

DAY: Returns the day of the month

MONTH: Returns the month of a specified date

YEAR: Returns the year of a specified date

EOMONTH: Returns on the last day of the month

WEEKDAY: Returns the day of the week

WEEKNUM: Returns the week number of a date

Calculate Date Difference:

DATEDIF: Returns the difference between two dates

EDATE: Returns a date N months before or after the start date

YEARFRAC: Calculates the fraction of the year between 2 dates

Calculate Workdays:

WORKDAY: Returns a date N working days in the future or the past

WORKDAY.INTL: Returns a date N weekdays from the start date with custom weekends

NETWORKDAYS: Returns the number of workdays between two dates

NETWORKDAYS.INTL: Returns the number of workdays between two dates with custom weekends

Excel DATE Function

DATE(year, month, day) returns a date's serial number based on your specified year, month, and day values.

When working with dates in Excel, DATE is the essential function to understand. The point is that other Excel date functions do not always can recognize dates entered in the text format. So, when performing date calculations in Excel, you'd better supply dates using the DATE function to ensure the correct results.

Here Are A Few Excel Date Formula Examples:

1. =DATE(2015, 5, 20): Returns a serial number corresponding to 20-May-2015.

2. =DATE(YEAR(TODAY()), MONTH(TODAY()), 1): Returns the first day of the current year and month.

3. =DATE(2015, 5, 20)-5: Subtracts 5 days from May 20, 2015.

Formula	Result	Explanation
=DATE(2015, 5, 20)	05/20/2015	Returns 20-May-2015
=DATE(YEAR(TODAY()), MONTH(TODAY()), 1)	05/01/2015	Returns the 1st day of the current year and month
=DATE(2015, 5, 20)-5	05/15/2015	Subtracts 5 days from May 20, 2015

Excel DATE Formula Examples

At first sight, the Excel DATE function looks very simple; however, it does have several specificities pointed out in the Excel DATE tutorial.

Below you will find a few more examples where the Excel DATE function is part of more extensive formulas:

- Subtracting two dates in Excel
- Adding or subtracting days to a date
- How to convert week number to date
- Find the first day of the month
- Calculate the number of days in a month

1. Excel DAYS360 Function

The Excel DAYS360 function returns the number of days between two dates based on a 360-day year, where all months are assumed to have 30 days. For example, the formula =DAYS360("1-Jan-2021","31-Dec-2021") returns 360 days.

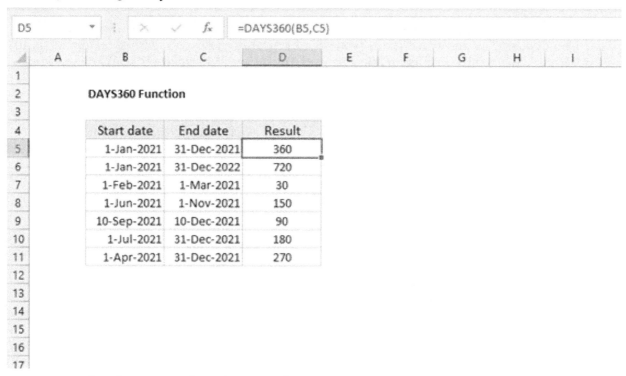

Purpose: Get days between 2 dates in a 360-day year

Return Value: A number represents days.

Syntax: =DAYS360 (start_date, end_date, [method])

Arguments

- **Start_date:** The start date.
- **End_date:** The end date.
- **Method:** [optional] Day count method. FALSE (default) = US method, TRUE = European method.

Usage notes

The DAYS360 function returns the number of days between two dates, based on a year where all months have 30 days. Both dates must be valid Excel dates or text values that can be parsed as dates. The DAYS360 function only works with whole numbers; time values are ignored.

Method

DAYS360 takes an optional argument called a method that can be set to either TRUE or FALSE. When the method is FALSE (default), DAYS360 uses a US method to compute days. When the start date is the last day of the month, it is treated as the 30th day of that month. When the end date is the last day of the month, and the start date is less than 30, the end date is treated as the 1st of the following month; otherwise, the end date is treated as the 30th of the same month.

DAYS360 uses a European method to calculate days if the process is set to TRUE. In this scheme, start and end dates equal to the 31st of a month are assigned to the 30th of the same month.

Examples

In the formula below, DAYS360 returns 360 days with a start date of January 1, 2021, and December 31, 2021.

=DAYS360("1-Jan-2021","31-Dec-2021") // returns 360

The result of 360 is based on 12 months * 30 days in each month.

Note: In general, storing and parsing text values that represent dates is a terrible form and should be avoided because it can introduce errors and parsing problems. Working with native Excel dates is a better approach.

With a start date of July 1, 2021, in A1, and an end date of December 31, 2021, in B1, the formula below returns 180:

=DAYS360(A1,B1) // returns 180

To create a date from scratch in a formula, use the DATE function. The formula below returns 90:

=DAYS360(DATE(2021,1,1),DATE(2021,4,1)) // returns 90

Notes

- The DAYS360 function only works with whole numbers and ignores time.
- If dates are not recognized, DAYS360 returns the #VALUE! Error.
- If dates are out of range, DAYS360 returns the #NUM! Error.

2. Excel DATEDIF Function

The Excel DATEDIF function returns the difference between two date values in years, months, or days. The DATEDIF (Date + Dif) function is a "compatibility" function from Lotus 1-2-3. It is only documented in Excel 2000, but you can use it in your formulas in all Excel versions since that time.

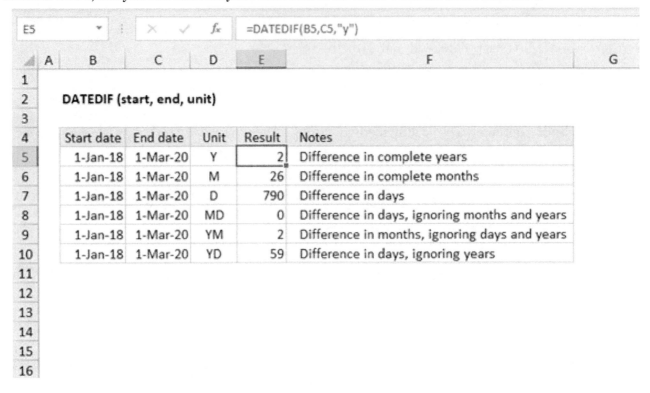

Note: Excel won't help you fill out the arguments for DATEDIF like other functions, but it will work when configured correctly.

Purpose: Get days, months, or years between two dates

Return Value: A number represents the time between two dates

Syntax: =DATEDIF (start_date, end_date, unit)

Arguments

- Start_date: Start date in Excel date serial number format.
- End_date: End date in Excel date serial number format.
- Unit: The time unit to use (years, months, or days).

Usage Notes

The DATEDIF (Date + Dif) function is a "compatibility" function from Lotus 1-2-3. For a long time, official documentation on DATEDIF was sparse. Even now (May 2021), Excel will not help you fill in arguments for DATEDIF like other functions. As the late Chip Pearson once wrote in his immortal words: DATEDIF is treated as the drunk cousin of the Formula family. Excel knows it lives a happy and valuable life but will not speak of it in polite conversation. Yet DATEDIF remains a beneficial function for specific problems.

Time Units

The DATEDIF function can calculate the time between a start_date and an end_date in years, months, or days. The time unit is specified with the unit argument, supplied as text. The table below summarizes available unit values and the result for each. Time units can be given in upper or lower case (i.e., "ym" is equivalent to "YM").

Unit Result

- "y" Difference in complete years
- "m" Difference in entire months
- "d" Difference in days
- "MD" Difference in days, ignoring months and years
- "ym" Difference in months, missing years
- "yd" Difference in days, missing years

Example 1 - Basic Usage

In the example shown above, column B contains the date January 1, 2016, and column C has the date March 1, 2018. In column E:

E5=DATEDIF(B5,C5,"y") // returns 2

E6=DATEDIF(B6,C6,"m") // returns 26

E7=DATEDIF(B7,C7,"d")// returns 790

Example 2 - Difference In Days

The DATEDIF function can calculate the difference between dates in days in three different ways: (1) total days, (2) days ignoring years, and (3) days ignoring months and years. The screenshot below shows all three methods, with a start date of June 15, 2015, and end date of September 15, 2021:

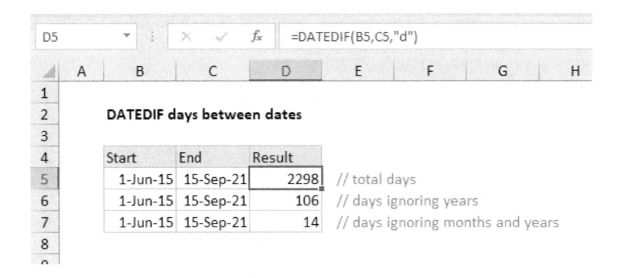

DATEDIF Difference In Days

The formulas used for these calculations are as follows:

=DATEDIF(B5,C5,"d") // total days

=DATEDIF(B6,C6,"yd") // days ignoring years

=DATEDIF(B7,C7,"md") // days ignoring months and years

Note: That because Excel dates are just large serial numbers, the first formula does not need DATEDIF and could be written as simply the end date minus the start date:

=C5-B5 // end-start = total days

Example 3 - Difference In Months

The DATEDIF function can calculate the difference between dates in months: (1) total complete months and (2) complete months ignoring years. The screenshot below shows both methods, with a start date of June 15, 2015, and end date of September 15, 2021:

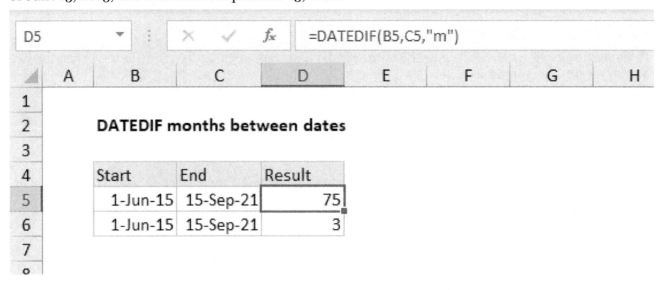

102 | Page

DATEDIF Difference In Months

=DATEDIF(B5,C5,"m") // complete months

=DATEDIF(B6,C6,"ym") // complete months ignoring years

DATEDIF always rounds months down to the last complete number of months. This means DATEDIF rounds the result down even when it is very close to the next whole month. In addition, DATEDIF may not work as expected when start and end dates are "end of month" dates. This example provides more information and alternatives.

Example 4 - Difference In Years

The DATEDIF function can calculate the difference between dates in whole years with just one method, shown below:

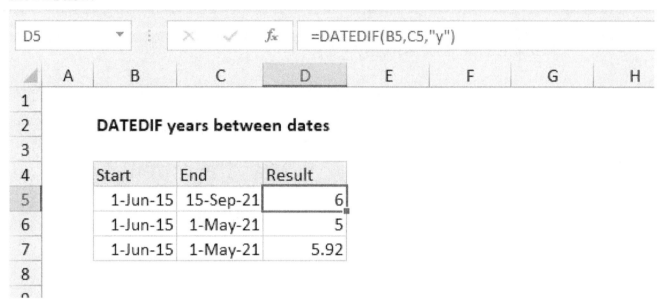

DATEDIF Difference In Years

=DATEDIF(B5,C5,"y") // complete years

=DATEDIF(B6,C6,"y") // complete years

=YEARFRAC(B7, C7) // fractional years with YEARFRAC

Notice in row 6 the difference is almost six years, but not quite. Because DATEDIF only calculates complete years, the result is still 5. In row 7, we use the YEARFRAC function to calculate a more accurate result.

Example 5 - Age From Birthday

who can use the DATEDIF function and the TODAY function to calculate the current age from a birth date? With a full birth date in A1, the formula is:

=DATEDIF(A1,TODAY(),"y")

Notes

- Excel will not help you fill in the DATEDIF function like other functions.
- DATEDIF will throw a #NUM error if the start_date is greater than the end_date. If you are working with a more complex formula where start dates and end dates may be unknown or out of bounds, you can trap the error with the IFERROR function or use MIN and MAX to sort out dates.

- Microsoft recommends not using the "MD" value for the unit because it "may result in a negative number, a zero, or an inaccurate result."

3. Excel EOMONTH Function

The Excel EOMONTH function returns the last day of the month, n months in the past or future. You can use EDATE to calculate expiration dates, due dates, and other dates that need to land on the last day of a month. Use a positive value for months to move forward in time, and a negative number to move back in time.

Date	Months	Result	Notes
30-Mar-2019	1	30-Apr-2019	Last day 1 month later
30-Mar-2019	-1	28-Feb-2019	Last day 1 month earlier
15-Feb-2019	3	31-May-2019	Last day 3 months later
15-Feb-2019	-6	31-Aug-2018	Last day 6 months earlier
15-Mar-2019	18	30-Sep-2020	Last day 18 months later
5-Jul-2018	24	31-Jul-2020	Last day 2 years later
12-Sep-2018	60	30-Sep-2023	Last day 5 years later

Purpose: Get last day of months in future or past

Return Value: Last day of month date

Syntax: =EOMONTH (start_date, months)

Arguments

- **Start_date:** A date that represents the start date in a valid Excel serial number format.
- **Months:** The number of months before or after start_date.

Usage Notes

The EOMONTH function returns the last day of the month a given number of months in the past or future. You can use EOMONTH to calculate expiration dates, due dates, and other dates that need to land on the last day of a month. The EOMONTH function takes two arguments: start_date and months. Start_date must be a valid Excel date. The months argument specifies how many months in the future or past to move – use a positive number to move forward in time, and a negative number to move back in time.

EOMONTH returns a serial number corresponding to an Excel date. To display the result as a date, apply a number format of your choice.

Example 1 - Basic Usage

With May 12, 2017 in cell B5:

=EOMONTH(B5,0) // returns May 31, 2017

=EOMONTH(B5,4) // returns Sep 30, 2017

=EOMONTH(B5,-3) // returns Feb 28, 2017

You can use EOMONTH to move through years as well:

=EOMONTH(B5,12) // returns May 31, 2018

=EOMONTH(B5,36) // returns May 31, 2020

=EOMONTH(B5,-24) // returns May 31, 2015

Example 2 - Last Day Of Current Month

To get the last day of the current month, combine the TODAY function with EOMONTH like this:

=EOMONTH(TODAY(),0) // last day of current month

The TODAY function returns the current date to the EOMONTH function. EOMONTH, with zero (0) for months, uses the current date to calculate the last day of the current month.

Example 3 - First Day Of Current Month

Although EOMONTH returns the last day of the month, you can use EOMONTH to get the first day month of the current month like this:

=EOMONTH(TODAY(),-1)+1 // first day of current month

See links below for more examples of how to use the EOMONTH function in formulas.

Notes
- For months, use a positive number for future dates and a negative number for past dates.
- EOMONTH will return the #VALUE error if the start date is not a valid date.
- If the start date has a fractional time attached, it will be removed.
- If the months argument contains a decimal value, it will be removed.
- To move any date n months into the future or past, see the EDATE function.
- EOMONTH returns a date serial number, which must be formatted as a date.

4. Excel DATEVALUE Function

The Excel DATEVALUE function converts a date as a text string into a valid Excel date. For example, the formula =DATEVALUE("3/10/1975") returns a serial number (27463) in the Excel date system that represents March 10, 1975. Proper Excel dates are more valuable than text dates since who can directly manipulate them with formulas and pivot tables.

	A	B	C	D
2		**DATEVALUE function**		
4		Input	Output	Formatted
5		3/10/1975	27463	10-Mar-1975
6		23-Aug-99	36395	23-Aug-1999
7		January 1, 2001	36892	1-Jan-2001
8		Dec 25, 2010	40537	25-Dec-2010
9		May 21, 2014	41780	21-May-2014
10		5/25/2017	42880	25-May-2017
11		March 2019	43525	1-Mar-2019
12		4/1	44287	1-Apr-2021
13		April 15	44301	15-Apr-2021
14		Nov 12	44512	12-Nov-2021
15		5-Sep-2021	#VALUE!	#VALUE!

C5: =DATEVALUE(B5)

Purpose: Convert the data in text format to a valid date

Return Value: A valid Excel time as a serial number

Syntax: =DATEVALUE (date_text)

Arguments

- **Date_text:** A valid date in text format.

Usage Notes

Sometimes, dates in Excel appear as text values that are not recognized as valid dates. The DATEVALUE function converts a date represented as a text string into a valid Excel date. Proper Excel dates are more valuable than text dates since they can be formatted as a date and directly manipulated with other formulas.

The DATEVALUE function takes just one argument, called date_text. If date_text is a cell address, the cell's value must be text. If date_text is entered directly into the formula, it must be enclosed in quotes.

Examples

To illustrate how the DATEVALUE function works, the formula below shows how the text "3/10/1975" is converted to the date serial number 27463 by DATEVALUE:

=DATEVALUE("3/10/1975") // returns 27463

Note: That DATEVALUE returns a serial number, 27463, representing March 10, 1975, in Excel's date system. Who must apply a date number format to display this number as a date?

In the example shown, column B contains dates entered as text values, except for B15, including a valid date. The formula in C5, copied down, is:

=DATEVALUE(B5)

Column C shows the number returned by DATEVALUE, and column D shows the exact number formatted as a date. Notice that Excel makes certain assumptions about missing day and year values. Missing days become the number 1, and the current year is used if no year value is available.

Alternative formula

Notice that the DATEVALUE formula in C15 fails with a #VALUE! Error because cell B15 already contains a valid date. This is a limitation of the DATEVALUE function. If you have a mix of good and invalid dates, you can try the simple formula below as an alternative:

=A1+0

The math operation of adding zero will cause Excel will try to coerce the value in A1 into a number. If Excel can parse the text into a valid date, it will return a valid serial number. If the date is already a valid Excel date (i.e., a serial number), adding zero will have no effect and generate no error.

Notes

- DATEVALUE will return a #VALUE error if date_text refers does not contain a date formatted as text.

5. Excel TODAY Function

The Excel TODAY function returns the current date, updated continuously when a worksheet is changed or opened. The TODAY function takes no arguments. You can format the value returned by TODAY with a date number format. If you need the current date and time, use the NOW function.

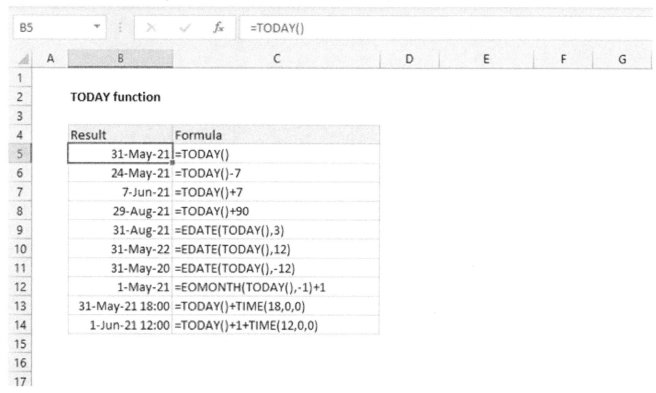

Purpose: Get the current date

Return Value: Excel date as a serial number

Syntax: =TODAY ()

Usage Notes

The TODAY function returns the current date and will continually update each time the worksheet is updated. Use F9 to force the worksheet to recalculate and update the value.

The value returned by the TODAY function is a standard Excel date. To display the result as a date:

- Apply a date number format.
- Optionally customize the number format as you like.
- Use the NOW function if you want the current date with a time value.

Examples

The TODAY function can be used independently or combined with other parts. The formulas below show how who can use the TODAY function in various ways:

- =TODAY() // current date
- =TODAY()-7 // one week in past
- =TODAY()+7 // one week in future
- =TODAY()+90 // 90 days from today
- =EDATE(TODAY(),3) // 3 months from today
- =EDATE(TODAY(),12) // 1 year from today
- =EDATE(TODAY(),-12) // 1 year in the past
- =EOMONTH(TODAY(),-1)+1 // first day of current month
- =TODAY()+TIME(18,0,0) // today at 6:00 PM
- =TODAY()+1+TIME(12,0,0) // tomorrow at noon

Static Date And Time

If you need a static date and time that won't change,

You can use the following shortcuts:

- Insert current date - Control + ;
- Insert current time - Control + Shift + :
- To enter both values in a single cell, join the date, space, and time.

Formatting Results

The result of TODAY is a serial number representing a valid Excel date. You can format the value returned by TODAY using any standard date format. You can use the TEXT function to build a text message that includes the current date:

="The current date is "&TEXT(TODAY(),"mmm d")

To return a message like "The current date is May 31".

6. Excel DAY Function

The Excel DAY function returns the day of the month as a number between 1 to 31 from a given date. You can use the DAY function to extract a day number from a date into a cell. You can also use the DAY function to extract and feed a day value into another function, like the DATE function.

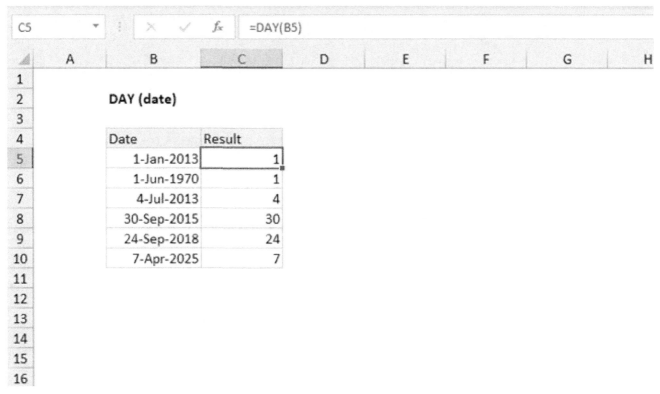

Purpose: Get the day as a number (1-31) from a date

Return Value: A number (1-31) represents the day component in a date.

Syntax: =DAY (date)

Arguments

- **Date:** A valid Excel date.

Usage Notes

The DAY function returns the day value on a given date as a number between 1 to 31 from a given date. For example, with the date January 15, 2019, in cell A1:

=DAY(A1) // returns 15

You can use the DAY function to extract a day number from a date into a cell. You can also use the DAY function to extract and feed a day value into another function, like the DATE function. For example, to change the year of a date in cell A1 to 2020, but leave the month and day as-is, you can use a formula like this:

=DATE(2020,MONTH(A1),DAY(A1))

7. Excel EDATE Function

The Excel EDATE function returns the date on the same day of the month, n months in the past or future. You can use EDATE to calculate expiration dates, maturity dates, and other due dates. Use a positive value for months to get a date in the future, and a negative value for dates in the past.

	D5			fx	=EDATE(B5,C5)	

EDATE function

Start	Months	Result	Notes
1-Feb-2018	1	1-Mar-2018	One month later
1-Feb-2018	-1	1-Jan-2018	One month earlier
15-Feb-2019	3	15-May-2019	Three months later
30-Mar-2019	-1	28-Feb-2019	Last day in Feb, not Feb 30
30-Mar-2019	12	30-Mar-2020	One year later
30-Mar-2019	24	30-Mar-2021	Two years later
1-Jun-2020	120	1-Jun-2030	10 years in the future
15-Sep-2020	-60	15-Sep-2015	5 years in the past

Purpose: Shift date n months in future or past

Return Value: New date as Excel serial number

Syntax: =EDATE (start_date, months)

Arguments

- **Start_date:** Start date as a valid Excel date.
- **Months:** Number of months before or after start_date.

Usage Notes

The EDATE function can add or subtract whole months from a date. You can use EDATE to calculate expiration dates, contract dates, due dates, anniversary dates, retirement dates, and other dates in the future or past. The EDATE function takes two arguments: start_date and months. Start_date must be a valid Excel date. The month's argument specifies how many months in the future or past to move – use a positive number to move forward in time, and a negative number to move back in time.

EDATE will return a serial number corresponding to a date. To display the result as a date, apply a number format of your choice.

Example 1 - Basic Usage

If A1 contains the date February 1, 2018, you can use EDATE like this:

=EDATE(A1,1) // returns March 1, 2018

=EDATE(A1,3) // returns May 1, 2018

=EDATE(A1,-1) // returns January 1, 2018

=EDATE(A1,-2) // returns December 1, 2017

Example 2 - 6 Months From Today

To use EDATE with today's date, you can combine it with the TODAY function. For example, to create a date exactly 6 months from today, you can use:

=EDATE(TODAY(),6) // 6 months from today

Example 3 - Move By Years

To use the EDATE function to move by years, multiply by 12. For example, to move the date forward 2 years, you can use either of these formulas:

=EDATE(A1,24) // forward 2 years

=EDATE(A1,2*12) // forward 2 years

The second form is handy when you already have a value for years in another cell and want to convert to months inside EDATE.

Example 4 - End Of Month

EDATE is clever about rolling "end of month" dates forwards or backwards, and will adjust year, month, and day values as necessary. For example EDATE will maintain the last day of month when a day is 31:

- =EDATE("31-Jan-2019",1) // returns 28-Feb-2019
- =EDATE("31-Jan-2019",2) // returns 31-Mar-2019
- =EDATE("31-Jan-2019",3) // returns 30-Apr-2019
- =EDATE("31-Jan-2019",4) // returns 31-May-2019
- =EDATE("31-Jan-2019",5) // returns 30-Jun-2019

EDATE will also respect leap years:

- =EDATE("31-Jan-2020",1) // returns 29-Feb-2020

However, EDATE will not maintain an end of the month when the day value is less than 31. For example:

=EDATE("28-Feb-2019",1) // returns 28-Mar-2019

If an end-of-month date is a requirement, the EOMONTH function is a better option.

Example 5 - EDATE With Time

The EDATE function will strip times from dates that include time (sometimes called a "DateTime"). To preserve the time in a date, you can use a formula like this:

=EDATE(A1,n)+MOD(A1,1)

Here, the MOD function is used to extract the time from the date in A1 and add it back to the result from EDATE.

8. Excel DATE Function

The Excel DATE function creates a valid date from the individual year, month, and day components. The DATE function is useful for assembling dates that need to change dynamically based on other values in a worksheet.

	A	B	C	D	E	F	G
1							
2		**DATE Function**					
3							
4		Year	Month	Day	Result		
5		1995	1	1	1-Jan-1995		
6		2010	1	1	1-Jan-2010		
7		2021	1	1	1-Jan-2021		
8		2021	2	1	1-Feb-2021		
9		2021	3	1	1-Mar-2021		
10		2021	4	15	15-Apr-2021		
11		2021	6	30	30-Jun-2021		
12		2021	7	10	10-Jul-2021		
13		2021	12	25	25-Dec-2021		
14		2021	12	31	31-Dec-2021		
15		2099	1	1	1-Jan-2099		
16							

E5 =DATE(B5,C5,D5)

Purpose: Create a date with year, month, and day

Return Value: A valid Excel date

Syntax: =DATE (year, month, day)

Arguments

- **Year:** Number for a year.
- **Month:** Number for a month.
- **Day:** Number for the day.

Usage Notes

The DATE function creates a date using individual year, month, and day arguments. Each argument is provided as a number, and a result is a serial number that represents a valid Excel date. Apply a date number format to display the output from the DATE function as a date.

In general, the DATE function is the safest way to create a date in an Excel formula, because year, month, and day values are numeric and unambiguous, in contrast to text representations of dates which can be misinterpreted.

Note: to move an existing date forward or backward in time, see the EDATE and EOMONTH.

Example 1 - Hard-Coded Numbers

For example, you can use the DATE function to create the dates January 1, 1999, and June 1, 2010 with the following syntax:

=DATE(1999,1,1) // returns Jan 1, 1999

=DATE(2010,6,1) // returns Jun 1, 2010

Example 2 - Cell Reference

The DATE function is useful for assembling dates that need to change dynamically based on other inputs in a worksheet. For example, with 2018 in cell A1, the formula below returns the date April 15, 2018:

=DATE(A1,4,15) // Apr 15, 2018

If A1 is then changed to 2019, the DATE function will return the date for April 15, 2019.

Example 3 - With SUMIFS, COUNTIFS

The DATE function can be used to supply dates as inputs to other functions like SUMIFS or COUNTIFS since you can easily assemble a date using year, month, and day values that come from a cell reference or formula result. For example, to count dates greater than January 1, 2019, in a worksheet where A1, B1, and C1 contain the year, month, and day values (respectively), you can use a formula like this:

=COUNTIF(range,">"&DATE(A1,B1,C1))

The result of COUNTIF will update dynamically when A1, B1, or C1 are changed.

Example 4 - The First Day Of The Current Year

To return the first day of the current year, you can use the DATE function like this:

=DATE(YEAR(TODAY()),1,1) // first of year

This is an example of nesting. The TODAY function returns the current date to the YEAR function. The YEAR function extracts the year and returns the result to the DATE function as the year argument. The month and day arguments are hard-coded as 1. The result is the first day of the current year, a date like "January 1, 2021".

Note: The DATE function returns a serial number and not a formatted date. In Excel's date system, dates are serial numbers. January 1, 1900, is number 1 and later dates are larger numbers. To display date values in a human-readable date format, apply the number format of your choice.

9. Excel WORKDAY Function

The Excel WORKDAY function takes a date and returns the nearest working day n days in the future or past. You can use the WORKDAY function to calculate things like ship dates, delivery dates, and completion dates that need to take into account working and non-working days.

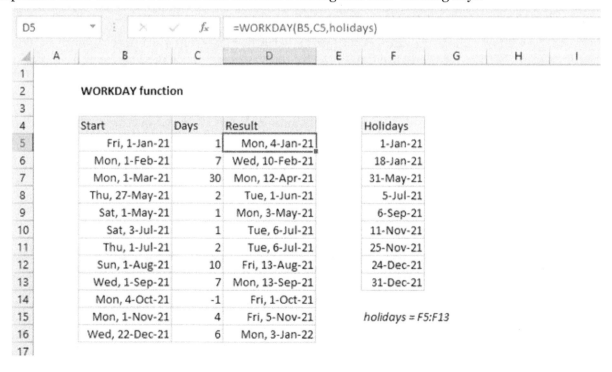

Purpose: Get a date n working days in the future or past

Return Value: A serial number representing a particular date in Excel.

Syntax: =WORKDAY (start_date, days, [holidays])

Arguments
- **Start_date:** The date from which to start.
- **Days:** The working days before or after start_date.
- **Holidays:** [optional] A list of dates that should be considered non-work days.

Usage Notes

The WORKDAY function returns the nearest working day n days in the future or past. WORKDAY can be used to calculate due dates, delivery dates, and other dates that should exclude non-working days.

The WORKDAY function takes three arguments: start_date, days, and holidays. Start_date must be a valid Excel date. The day's argument is the number of days in the future or past to calculate a workday. Use a positive number for days to calculate future dates and a negative number for past dates. The holiday is an optional argument to specify non-working days. Holidays should be provided as a range that contains valid Excel dates. If holidays are not provided, WORKDAY will treat only Saturdays and Sundays as non-working days.

When calculating a result, WORKDAY does not include the start date as a workday.

Example 1 - Basic Usage

In the formula below, WORKDAY is given Friday, January 1, 2021, for start_date, 1 for days, and F5:F13 for holidays. The result is Monday, January 4, 2021, since Saturday and Sunday are excluded:

=WORKDAY("1-Jan-2021",1,F5:F13)// returns 4-Jan-2021

If the start date is moved back one day to Thursday, December 31, 2021, the result is the same, since January 1 is a holiday, and Saturday and Sunday are also excluded:

=WORKDAY("31-Dec-2020",1,F5:F13) // returns 4-Jan-2021

Example 2 - Worksheet As Shown

In the worksheet shown above, Column B contains a variety of different start dates, column C contains the number of days to move, and "holidays" are the named range F5:F13. The formula in column D (copied down) is:

=WORKDAY(B5,C5,holidays)

At each row, WORKDAY returns the nearest workday in column D, based on the given start date and days to offset.

Weekends

By default, WORKDAY will exclude weekends (Saturday and Sunday).

10. Excel YEAR Function

The Excel YEAR function returns the year component of a date as a 4-digit number. You can use the YEAR function to extract a year number from a date into a cell or to extract and feed a year value into another formula, like the DATE function.

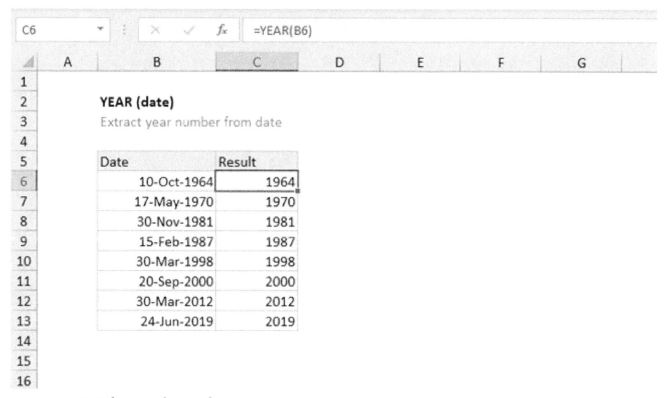

Purpose: Get the year from a date
Return Value: Year as a 4-digit number
Syntax: =YEAR (date)
Arguments
- **Date:** A valid Excel date.

Usage Notes

The YEAR function extracts the year from a given date as a 4-digit number. For example:

=YEAR("23-Aug-2012") // returns 2012

=YEAR("11-May-2019") // returns 2019

You can use the YEAR function to extract a month number from a date into a cell, or to feed a month number into another function like the DATE function:

=DATE(YEAR(A1),1,1) // first of same year

11. Excel MONTH Function

The Excel MONTH function extracts the month from a given date as a number between 1 to 12. You can use the MONTH function to extract a month number from a date into a cell or to feed a month number into another function like the DATE function.

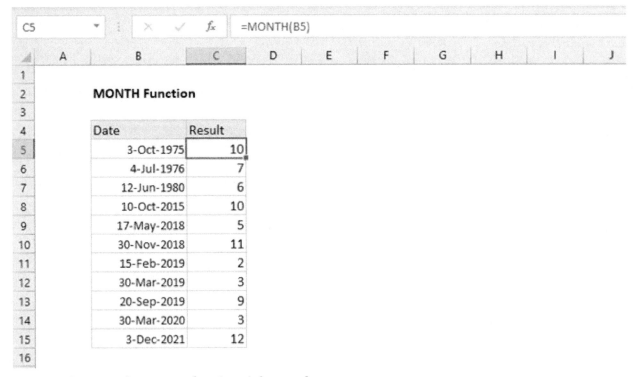

Purpose: Get month as a number (1-12) from a date

Return Value: A number between 1 and 12.

Syntax: =MONTH (serial_number)

Arguments

- **Serial_number:** A valid Excel date.

Usage Notes

The MONTH function extracts the month from a given date as a number between 1 to 12. For example, given the date "June 12, 2021", the MONTH function will return 6 for June. MONTH takes just one argument, serial_number, which must be a valid Excel date.

Dates can be supplied to the MONTH function as text (e.g. "13-Aug-2021") or as native Excel dates, which are large serial numbers. To create a data value from scratch with separate year, month, and day inputs, use the DATE function.

The MONTH function will "reset" every 12 months (like a calendar). To work with month durations larger than 12, use a formula to calculate months between dates.

The MONTH function returns a number. If you need the month name, see this example.

Examples

To use the MONTH function, supply a date:

=MONTH("23-Aug-2012") // returns 8

=MONTH("11-May-2019") // returns 5

With the date "September 15, 2017" in cell A1, MONTH returns 9:

=MONTH(A1) // returns 9

You can use the MONTH function to extract a month number from a date into a cell or to feed a month number into another function like the DATE function. The formula below extracts the month from the date in cell A1 and uses the TODAY and DATE functions to create a date on the first day of the same month in the current year.

=DATE(YEAR(TODAY(),MONTH(A1),1) // same month current year

Time Functions
What Is The TIME Function?

The TIME function is categorized under Excel DATE/TIME functions. TIME helps us create a time with individual hour, minute, and second components.

Formula

=TIME(hour, minute, second)

The TIME function uses the following arguments:

1. Hour: This can be any number between 0 and 32767, representing the hour. The point to be noted for this argument is that if the hour value is larger than 23, it will be divided by 24. The remainder of the division will be used as the hour value. For better understanding, TIME(24,0,0) will be equal to TIME(0,0,0), TIME (25,0,0) means TIME(1,0,0) and TIME(26,0,0) will be equal to TIME(2,0,0) and so on.

2. Minute: This can be any number between 0 and 32767, representing the minute. For this argument, you should note that if the minute value is larger than 59, every 60 minutes will add up to 1 hour in the preexisting hour value. For better understanding, TIME(0,60,0) will be equal to TIME(1,0,0) and TIME(0,120,0) will be equal to TIME(2,0,0) and so on.

3. Second: This can be any number between 0 and 32767, representing the second. For this argument, you should note that if the second value exceeds 59, every 60 seconds will add 1 minute to the preexisting minute value. For better understanding, TIME(0,0,60) will be equal to TIME(0,1,0) and TIME(0,0,120) will be equal to TIME(0,2,0) and so on.

1. **Excel TIME function**

The Excel TIME function is a built-in function that allows you to create a time with individual hour, minute, and second components. The TIME function is useful when you want to assemble a proper time inside another formula.

	A	B	C	D	E	F
1						
2		TIME function				
3						
4		Hour	Minute	Second	Result	Raw value
5		6	0	0	6:00 AM	0.25
6		12	0	0	12:00 PM	0.5
7		18	0	0	6:00 PM	0.75
8		24	0	0	12:00 AM	0
9		48	0	0	12:00 AM	0
10		6	30	0	6:30 AM	0.270833
11		6	60	0	7:00 AM	0.291667
12		24	-1	0	11:59 PM	0.999306
13		24	-60	0	11:00 PM	0.958333
14		0	60	0	1:00 AM	0.041667
15		0	120	0	2:00 AM	0.083333

Formula bar: E5 =TIME(B5,C5,D5)

How To Open The TIME Function In Excel?

You can simply enter the desired TIME formula in the required cell to attain a return value on the argument.

You can manually open the TIME formula dialogue box in the spreadsheet and enter the logical values to attain a return value.

Consider the screenshot below to see the Formula of TIME option under the Date & Time Function in the Excel menu.

Purpose: Create a time with hours, minutes, and seconds

Return Value: A decimal number represents a particular time in Excel.

Syntax: =TIME (hour, minute, second)

Arguments

- **Hour:** The hour for the time you wish to create.
- **Minute:** The minute for the time you want to create.
- **Second:** The second for the time you want to make.

Usage Notes

The TIME function creates a valid Excel time based on supplied values for hour, minute, and second. Like all Excel time, a result is a number that represents a fractional day. The TIME function will only return time values up to one full day, between 0 (zero) to 0.99999999, or 0:00:00 to 23:59:59. To see results formatted as time, apply a time-based number format.

Examples

=TIME(3,0,0) // 3 hours

=TIME(0,3,0) // 3 minutes

=TIME(0,0,3) // 3 seconds

=TIME(8,30,0) // 8.5 hours

The TIME function can interpret units in larger increments. For example, both of the formulas below return a result of 2 hours:

=TIME(0,120,0) // 2 hours

=TIME(0,0,7200) // 2 hours

However, when the total time reaches 24 hours, the TIME function will "reset" to zero.

=TIME(12,0,0) // 12 hours

=TIME(36) // 12 hours

In this way, TIME behaves like a 24-hour clock that resets when it crosses midnight. Notably, TIME will not handle numeric inputs larger than 32,767. For example, even though there are 86,400 seconds in a day, the following formula (which represents 12 hours) will fail with a #NUM! Error:

=TIME(0,0,43200) // returns #NUM!

As a workaround, you can convert hours, minutes, and seconds directly to Excel time with a formula:

=hours/24+minutes/1440+seconds/86400

The result is the same as the TIME function up to 24 hours. Over 24 hours, this formula will continue to accumulate time, unlike the TIME function.

Things To Remember About The TIME Function

TIME was introduced in MS Excel 2000 and is available in all later versions.

#NUM! Error: Occurs if the given hour arguments evaluate an adverse time, e.g., if the allotted hours are less than 0.

#VALUE! Error: Occurs when any of the given arguments is non-numeric.

2. **Excel TIME VALUE Function**

The Excel TIME VALUE function converts a time represented as text into a proper Excel time. For example, the formula =TIMEVALUE("9:00 AM") returns 0.375, the numeric representation of 9:00 AM in Excel's time system. Numeric time values are more valuable than text since who can directly manipulate them with formulas and pivot tables.

	A	B	C	D
2		**TIMEVALUE function**		
4		Input	Output	Formatted
5		12:00 PM	0.5	12:00 PM
6		6:00 PM	0.75	6:00 PM
7		21:00	0.875	9:00 PM
8		6:00	0.25	6:00 AM
9		1-Jan-21 12:00	0.5	12:00 PM
10		6/20/1970 9:00 PM	0.875	9:00 PM
11		36:00	0.5	12:00:00
12		1:40:45	0.069965278	1:40:45
13		0:10	0.006944444	0:10:00
14		0:0:10	0.000115741	0:00:10
15		12:00 PM	#VALUE!	#VALUE!

Cell C5: =TIMEVALUE(B5)

Purpose: Get a valid time from a text string

Return Value: A valid Excel time as a decimal number

Syntax: =TIMEVALUE (time_text)

Arguments

- **Time_text:** A date and/or time in a text format recognized by Excel.

Usage Notes

Sometimes, times in Excel appear as text values that are not appropriately recognized as time. The TIME VALUE function is meant to parse a time that appears as a text value into a valid Excel time. A native Excel time is more valuable than text because it is a numeric value that can be formatted as time and directly manipulated in a formula.

The TIME VALUE function takes just one argument, called time_text. If time_text is a cell address, the value in the cell must be text. If time_text is entered directly into the formula, it must be enclosed in double-quotes ("). Time_text should be supplied in a text format that Excel can recognize, for example, "6:45 PM" or "18:45". TIME VALUE ignores dates if present in a text string.

The TIME VALUE function creates a time in serial number format from a date and time in an Excel text format. TIME VALUE will return a decimal number between 0 and 0.99988426, representing 12:00:00 AM to 11:59:59 PM. Because the maximum value returned by TIME VALUE is less than 1, hours will reset every 24 hours (like a clock).

Essential Characteristics Of The TIME VALUE Function

The TIME VALUE function parses the text string inserted in the time_text argument to create a native English time value.

The time_text argument may be supplied either as a valid text string or a cell reference containing a valid text string. If the value is provided directly into the formula, you must enclose the text string in double-quotes.

The TIME VALUE function ignores dates in the supplied value.

The supplied value must be valid, i.e., "10:11:12 PM" or "22:11:12".

The output of the TIME VALUE function resets to 0 every 24 hours.

The TIME VALUE function always returns a decimal value between 0 (which represents midnight) and 0.99988426 (which means 23:59:59).

Examples

The formulas below show the output from TIMEVALUE:

=TIMEVALUE("12:00") // returns 0.5

=TIMEVALUE("12:00 PM") // returns 0.5

=TIMEVALUE("18:00") // returns 0.75

Apply a time number format to display the output from TIME VALUE as a formatted time.

Alternative Formula

Notice that the TIME VALUE formula in C15 fails with a #VALUE! Error because cell B15 already contains a valid time. This is a limitation of the TIME VALUE function. If you have a mix of good and invalid dates, you can use the simple formula below as an alternative:

=A1+0

The math operation of adding zero will cause Excel will try to coerce the value in A1 into a number. If Excel can parse the text into a proper time, it will return a reasonable time as a decimal number. If the time is already a good Excel time, adding zero will have no effect and generate no error.

Notes: TIME VALUE will return a #VALUE error if time_text does not contain time formatted as text.

3. **Excel NOW Function**

The Excel NOW function returns the current date and time, updated continuously when a worksheet is changed or opened. The NOW function takes no arguments. You can format the value returned by NOW as a date or date with time by applying a number format.

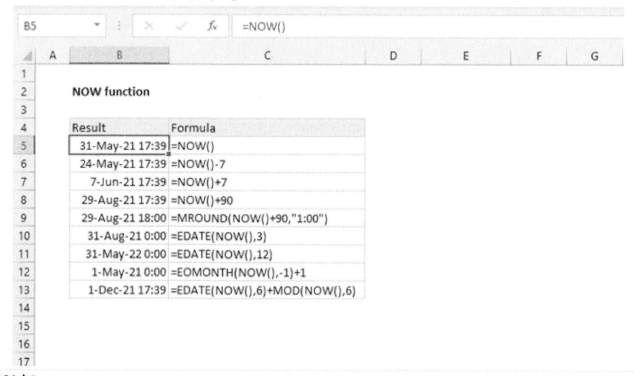

Purpose: Get the current date and time

Return Value: A number representing the current date and time in Excel.

Syntax: =NOW ()

Usage Notes

NOW takes no parameters but requires empty parentheses. The value returned by NOW will continually update each time the worksheet is updated, for example, each time a value is entered or changed. Use F9 to force the worksheet to recalculate and update the value.

The value returned by the NOW function is a standard Excel date, including a fractional value for time. To display the result as a date:

1. Apply a date number format.

2. Optionally customize the number format to include the time.

3. Use the TODAY function if you want the current date without a time value.

Examples

The examples below show how who can use the NOW function in various ways:

=NOW() // current date and time

=NOW()-7 // last week same time

=NOW()+7 // next week same time

=NOW()+90 // 90 days from now

=MROUND(NOW()+90,"1:00") // 90 days from now to nearest hour

=EDATE(NOW(),3) // 3 months from now, time removed

=EDATE(NOW(),12) // 12 months from now, time removed

=EOMONTH(NOW(),-1)+1 // first day of current month

=EDATE(NOW(),6)+MOD(NOW(),6) // 6 months from now, time preserved

Static Date And Time

If you need a static date and time that won't change,

you can use the following shortcuts:

- Insert current date - Control + ;
- Insert current time - Control + Shift + :
- To enter both values in a single cell, join the date, space, and time.

Formatting Results

The result of NOW is a serial number representing an Excel date and time. You can format the value returned by TODAY using any standard date format. You can use the TEXT function to build a text message that includes the current date:

="The date is "&TEXT(NOW(),"mmm d")&" and the time is "&
TEXT(NOW(),"h:mm AM/PM")

To return a text string like "The date is May 31 and the time is 6:10 PM".

CHAPTER 8: STATISTICAL FUNCTIONS

A statistical function, such as Mean, Median, or Variance, summarizes a sample of values by a single value. By default, they expect their parameter(s) to be a probabilistic value represented by a random sample of values over the Run index. But, you can also apply a statistical function over an array of data indexes by specifying that index as an optional parameter.

Statistical Functions In Excel With Examples

To begin with, statistical function in Excel, let's first understand what is statistics and why we need it? So, statistics is a branch of sciences that can give a property to a sample. It deals with collecting, organizing, analyzing, and presenting the data. One of the great mathematicians, Karl Pearson, also the father of modern statistics, quoted that "statistics is the grammar of science."

We used statistics in every industry, including business, marketing, governance, engineering, health, etc. So, in short, statistics are a quantitative tool to understand the world in a better way.

For example, the government studies the demography of their country before making any policy, and the demography can only check with the help of statistics. We can take another example of making a movie or any campaign. It is essential to understand your audience, and there too, we used statistics as our tool.

Commonly Used Statistical Functions

Function Output

- ABS: The absolute value of a number
- AVERAGE: The average or arithmetic mean for a group of numbers
- COUNT: The number of cell locations in a range that contain a numeric character
- COUNTA: The number of cell locations in a range that have a text or numeric character
- MAX: The highest numeric value in a group of numbers
- MEDIAN: The middle number in a group of numbers (half the numbers in the group are higher than the median, and half the numbers in the group are lower than the median)
- MIN: The lowest numeric value in a group of numbers
- MODE: The number that appears most frequently in a group of numbers
- PRODUCT: The result of multiplying all the values in a range of cell locations
- SQRT: The positive square root of a number
- STDEV.S: The standard deviation for a group of numbers based on a sample
- SUM: The total of all numeric values in a group

Ways To Approach Statistical Function In Excel:

In Excel, we have a range of statical functions, and we can perform basic mead, median mode to more complex statistical distribution, and probability test. To understand statistical Functions, we will divide them into two sets:

- Basic statistical function
- Intermediate Statistical Function.

Statistical Function In Excel

Excel is the best tool to apply statistical functions. As discussed above, we first discuss the essential statistical function, then study the intermediate statistical function. Throughout the book, we will take data, and by using it, we will understand the statistical function.

So, let's take random data of a book store that sells textbooks for classes 11th and 12th.

	A	B	C	D	E	F
1	Textbooks	Quantity	Cost	Discount	Revenue	
2	Maths	321	250	20%	16050	
3	English	500	180		72000	
4	Hindi	200	120		18000	
5	Physics	620	420	40%	133080	
6	Chemistry	500	300	10%	13500	
7	Biology	300	128	5%	9500	
8	Accounts	200	200	20%	16050	
9	Economics	180	250	50%	1015000	
10	Sociology	150	120	15%	5760	
11						

Example Of Statistical Function.

Basic Statistical Function

These are some most common and practical functions. These include the COUNT function, COUNTA function, COUNTBLANK function, and COUNTIFS function. Let's discuss one by one:

1. COUNT Function

The COUNT function counts the number of cells containing a number. Always remember one thing it will only count the number.

Formula for COUNT function = COUNT(value1, [value2], …)

D2 =COUNT(D2:D11)

	A	B	C	D	E	F
1	Textbooks	Quantity	Cost	Discount	Revenue	
2	Maths	321	250	20%	16050	
3	English	500	180		72000	
4	Hindi	200	120		18000	
5	Physics	620	420	40%	133080	
6	Chemistry	500	300	10%	13500	
7	Biology	300	128	5%	9500	
8	Accounts	200	200	20%	16050	
9	Economics	180	250	50%	1015000	
10	Sociology	150	120	15%	5760	
11				=COUNT(D2:D11		
12				COUNT(**value1**, [value2], …)		
13						

Thus, there are **7 textbooks** that have a discount out of 9 books.

2. COUNTA Function

This function will count everything and the number of cells containing any information, including numbers, error values, and empty text.

Formula for COUNTA function = COUNT(value1, [value2], …)

	A	B	C	D	E
1	Textbooks	Quantity	Cost	Discount	Revenue
2	Maths	321	250	20%	16050
3	English	500	180		72000
4	Hindi	200	120		18000
5	Physics	620	420	40%	133080
6	Chemistry	500	300	10%	13500
7	Biology	300	128	5%	9500
8	Accounts	200	200	20%	16050
9	Economics	180	250	50%	1015000
10	Sociology	150	120	15%	5760
11				=COUNTA(D2:D10	
12				COUNTA(**value1**, [value2], …)	

So, there are a total of 9 subjects that being sold in the store

3. COUNTBLANK Function

COUNTBLANK function, as the term, suggest it will only count blank or empty cells.

Formula for COUNTBlANK function = COUNTBLANK(range)

	A	B	C	D	E
1	Textbooks	Quantity	Cost	Discount	Revenue
2	Maths	321	250	20%	16050
3	English	500	180		72000
4	Hindi	200	120		18000
5	Physics	620	420	40%	133080
6	Chemistry	500	300	10%	13500
7	Biology	300	128	5%	9500
8	Accounts	200	200	20%	16050
9	Economics	180	250	50%	1015000
10	Sociology	150	120	15%	5760
11				=COUNTBLANK(D2:D10	
12				COUNTBLANK(**range**)	

There are 2 subjects that don't have any discount.

4. COUNTIFS Function

COUNTIFS function is the most used function in Excel. The function will work on one or more than one condition in a given range and counts the cell that meets the condition.

Formula for COUNTIFS function = COUNTIFS (range1, criteria1, [range2], [criteria2], …)

Intermediate Statistical Function

Let's discuss some intermediate statistical functions in Excel. These functions are used more often by the analyst. It includes the AVERAGE function, MEDIAN function, MODE function, STANDARD DEVIATION function, VARIANCE function, QUARTILES function, and CORRELATION function.

1. AVERAGE Value1, [Value2], …)

The AVERAGE function is one of the most used intermediate functions. The function will return the arithmetic mean or an average of the cell in a given range.

Formula for AVERAGE function = AVERAGE(number1, [number2], …)

	A	B	C	D	E
1	Textbooks	Quantity	Cost	Discount	Revenue
2	Maths	321	250	20%	16050
3	English	500	180		72000
4	Hindi	200	120		18000
5	Physics	620	420	40%	133080
6	Chemistry	500	300	10%	13500
7	Biology	300	128	5%	9500
8	Accounts	200	200	20%	16050
9	Economics	180	250	50%	1015000
10	Sociology	150	120	15%	5760
11					=AVERAGE(E2:E10

So the average total revenue is Rs.144326.6667

2. AVERAGEIF Function

The function will return the arithmetic mean or an average of the cell in a given range that meets the given criteria.

Formula for AVERAGEIF function = AVERAGEIF(range, criteria, [average_range])

3. MEDIAN Function

The MEDIAN function will return the central value of the data. Its syntax is similar to the AVERAGE function.

Formula for MEDIAN function = MEDIAN(number1, [number2], …)

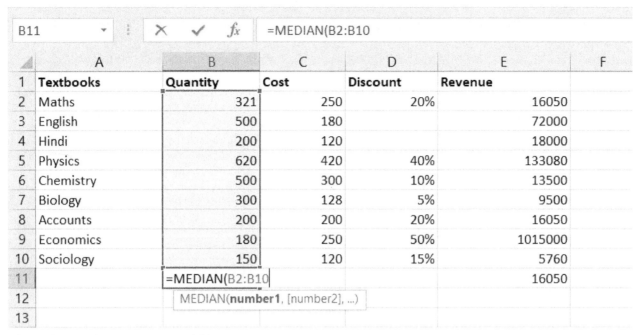

Thus, the median quantity sold is 300.

4. MODE Function

The MODE function will return the most frequent value of the cell in a given range.

Formula for MODE function = MODE.SNGL(number1,[number2],…)

Thus, the most frequent or repetitive cost is Rs. 250.

5. Standard Deviation

This function helps us determine how much-observed value deviated from or varied from the average. This function is one of the applicable functions in Excel.

Formula for STANDARD DEVIATION function = STDEV.P(number1,[number2],…)

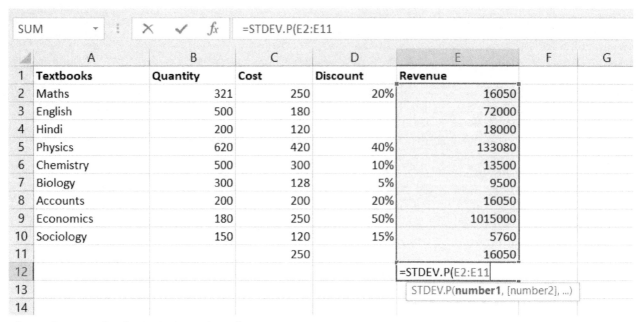

Thus, the Standard Deviation of total revenue =296917.8172

6. VARIANCE Function

To understand the VARIANCE function, we first need to know what is a variance? The variance will determine the degree of variation in your data set. The more data is spread it means, the more conflict is.

Formula for VARIANCE function = VAR(number1, [number2], ...)

So, the variance of Revenue= 97955766832

7. QUARTILES Function

The quartile divides the data into four parts, just like the median, which divides the data into two equal parts. So, the Excel QUARTILES function returns the quartiles of the dataset. It can replace the minimum, first, second, third, and max values. Let's see the syntax :

The formula for QUARTILES function = QUARTILE (array, quart)

	A	B	C	D	E	F
1	Textbooks	Quantity	Cost	Discount	Revenue	
2	Maths	321	250	20%	16050	
3	English	500	180		72000	
4	Hindi	200	120		18000	
5	Physics	620	420	40%	133080	
6	Chemistry	500	300	10%	13500	
7	Biology	300	128	5%	9500	
8	Accounts	200	200	20%	16050	
9	Economics	180	250	50%	1015000	
10	Sociology	150	120	15%	5760	
11			250		16050	
12					=QUARTILE.INC(E2:E11,1	
13					QUARTILE.INC(array, **quart**)	

So, the first quartile = 14137.5

8. CORRELATION Function

CORRELATION function help to find the relationship between the two variables. The analyst mainly uses this function to study the data. The range of the CORRELATION coefficient lies between -1 to +1.

Formula for CORRELATION function = CORREL(array1, array2)

	A	B	C	D	E	F
1	Textbooks	Quantity	Cost	Discount	Revenue	
2	Maths	321	250	20%	16050	
3	English	500	180		72000	
4	Hindi	200	120		18000	
5	Physics	620	420	40%	133080	
6	Chemistry	500	300	10%	13500	
7	Biology	300	128	5%	9500	
8	Accounts	200	200	20%	16050	
9	Economics	180	250	50%	1015000	
10	Sociology	150	120	15%	5760	
11					=CORREL(D2:D10,E2:E10	
12					CORREL(array1, **array2**)	

So, the correlation coefficient between discount and revenue of store = 0.802428894. Since it is a positive number, thus we can conclude discount is positively related to revenue.

9. MAX Function

The MAX function will return the enormous numeric value within a given data set or an array.

Formula for MAX function = MAX (number1, [number2], ...)

| B11 | ▼ | : | × | ✓ | fx | = MAX(B2:B10) |

	A	B	C	D	E	F
1	Textbooks	Quantity	Cost	Discount	Revenue	
2	Maths	321	250	20%	16050	
3	English	500	180		72000	
4	Hindi	200	120		18000	
5	Physics	620	420	40%	133080	
6	Chemistry	500	300	10%	13500	
7	Biology	300	128	5%	9500	
8	Accounts	200	200	20%	16050	
9	Economics	180	250	50%	1015000	
10	Sociology		150	120	15%	5760
11		= MAX(B2:B10)				
12						
13						

The maximum quantity of textbooks is Physics, 620 in number.

10. MIN Function

The MIN function will return the smallest numeric value within a given data set or an array.

Formula for MAX function = MAX (number1, [number2], ...)

| B11 | ▼ | : | × | ✓ | fx | =MIN(B2:B10 |

	A	B	C	D	E	F
1	Textbooks	Quantity	Cost	Discount	Revenue	
2	Maths	321	250	20%	16050	
3	English	500	180		72000	
4	Hindi	200	120		18000	
5	Physics	620	420	40%	133080	
6	Chemistry	500	300	10%	13500	
7	Biology	300	128	5%	9500	
8	Accounts	200	200	20%	16050	
9	Economics	180	250	50%	1015000	
10	Sociology	150	120	15%	5760	
11		=MIN(B2:B10				
12		MIN(**number1**, [number2], ...)				

The minimum number of the book available in the store = is 150(Sociology)

11. LARGE Function

The LARGE function is similar to the MAX function, but the only difference is it returns the nth most enormous value within a given set of data or an array.

The formula for LARGE function = LARGE (array, k)

Let's find the most expensive textbook using a significant function, where k = 1

	A	B	C	D	E
			fx	=LARGE(C2:C10,1	
	A	B	C	D	E
1	Textbooks	Quantity	Cost	Discount	Revenue
2	Maths	321	250	20%	16050
3	English	500	180		72000
4	Hindi	200	120		18000
5	Physics	620	420	40%	133080
6	Chemistry	500	300	10%	13500
7	Biology	300	128	5%	9500
8	Accounts	200	200	20%	16050
9	Economics	180	250	50%	1015000
10	Sociology	150	120	15%	5760
11			=LARGE(C2:C10,1		
12			LARGE(array, k)		

The most expensive textbook is Rs. 420.

12. SMALL Function

The SMALL function is similar to the MIN function, but the only difference is it returns the nth smallest value within a given set of data or an array.

Formula for SMALL function = SMALL (array, k)

Similarly, we can find the second least expensive book using the SMALL function.

	A	B	C	D	E
			fx	=SMALL(C2:C10,2	
	A	B	C	D	E
1	Textbooks	Quantity	Cost	Discount	Revenue
2	Maths	321	250	20%	16050
3	English	500	180		72000
4	Hindi	200	120		18000
5	Physics	620	420	40%	133080
6	Chemistry	500	300	10%	13500
7	Biology	300	128	5%	9500
8	Accounts	200	200	20%	16050
9	Economics	180	250	50%	1015000
10	Sociology	150	120	15%	5760
11			=SMALL(C2:C10,2		
12			SMALL(array, k)		

Thus, Rs. 120 is the least cost price.

Round

What is the ROUND Function?

The ROUND Function is categorized under Excel Math and Trigonometry functions. The function will round up a number to a specified number of digits. Unlike the ROUNDUP and ROUNDDOWN functions, the ROUND function can round either up or down.

This function is helpful as it helps round a number and eliminates the least significant digits, simplifying the notation but keeping close to the original value.

Formula

=ROUND(number,num_digits)

Arguments

The Function Uses The Following Arguments:

- **Number (Required Argument):** This is a natural number we wish to round.
- **Num_Digits (Required Argument):** This is the number of digits to which we want to round the number.

Now, If The Num_Digits Argument Is:

- A positive value greater than zero specifies the number of digits to the right of the decimal point.
- Equal to zero, it specifies rounding to the nearest integer.
- A negative value that is less than zero specifies the number of digits to the left of the decimal point.

This list illustrates three functions to round numbers in Excel. ROUND, ROUNDUP, and ROUNDDOWN.

Before your start: if you round a number, you lose precision. If you don't want this, show fewer decimal places without changing the number itself.

The ROUND function in Excel rounds a number to a specified number of digits. The ROUND function rounds up or down. 1, 2, 3, and 4 get rounded down. 5, 6, 7, 8, and 9 get rounded up.

1. For example, round a number to three decimal places.

	A	B
	B1	=ROUND(A1,3)
1	114.7261	114.726
2		

Note: 114.7261, 114.7262, 114.7263 and 114.7264 get rounded down to 114.726 and 114.7265, 114.7266, 114.7267, 114.7268 and 114.7269 get rounded up to 114.727.

2. Round a number to two decimal places.

	A	B
	B1	=ROUND(A1,2)
1	114.7261	114.73
2		

3. Round a number to one decimal place.

B1			✗	✓	fx	=ROUND(A1,1)				
	A	B	C	D	E	F	G	H	I
1	114.7261	114.7							
2									

4. Round a number to the nearest integer.

B1			✗	✓	fx	=ROUND(A1,0)				
	A	B	C	D	E	F	G	H	I
1	114.7261	115							
2									

5. Round a number to the nearest 10.

B1			✗	✓	fx	=ROUND(A1,-1)				
	A	B	C	D	E	F	G	H	I
1	114.7261	110							
2									

6. Round a number to the nearest 100.

B1			✗	✓	fx	=ROUND(A1,-2)				
	A	B	C	D	E	F	G	H	I
1	114.7261	100							
2									

7. Round a number to the nearest 1000.

B1			✗	✓	fx	=ROUND(A1,-3)				
	A	B	C	D	E	F	G	H	I
1	114.7261	0							
2									

8. Round a negative number to one decimal place.

B1			✗	✓	fx	=ROUND(A1,1)				
	A	B	C	D	E	F	G	H	I
1	-114.7261	-114.7							
2									

9. Round a negative number to the nearest integer.

RoundUp

The ROUNDUP function in Excel always rounds a number up (away from zero). 1, 2, 3, 4, 5, 6, 7, 8, and 9 get rounded up.

1. For example, round a number up to three decimal places.

Note: 114.7261, 114.7262, 114.7263, 114.7264, 114.7265, 114.7266, 114.7267, 114.7268 and 114.7269 get rounded up to 114.727.

2. Round a number up to two decimal places.

3. Round a number up to one decimal place.

4. Round a number up to the nearest integer.

5. Round a number up to the nearest 10.

| B1 | =ROUNDUP(A1,-1) |

	A	B
1	114.7261	120

6. Round a number up to the nearest 100.

| B1 | =ROUNDUP(A1,-2) |

	A	B
1	114.7261	200

7. Round a number up to the nearest 1000.

| B1 | =ROUNDUP(A1,-3) |

	A	B
1	114.7261	1000

8. Round a negative number up to one decimal place.

| B1 | =ROUNDUP(A1,1) |

	A	B
1	-114.7261	-114.8

Note: Remember, the ROUNDUP function rounds a number up (away from zero).

9. Round a negative number up to the nearest integer.

Again, the ROUNDUP function rounds a number up (away from zero).

RoundDown

The ROUNDDOWN function in Excel always rounds a number down (toward zero). 1, 2, 3, 4, 5, 6, 7, 8, and 9 get rounded down.

1. For example, round a number down to three decimal places.

B1			✓	fx	=ROUNDDOWN(A1,3)				
	A	B	C	D	E	F	G	H	I
1	114.7261	114.726							
2									

Note: 114.7261, 114.7262, 114.7263, 114.7264, 114.7265, 114.7266, 114.7267, 114.7268 and 114.7269 get rounded down to 114.726.

2. Round a number down to two decimal places.

B1			✓	fx	=ROUNDDOWN(A1,2)				
	A	B	C	D	E	F	G	H	I
1	114.7261	114.72							
2									

3. Round a number down to one decimal place.

B1			✓	fx	=ROUNDDOWN(A1,1)				
	A	B	C	D	E	F	G	H	I
1	114.7261	114.7							
2									

4. Round a number down to the nearest integer.

B1			✓	fx	=ROUNDDOWN(A1,0)				
	A	B	C	D	E	F	G	H	I
1	114.7261	114							
2									

5. Round a number down to the nearest 10.

B1			✓	fx	=ROUNDDOWN(A1,-1)				
	A	B	C	D	E	F	G	H	I
1	114.7261	110							
2									

6. Round a number down to the nearest 100.

B1			✓	fx	=ROUNDDOWN(A1,-2)				
	A	B	C	D	E	F	G	H	I
1	114.7261	100							
2									

7. Round a number down to the nearest 1000.

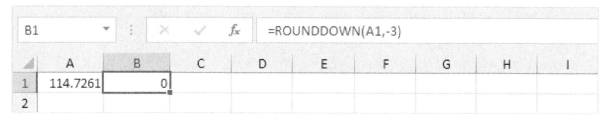

8. Round a negative number down to one decimal place.

Note: Remember, the ROUNDDOWN function rounds a number down (toward zero).

9. Round a negative number down to the nearest integer.

Note: Again, the ROUNDDOWN function rounds a number down (toward zero).

What is the SQRT Function?

The SQRT Function is an Excel Math and Trigonometry function. It will provide the square root of a positive number. The function was introduced in MS Excel 2010.

Formula

=SQRT(number)

Arguments

The SQRT Function Uses The Following Argument:

- **Number (Required Argument):** This is the number for which we wish to find out the square root. It must be a positive number, an Excel formula, or a function that results in a positive number.

How To Use The SQRT Function In Excel?

To understand the uses of the SQRT function, let's consider a few examples:

Example 1

Suppose we wish to find the square root of the following numbers:

- 25
- 49
- 900
- 121
- 100

The formula used would be =SQRT(reference). We will get the following results:

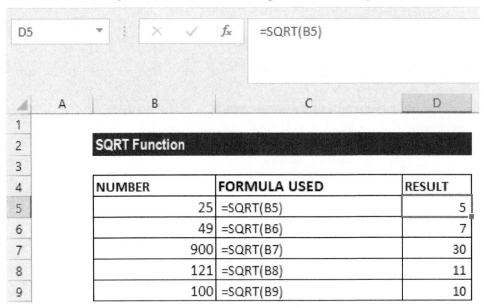

Example 2

If a number provided by a user is negative, the SQRT function will return the #NUM! Error. The square root of a negative number does not exist among the set of real numbers. There is no way to square a number and get a negative result.

However, if we wish to take the square root of a negative number as a positive number, we need to use the ABS function. We will wrap the source number in the ABS function, which will return the absolute value of a number and ignore the positive or negative sign of the given number:

Suppose we are given the data below:

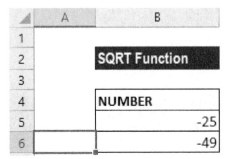

To find the SQRT, we will use the formula =SQRT(ABS(ref)), as shown below:

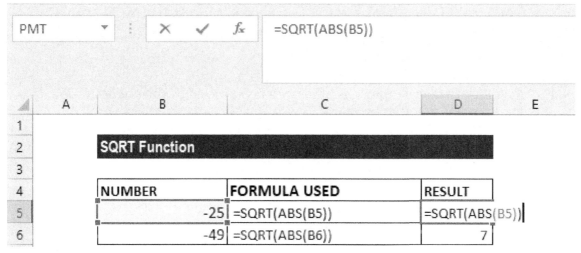

We get the result below:

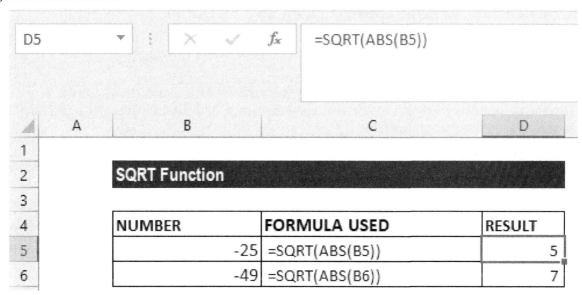

Things To Remember About The SQRT Function

- #NUM! Error – Occurs when the supplied number argument is opposing.
- Depending on the user's requirement, who can use the SQRT function and the ABS, ROUND, ROUNDUP, and ROUNDDOWN parts.
- SQRT is similar to the POWER function. However, the POWER function works like an exponent in a standard math equation. For example, for the number 25, we will provide the formula =SQRT(25) and =POWER(25, 1/2).

CHAPTER 9: MS EXCEL FINANCIAL FUNCTIONS

What Are Financial Functions In Excel

Everybody does not use financial Functions, which are mainly used by finance professionals, especially banking and financial company employees.

What would be the net present value of your investment as today will be calculated using the NPV function, what is the Internal Rate of Return of an investment will be calculated by IRR function, addition to this function you can also learn XIRR, MIRR as well. When it comes to money borrowing, you will use EMI calculation formulas like PMT, FV, RATE, PRICE, and PV functions.

The excel financial functions have been made available to execute a variety of financial calculations, including yield calculations, investment valuations, interest rates, internal rate of return, asset depreciation, and payments. However, these financial functions can be classified into different categories to enable you to stumble on the required function.

There Are Generally Four Interrelated quantities That Include:

1. Present Value (PV) equivalent to the value of the load or savings today. This function estimates the loan size that could be paid off provided a periodic payment over a provided total number of payments and a provided regular interest rate.

2. Interest Rate per period (RATE) equivalent to the interest rate, generally monthly. This function calculates the periodic interest rate required to pay off a provided present value with a provided regular payment and a total number of payments.

3. Number of payment periods (NPER) equivalent to several payment periods. This function evaluates the total number of payment periods required to pay off a given present value with a provided payment and periodic interest rate.

4. Periodic payment (PMT) is equivalent to the payment per period. This function calculates the fixed periodic payment with a given present value, regular interest rate, and the total number of payments.

1. PV Function In Excel

PV Function also expands as Present Value, which is quite a useful function available under a financial category in excel; it is used to find out the present value at any point of the period of borrowed or invested amount and consider the interest rate a monthly basis. This is a valuable function for calculating how much we need to invest or pay to complete the due with the interest rate applicable at the time.

What Is The PV Function?

The PV function is a widely used financial function in Microsoft Excel. It calculates the present value of a loan or an investment. PV is used to calculate the dollar value of future payments in the present time. We assume periodic, fixed payments and a fixed interest rate for multiple payments. Alternatively, the function can also calculate the current value of a single future value.

The Excel PV function is a financial function that returns the present value of an investment. You can use the PV function to get the value in today's dollars of a series of future payments, assuming periodic, constant payments and a constant interest rate.

The Formula For PV In Excel

Again, the formula for calculating PV in Excel is

=PV(rate, nper, pmt, [fv], [type]).

The PV Function Uses The Following Arguments:

Rate: (Required Argument): The interest rate per compounding period. A loan with a 12% annual interest rate and monthly required payments would have a monthly interest rate of 12%/12 or 1%. Therefore, the rate would be 1%.

Nper: (Required Argument): The number of payment periods. For example, a 3-year loan with monthly payments would have 36 periods. Therefore, nper would be 36 months.

Pmt: (Required Argument): The fixed payment per period.

Fv: (Optional Argument): An investment's future value at the end of all payment periods (nper). If there is no input for fv, Excel will assume the information is 0.

Type: (Optional Argument): Type indicates when payments are issued. There are only two inputs, 0 and 1. If type is omitted or 0 is the input, payments are made at period end. If set to 1, payments are made at the period beginning.

Notes:
- All the payments are constant and cannot be changed over a period.
- Constant rate of interest throughout the loan period.
- We need to mention the outflow in negative and inflow in positive numbers.

Things To Remember About The PV Function In Excel
- The PV function in excel uses a specific order of values (the rate, nper, pmt, fv, type) and is separated by "If any of the arguments are not provided, PV in excel function can be left blank. As in example 3, it is PV(B4,B5,,B6,0).
- The rate is the interest/return rate per period, different from the annual rate.
- PV in excel function allows cash flows either at the beginning or end of the period.
- The PV excel function has constant cash flow and a constant interest rate.

How To Use PV Function In Excel - Formula Examples

The following examples will give you insight into how the Excel PV function works in different scenarios so that you can adjust the basic formula for your specific task.

Calculate PV Of Annuity

Let's say you bought an annuity in which a regular payment of $200 is to be made to the insurance company at the start of every month for the next ten years. The annuity earns a 9% annual interest compounded monthly. The question is - how much is this annuity worth now?

To begin with, enter all the data in separate cells:
- Annual interest rate (B2): 9%
- Number of years (B3): 10
- Monthly payment (B4): -200
- Annuity type (B5): 1
- Number of periods per year (B6): 12

The interest rate (rate) and payment (PMT) are for different periods. To do PV right, we need to make a couple of conversions:

To convert an annual interest rate to a periodic rate, divide the annual rate by the number of periods per year:

rate = annual interest rate / no. of periods per year

To get the total number of periods, multiply the annuity term in years by the number of periods per year:

nper = no. of years * no. of periods per year

Since we have a monthly annuity, we can divide and multiply by 12 or by cell B6, in which this number is entered.

The complete PV formula in B8 is:

=PV(B2/B6, B3*B6, B4, B5)

	A	B
1	Description	Value
2	Annual interest rate	9%
3	Annuity term in years	10
4	Periodic payment	-$200
5	Annuity type	1
6	Periods per year	12
7		
8	Present value	$15,906.75

Formula shown: =PV(B2/B6, B3*B6, B4,, B5)

Similarly, you can calculate the present value of a weekly, quarterly or semiannual annuity. For this, change the number of periods per year in the corresponding cell:

- Weekly: 52
- Monthly: 12
- Quarterly: 4
- Semiannual: 2
- Annual: 1

Calculate PV of Investment Based On Its Future Value

In this example, we will find the present value of an investment that will pay $50,000 in 5 years, with an annual interest rate of 7%. The goal is to determine how much money we need to invest today to reach the target amount at the end of the investment period.

As usual, we input the annuity data in separate cells:

- Annual interest rate (B2): 7%
- Number of years (B3): 5
- Future value (B4): 50,000
- Annuity type (B5): 0

Assuming the interest rate is compounded annually, the present value formula is as simple as this:

=PV(B2, B3, B4, B5)

Please pay attention that the Pmt argument is omitted in this case because it's supposed to be a single lump-sum investment without additional periodic payments.

As shown in the screenshot below, the result of the PV formula is harmful because it's an outflow, i.e., the money you'd invest now to earn the target amount in the future.

	A	B
1	Description	Value
2	Annual interest rate	7%
3	No. of years	5
4	Future value	$50,000
5	Annuity type	0
6		
7	Present value	-$35,649.31

B7 =PV(B2, B3, , B4, B5)

But what if we have several proposals from various investment firms and want to compare the effect of different compounding periods?

In this case, we type the number of compounding periods per year in cells E2:E6, as shown in the image below. Then, we enter the below formula in F2 and drag it down through F6:

=PV($B$2/E2, $B$3* E2, ,$B$4)

The constant data such as the interest rate ($B$2), annuity term ($B$3), future value ($B$4), and type ($B$5) must be supplied as absolute references so that the formula copies correctly to the below cells.

F2 =PV($B$2/E2, $B$3* E2, ,$B$4, $B$5)

	A	B	C	D	E	F
1	Description	Value		Compounded	Periods per year	Present value
2	Annual interest rate	7%		Weekly	52	($35,242.70)
3	No. of years	5		Monthly	12	($35,270.25)
4	Future value	$50,000		Quarterly	4	($35,341.23)
5	Annuity type	0		Semiannually	2	($35,445.94)
6				Annually	1	($35,649.31)

Looking at the results, you may notice an inverse relationship between the calculated PV (absolute value ignoring the sign) and the number of compounding periods. The best deal for us is weekly compounding - by investing the smallest amount of money now, we will get the same $50,000 in 5 years.

Difference Between NPV And PV Formula In Excel

Besides PV, in finance, there is one more term, called NPV, that discounts future cash flows by an expected rate of return to estimate their current value. Though these two terms have a lot in common, they differ significantly.

1. Present value (PV): Refers to future cash inflows in a given period.

2. Net present value (NPV): Is the difference between the present value of cash inflows and the present value of cash outflows. In other words, NPV considers the initial investment, making the current value a net figure.

In Microsoft Excel, There Are Two Main Differences Between The PV And NPV Functions:

The PV function can only calculate constant cash flows that do not change over the entire lifetime of an annuity. The NPV function can calculate variable cash flows.

PV Works for both regular annuity and annuity due. NPV can only process cash flows at the end of each period.

Special Considerations

For the PV formula in Excel, adjustments must be made if the interest rate and payment amount are based on different periods. A widespread change needed to make the PV formula in Excel work is changing the annual interest rate to a period rate. That's done by dividing the annual rate by the number of periods per year.

For example, if your payment for the PV formula is made monthly, you'll need to convert your annual interest rate to monthly by dividing by 12. For NPER, which is the number of periods, if you're collecting an annuity payment monthly for four years, the NPER is 12 times 4, or 48.

What Is The Difference Between Present Value (PV) And Future Value (FV)?

The present value uses the time value of money to discount future amounts of money or cash flows to what they are worth today. This is because cash today tends to have greater purchasing power than the same amount of money in the future. Taking the same logic in the other direction, future value (FV) takes the value of money today and projects what its buying power would be at some point in the future.

Why Is Present Value Important?

Present value is essential to price assets or investments today that will be sold in the future or have returns or cash flows that will pay in the future. Because transactions take place in the present, those future cash flows or returns must be considered using the value of today's money.

When Might You Need To Calculate Present Value?

Present value calculations are pretty standard. Any asset that pays interest, such as a bond, annuity, lease, or real estate, will be priced using its net present value. Stocks are also often priced based on the current value of their future profits or dividend streams using discounted cash flow (DCF) analysis.

NPV Vs. PV Formula In Excel

While calculating PV in Excel, you can also calculate the net present value (NPV). Present value is discounted future cash flows. The net current worth is the difference between PV of cash flows and PV of cash outflows.

The big difference between PV and NPV is that NPV considers the initial investment. The NPV formula for Excel uses the discount rate and series of cash outflows and inflows.

Critical Differences Between NPV And PV:

PV can be used for regular annuities (payments at the end of the period) and annuities due (payments at the beginning of the period).

NPVs can only be used for payments or cash flows at the end of the period.

2. NPV Functions

What Is Net Present Value (NPV)?

Net present value (NPV) is the difference between the present value of cash inflows and the current value of cash outflows. NPV is used in capital budgeting and investment planning to analyze the profitability of a projected investment or project. NPV is the result of calculations used to find today's value of a future stream of payments.

Formula

=NPV(rate,value1,[value2],...)

Arguments

The NPV function uses the following arguments:

Rate (Required Argument): This is the discount rate over the length of the period.

Value 1, Value 2: Value1 is a required option. They are numeric values that represent a series of payments and income where:

- Negative payments represent outgoing payments.
- Positive payments represent incoming payments.

How To Use The NPV Function In Excel?

To understand the uses of the function, let's consider a few examples:

Example – Using The Function

Suppose we are given the following data on cash inflows and outflows:

	A	B	C	D
1				
2		**NPV Function**		
3				
4				
5		Period	Cashflow	
6		0	(800)	
7		1	100	
8		2	200	
9		3	300	
10		4	400	
11		5	500	
12				
13		Required return	10%	

The required rate of return is 10%. To calculate the NPV, we will use the formula below:

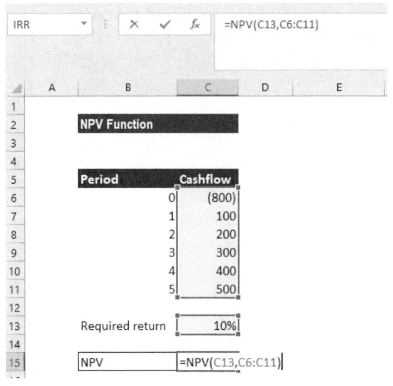

We get the result below:

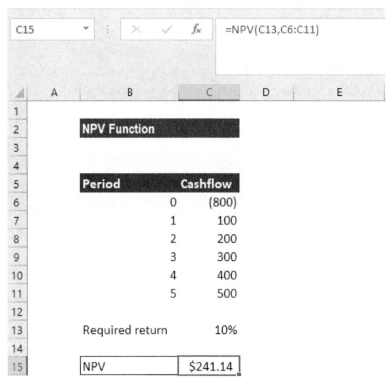

The NPV formula is based on future cash flows if the first cash flow occurs at the start of the first period, who must add the first value to the NPV result, not included in the values arguments.

Some Important Things To Know When Using The NPV Function In Excel:
- The NPV function considers all these values are evenly spaced out (i.e., have the same time interval between each value).
- The order of the values matter, so if you change the order and keep the same values, the final result would be different.
- The formula considers that the inflow/outflow occurs at the end of the period.
- It only considers the numeric values, and if there are blanks or text values, who would ignore these.

The most important thing to remember is that you can only use this formula when your regular flow of inflows and outflows. For example, if the inflow/outflow happens at the end of the year, it should be the same for all the values.

What Net Present Value Can Tell You

NPV accounts for the time value of money and can be used to compare similar investment alternatives.

The NPV relies on a discount rate derived from the cost of the capital required to invest and who should avoid any project or investment with a negative NPV. A critical drawback of NPV analysis is that it makes assumptions about future events that may not be reliable.

NPV looks to assess the profitability of a given investment because a dollar in the future is not worth the same as a dollar today. Money loses value over time due to inflation. However, a dollar today can be invested and earn a return, making its future value possibly higher than a dollar received at the same point.

NPV seeks to determine the present value of an investment's future cash flows above the investment's initial cost. The discount rate element of the NPV formula discounts the future cash flows to the present-day value. If subtracting the initial cost of the investment from the sum of the cash flows in the present day is positive, then the investment is worthwhile.

For example, an investor could receive $100 today or a year later. Most investors would not be willing to postpone receiving $100 today. However, what if an investor could choose to receive $100 today or $105 in one year? The 5% rate of return (RoR) for waiting one year might be worthwhile for an investor unless another investment could yield a greater than 5% over the same period.

If an investor knew they could earn 8% from a relatively safe investment over the next year, they would choose to receive $100 today and not the $105 in a year, with the 5% rate of return. In this case, 8% would be the discount rate.

Positive vs. Negative NPV

A positive NPV indicates that the projected earnings generated by a project or investment in current dollars exceeds the anticipated costs, also in current dollars. It is assumed that an investment with a positive NPV will be profitable.

An investment with a negative NPV will result in a net loss. This concept is the basis for the Net Present Value Rule, which dictates who should consider only investments with positive NPV values.

Calculating Net Present Value

Money in the present is worth more than the same amount in the future due to inflation and possible earnings from alternative investments that who could make during the intervening time. In other words, a dollar earned in the future won't be worth as much as one achieved in the present. The discount rate element of the NPV formula is a way to account for this.

For example, assume that an investor could choose a $100 payment today or in a year. A rational investor would not be willing to postpone payment. However, what if an investor could choose to receive $100 today or $105 in a year? If the payer was reliable, that extra 5% might be worth the wait, but only if there wasn't anything else the investors could do with the $100 that would earn more than 5%.

An investor might be willing to wait a year to earn an extra 5%, but that may not be acceptable for all investors. In this case, the 5% is the discount rate, which will vary depending on the investor. If an investor knew they could earn 8% from a relatively safe investment over the next year, they would not be willing to postpone payment for 5%. In this case, the investor's discount rate is 8%.

A company may determine the discount rate using the expected return of other projects with a similar level of risk or the cost of borrowing the money needed to finance the project. For example, a company may avoid a project expected to return 10% per year if it costs 12% to finance it, or an alternative project is expected to produce 14% per year.

Imagine a company can invest in equipment that will cost $1,000,000 and is expected to generate $25,000 a month in revenue for five years. The company has the capital available for the equipment and could alternatively invest it in the stock market for an expected return of 8% per year. The managers feel that buying the equipment or investing in the stock market are similar risks.

Steps To Calculate NPV In Excel

There are two methods to calculate the NPV in the Excel sheet. First, you can use the basic formula, calculate the present value of each component for each year individually, and then sum all of them up together. Second, you can use the in-built Excel function, which can be accessed using the "NPV" formula.

Using Present Value For NPV Calculation In Excel

Using the figures quoted in the above example, we assume that the project will need an initial outlay of $250,000 in year zero. From the second year (year one) onwards, the project starts generating inflows of $100,000, and they increase by $50,000 each year until year five, when the project gets over. THE COMPANIES USE the WACC, or a weighted average cost of capital, as the discount rate when budgeting for a new project and is assumed to be 10 percent throughout the project tenure.

The present value formula is applied to each cash flow from year zero to year five. For example, the cash flow of -$250,000 in the first year leads to the same present value during year zero, while the inflow of $100,000 during the second year (year 1) leads to a current value of $90,909. It indicates that a one-year future influx of $100,000 is worth $90,909 at year zero, and so on.

	A	B	C	D	E	F	G
1							
2		WACC	10%			Method - 1: Using Basic PV Formula	
3			Year			PV-Formula	Present Value
4		2017-A	0	-$250,000		=D4/((1+$C$2)^C4)	-$250,000
5		2018-P	1		$100,000	=E5/((1+$C$2)^C5)	$90,909
6		2019-P	2		$150,000	=E6/((1+$C$2)^C6)	$123,967
7		2020-P	3		$200,000	=E7/((1+$C$2)^C7)	$150,263
8		2021-P	4		$250,000	=E8/((1+$C$2)^C8)	$170,753
9		2022-P	5		$300,000	=E9/((1+$C$2)^C9)	$186,276
10		Sum-PV					$472,169

Calculating the present value for each of the years and then summing those up gives the NPV value of $472,169, as shown in the above screenshot of the Excel with the described formulas.

Using Excel NPV Function For NPV Calculation In Excel

The second method uses the in-built Excel formula "NPV." It takes two arguments, the discounting rate (represented by WACC) and the series of cash flows from year 1 to the last year. Who should take care not to include the year zero cash flow in the formula, also indicated by the initial outlay?

	A	B	C	D	E	F	G
1							
2		WACC	10%			Method - 1 : Using Basic PV Formula	
3			Year			PV-Formula	Present Value
4		2017-A	0	-$250,000		=D4/((1+$C$2)^C4)	-$250,000
5		2018-P	1		$100,000	=E5/((1+$C$2)^C5)	$90,909
6		2019-P	2		$150,000	=E6/((1+$C$2)^C6)	$123,967
7		2020-P	3		$200,000	=E7/((1+$C$2)^C7)	$150,263
8		2021-P	4		$250,000	=E8/((1+$C$2)^C8)	$170,753
9		2022-P	5		$300,000	=E9/((1+$C$2)^C9)	$186,276
10		Sum-PV					$472,169
11							
12						Method - 2 : Using in-built Excel NPV Formula	
13		NPV Formula					=NPV($C$2,E5:E9)
14		NPV Formula Result					$722,169
15		Initial Outlay					($250,000)
16		NPV Value				NPV Formula + Initial Outlay	$472,169

The NPV formula for the above example comes to $722,169. To compute the final NPV, one needs to decrease the initial outlay from the value obtained from the NPV formula. It leads to NPV = ($722,169 - $250,000) = $472,169.

This computed value matches the one obtained from the first method using PV value.

3. FV Functions

What Is Future Value?

The value of the investment at a particular date in the future is equivalent in value to a specified sum today.

Where:

I = Invested Amount

R = Interest Rate

T = number of periods

What Is The Excel FV Function?

The FV Function Excel formula is categorized under Financial functions. This function helps calculate the future value of an investment.

The FV function helps calculate the future value of investments made by a business, assuming periodic, constant payments with a regular interest rate. It helps evaluate low-risk assets such as certificates of deposit or fixed rate annuities with low-interest rates. Who can also use it about interest paid on loans? The function is available in all versions of Excel 365, Excel 2019, Excel 2016, Excel 2013, Excel 2010, and Excel 2007.

The Formula

=FV(rate,nper,pmt,[pv],[type])

This Function Uses The Following Arguments:

1. Rate (Required View): This is the interest rate for each period.

2. Nper (Necessary Argument): The total number of payment periods.

3. Pmt (Optional Argument): This specifies the payment per period. If we omit this argument, we need to provide the PV argument.

4. PV (Optional Argument): This specifies the present value (PV) of the investment/loan. The PV argument, if omitted, defaults to zero. If we forget the argument, we need to provide the Pmt argument.

5. Type (Optional Argument): This defines whether payments are made at the start or end of the year. The argument can either be 0 (the fee is made at the end of the period) or 1 (the payment is made at the start of the period).

Four Things To Remember About The Excel FV Function

To correctly build an FV formula in your worksheets and avoid common errors, please keep in mind these usage notes:

1. For any inflows such as dividends or other earnings, use positive numbers. Use negative numbers for outflows such as deposits to saving or investing accounts.

2. If the present value (PV) is zero or omitted, who must include the payment amount (PMT), and vice versa.

3. The rate argument can be expressed as a percentage or decimal number, e.g., 8% or 0.08.

4. To get the correct future value, you must be consistent with nper and rate. For instance, if you make three yearly payments at an annual interest rate of 5%, use 3 for nper and 5% for rate. If you do a series of monthly investments for three years, then use 3*12 (36 payments) for nper and 5%/12 for rate.

Basic Future Value Formula In Excel

This example shows how to use the FV function in Excel in its simplest form to calculate the future value, given a periodic interest rate, the total number of periods, and a constant payment amount per period.

- Periodic interest rate (rate): C2
- Number of periods (nper): C3
- Payment amount (PMT): C4

You will make a yearly $1,000 payment for ten years with an annual interest rate of 6%. It is assumed to be a regular annuity where all payments are made at the end of the year.

To find the future value, configure the FV function in this way:

=FV(C2, C3, C4)

Please notice that pmt is a negative number because this money is paid out.

	A	B	C
1	Description	Argument	Value
2	Periodic interest rate	rate	6%
3	No. of periods	nper	10
4	Periodic payment	pmt	-$1,000
5			
6	Future value		$13,180.79

C6 = =FV(C2, C3, C4)

If a positive number represents the payment, don't forget to put the minus sign right before the pmt argument:

=FV(C2, C3, -C4)

	A	B	C
1	Description	Argument	Value
2	Periodic interest rate	rate	6%
3	No. of periods	nper	10
4	Periodic payment	pmt	$1,000
5			
6	Future value		$13,180.79

Basic Future Value Formula In Excel

How To Calculate Future Value In Excel - Formula Examples

The basic Excel FV formula is straightforward, right? Now, let's look at how to tweak it to handle a couple of most common scenarios.

FV Formula For Periodic Payments

When investing money through a series of regular savings, you are often provided with an annual interest rate and the investment term defined in years. In contrast, the payments must be made weekly, monthly, quarterly, or semiannually. In such situations, the rate and per unit must be consistent.

To convert an annual interest rate to a periodic rate, divide the annual rate by the number of periods per year:

- Monthly payments: rate = annual interest rate / 12
- Quarterly payments: rate = annual interest rate / 4
- Semiannual payments: rate = annual interest rate / 2

To get the total number of periods, multiply the term in years by the number of periods per year:

- Monthly payments: nper = no. of years * 12
- Quarterly payments: nper = no. of years * 4
- Semiannual payments: nper = no. of years * 2

Now, let's see how it works in practice. Suppose you monthly invest $200 for three years with an annual interest rate of 6%. The source data is input into these cells:

- Annual interest rate (B2): 6%
- No. of years (B3): 3
- Monthly payment (B4): -200
- Periods per year (B5): 12

To calculate the future value of this investment, the formula in B7 is:

=FV(B2/B5, B3*B5, B4)

As shown in the image below, the same formula determines the future value based on quarterly savings equally well:

Monthly payments   *Quarterly payments*

	A	B
1	Description	Value
2	Annual interest rate	6%
3	No. of years	3
4	Periodic payment	-$200
5	Periods per year	12
6		
7	Future value	$7,867.22

`=FV(B2/B5, B3*B5, B4)`

	A	B
1	Description	Value
2	Annual interest rate	6%
3	No. of years	3
4	Periodic payment	-$2,000
5	Periods per year	4
6		
7	Future value	$26,082.42

`=FV(B2/B5, B3*B5, B4)`

FV Formula For A Lump-Sum Investment

If you choose to invest the money as a one-time lump sum payment, the future value formula is based on the present value (PV) rather than the periodic payment (PMT).

So, we set up our sample data as follows:

- Annual interest rate (C2): 7%
- No. of years (C3): 5
- Present value (C4): -1000

The formula to calculate the future value of the investment is:

`=FV(C2, C3, ,C4)`

C6   fx   `=FV(C2, C3, ,C4)`

	A	B	C
1	Description	Argument	Value
2	Annual interest rate	rate	7%
3	No. of years	nper	5
4	Investment	pv	-$1,000
5			
6	Future value		$1,402.55

Please Notice That:

- The investment amount (PV) is a negative number because it's an outflow.
- The pmt argument is 0 or omitted.

If the compounding periods for your investment are not annual, then to determine the future value accurately, you need to make the following adjustments to the formula:

- For rate, divide an annual interest rate by the number of compounding periods per year.
- For nper, multiply the number of years by the number of compounding periods per year.

For example, let's find the future value of the above investment with an interest rate compounded monthly. For this, we divide an annual interest rate (C2) by 12 and multiply the number of years (C3) by 12:

=FV(C2/12, C3*12, ,C4)

or

=FV(C2/C5, C3*C5, ,C4)

Where C5 is the number of compounding periods per year:

	A	B	C
1	Description	Argument	Value
2	Annual interest rate	rate	7%
3	No. of years	nper	5
4	Investment	pv	-$1,000
5			
6	Future value		$1,402.55

Formula in C6: =FV(C2, C3, ,C4)

Get Future Value For Different Compounding Periods

To compare the amount of growth generated by various compounding periods, you need to supply different rates and nper to the FV function. To have all calculations performed with a single formula, do the following:

- Input the number of compounding periods per year in B2.
- Arrange your data, as shown in the image below.
- Enter the following formula in C2 and drag it down through C6:
  =FV($F$2/B2, $F$3*B2, ,$F$4)

Please pay attention that we lock the annual interest rate ($F$2), the number of years ($F$3), and the investment amount ($F$4) references with the dollar sign ($), so they won't shift when copying down the formula.

	A	B	C	D	E	F
1	Compounded	Periods per year	Future value			
2	Weekly	52	$1,283.87		Annual interest rate	5%
3	Monthly	12	$1,283.36		No. of years	5
4	Quarterly	4	$1,282.04		Investment	-$1,000
5	Semiannually	2	$1,280.08			
6	Annually	1	$1,276.28			

Formula in C2: =FV($F$2/B2, $F$3*B2, ,$F$4)

Make A Future Value Calculator In Excel.

If your goal is to build a universal FV calculator that works for periodic and lump-sum payments with either annuity type, you will need to use the Excel FV function in its complete form.

For starters, allocate cells for all the arguments, including the optional ones, shown in the screenshot below. And then, define the arguments in this way:

Rate (periodic interest rate): B2/ B7 (annual interest rate / periods per year)

Nper (total number of payment periods): B3*B7 (number of years * periods per year)

Pmt (periodic payment amount): B4

Pv (initial investment): B5

Type (when payments are due): B6

Compounding periods per year: B7

Putting the arguments together, we get this formula:

=FV(B2/B7, B3*B7, B4, B5, B7)

Suppose you wish to save some money for renovating your house in 5 years. You deposit $3,000 to your saving account at an interest rate of 7% compounded monthly. Furthermore, you will add $100 at the beginning of each month. How much money will there be in your saving account in 5 years? According to our Excel FV calculator - around $11,500.

	Description	Value
1	Description	Value
2	Annual interest rate	7%
3	No. of years	5
4	Periodic payment	-$100
5	Initial investment	-$3,000
6	When payments are due	1
7	Compounding periods per year	12
8		
9	Future value	$11,453.93

When setting up a future value calculator for other users, there are a few things to take notice of:

- Both pmt and PV should be negative numbers because they represent an outflow. If positive numbers are entered in the corresponding cells, put the minus sign before these arguments directly in the formula.
- If pmt is zero or omitted, specify the present value (PV) and vice versa.
- For type, consider creating a drop-down list to only allow 0 and 1 values. This will help you prevent accidental mistakes that users could make.
- The Compounding periods per year cell (B7) must have a number other than zero; otherwise, the formula will return a #DIV/0 error. If an interest rate is compounded annually, enter 1 in that cell.

Excel FV Function Is Not Working.

If an FV formula results in an error or yields a wrong result, in all likelihood, that will be one of the following.

1. #VALUE! error

It may occur if one or more arguments are non-numeric. Check if any of the numbers referenced in your formula are formatted as text to fix the error. If some are, then convert text values to numbers.

2. FV function returns an incorrect future value.

If the returned future value is negative or much lower than expected, most likely, either the pmt or PV argument or both are represented by positive numbers. Please remember that who should use negative numbers for all outgoing payments.

4. The PMT Functions

The PMT function is a financial function that returns periodic payments. You can use the PMT function to figure out payments for a loan, given the loan amount, the number of periods, and the interest rate.

What Is The PMT Function In Excel?

The Excel PMT function is a financial function that calculates the payment for a loan based on a constant interest rate, the number of periods, and the loan amount.

"PMT" stands for "payment," hence the function's name.

For example, if you are applying for a two-year car loan with an annual interest rate of 7% and a loan amount of $30,000, a PMT formula can tell you your monthly payments.

Usage Notes

who can use the PMT function to figure out the future payments, assuming constant payments and a constant interest rate?

For example, if you borrow $10,000 on a 24-month loan with an annual interest rate of 8 percent, PMT can tell you what your monthly payments are and how much Principal and interest you are paying each month.

Notes:

The payment returned by PMT includes Principal and interest but will not include any taxes, reserve payments, or fees.

Be sure you are consistent with the units you supply for rate and per. If you make monthly payments on a three-year loan at an annual interest rate of 12 percent, use 12%/12 for the speed and 3*12 for nper. For yearly payments on the same loan, use 12 percent for rate and 3 for nper.

For The PMT Function To Work Correctly In Your Worksheets, Please Keep In Mind These Facts:

- In line with the general cash flow model, the payment amount is output as a negative number because it's a cash outflow.
- The value returned by the PMT function includes Principal and interest but does not include any fees, taxes, or reserve payments that may be associated with a loan.
- A PMT formula in Excel can compute a loan payment for different payment frequencies such as weekly, monthly, quarterly, or annually. This example shows how to do it correctly.
- The PMT function is available in Excel for Office 365, Excel 2019, Excel 2016, Excel 2013, Excel 2010, and Excel 2007.

Excel PMT Function - Syntax And Primary Uses

The PMT function has the following arguments:

- PMT(rate, nper, pv, [fv], [type])

Where:

Rate (Required): The constant interest rate per period. It can be supplied as a percentage or decimal number.

For example, if you make annual payments on a loan at an annual interest rate of 10 percent, use 10% or 0.1 for speed. If you make monthly payments on the same loan, use 10%/12 or 0.00833 for the rate.

Nper (Required): The number of payments for the loan, i.e., the total number of periods over who should pay the loan.

For example, if you make annual payments on a 5-year loan, supply 5 for nper. If you make monthly payments on the same loan, multiply the number of years by 12, and use 5*12 or 60 for nper.

Pv (Required): The present value, i.e., the total amount that all future payments are worth now. In the case of a loan, it's simply the original amount borrowed.

Fv (Optional): The future value or the cash balance you wish to have after the last payment. If omitted, the loan's future value is assumed to be zero (0).

Type (Optional): Specifies when the payments are due:
- 0 or omitted: Payments are due at the end of each period.
- 1: Payments are due at the beginning of each period.

For example, if you borrow $100,000 for five years with an annual interest rate of 7%, the following formula will calculate the annual payment:

=PMT(7%, 5, 100000)

To find the monthly payment for the same loan, use this formula:

=PMT(7%/12, 5*12, 100000)

Or, you can enter the known components of a loan in separate cells and reference those cells in your PMT formula. With the interest rate in B1, no. of years in B2, and loan amount in B3, the formula is as simple as this:

=PMT(B1, B2, B3)

Please remember that the payment is returned as a negative number because this amount will be debited (subtracted) from your bank account.

By default, Excel displays the result in the currency format, rounded to 2 decimal places, highlighted in red, and enclosed in parenthesis, as shown in the left part of the image below. The image on the right shows the same result in the General format.

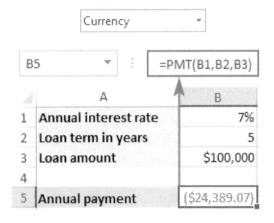 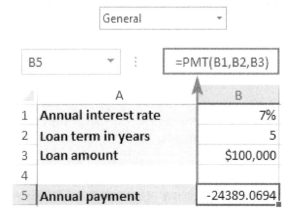

PMT Function In Excel

If you'd like to have the payment as a positive number, put a minus sign before either the entire PMT formula or the PV argument (loan amount):

=-PMT(B1, B2, B3)

or

=PMT(B1, B2, -B3)

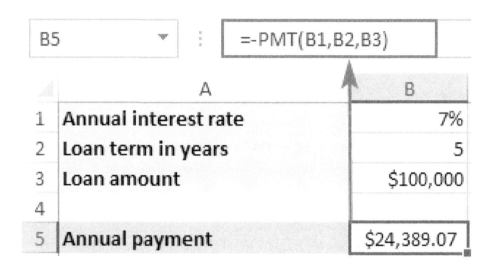

Tip: To calculate the total amount paid for the loan, multiply the returned PMT value by the number of periods (nper value). In our case, we'd use this equation: 24,389.07*5 and find that the total amount equals $121,945.35.

How To Use PMT Function In Excel - Formula Examples

Below you will find a few more examples of an Excel PMT formula that show how to calculate other periodic payments for a car loan, home loan, mortgage loan, and the like.

The Complete Form Of The PMT Function In Excel

For the most part, you can omit the last two arguments in your PMT formulas (like we did in the above examples) because their default values cover the most typical uses cases:

- Fv omitted - implies zero balance after the last payment.
- Type missed - payments are due at the end of each period.

If your loan conditions are different from the defaults, then use the complete form of the PMT formula.

As an example, let's calculate the number of annual payments based on these input cells:

- B1 - annual interest rate
- B2 - loan term (in years)
- B3 - loan amount
- B4 - future value (balance after the last payment)
- B5 - annuity type:
    i. 0 (regular annuity) - payments are made at the end of each year.
    ii. 1 (allowance due) - payments are made at the beginning of the period, e.g., rent or lease payments.

Supply these references to your Excel PMT formula:

=PMT(B1, B2, B3, B4, B5)

And you will have this result:

	A	B	C	D	E	F
1	Annual interest rate	7%				
2	Loan term in years	5				
3	Loan amount	$100,000				
4	Future value	$0				
5	When payments are due		1 <-- 0 - end of period; 1 - beginning of period			
6						
7	Annual payment	($22,793.52)				

B7 = =PMT(B1,B2,B3,B4,B5)

Calculate Weekly, Monthly, Quarterly, And Semiannual Payments

Depending on the payment frequency, you need to use the following calculations for rate and nper arguments:

- For rate, divide the annual interest rate by the number of payments per year (which is equal to the number of compounding periods).
- For nper, multiply the number of years by the number of payments per year.

The below table provides the details:

Payment Frequency	Rate	Nper
Weekly	annual interest rate / 52	years * 52
Monthly	annual interest rate / 12	years * 12
Quarterly	annual interest rate / 4	years * 4
Semi-annual	annual interest rate / 2	years * 2

For instance, to find the amount of a periodic payment on a $5,000 loan with an 8% annual interest rate and a duration of 3 years, use one of the below formulas.

Weekly payment:

=PMT(8%/52, 3*52, 5000)

Monthly payment:

=PMT(8%/12, 3*12, 5000)

Quarterly payment:

=PMT(8%/4, 3*4, 5000)

Semiannual payment:

=PMT(8%/2, 3*2, 5000)

In all cases, the balance after the last payment is assumed to be $0, and the payments are due at the end of each period.

The screenshot below shows the results of these formulas:

	A	B	C	D
1	Annual interest rate	8%		
2	Loan term in years	3		
3	Loan amount	$5,000		
4				
5	Weekly payment	($36.08)	=PMT(B1/52,B2*52,B3)	
6	Monthly payment	($156.68)	=PMT(B1/12,B2*12,B3)	
7	Quarterly payment	($472.80)	=PMT(B1/4,B2*4,B3)	
8	Semi-annual payment	($953.81)	=PMT(B1/2,B2*2,B3)	

How To Make A PMT Calculator In Excel

Before you go ahead and borrow money, it stands to reason to compare different loan conditions to find the options that suit you most. For this, let's create our own Excel loan payment calculator.

1. To begin with, enter the loan amount, interest rate, and loan term in separate cells (B3, B4, B5, respectively).

2. To be able to choose different periods and specify when the payments are due, create drop-down lists with the following predefined options (B6 and B7):

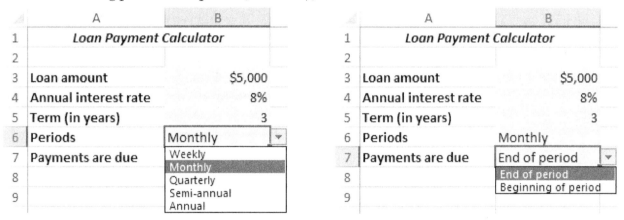

3. Set up the lookup tables for Periods (E2:F6) and Payments are Due (E8:F9), as shown in the screenshot below. It is essential that text labels in the lookup tables exactly match the items of the corresponding drop-down list. In the cells next to the drop-down lists, enter the following IFERROR VLOOKUP formulas that will pull the number from the lookup table corresponding to the item selected in the drop-down list.

The formula for Periods (C6):

=IFERROR(VLOOKUP(B6, E2:F6, 2, 0), "")

The formula for Payments are Due (C7):

=IFERROR(VLOOKUP(B7, E8:F9, 2, 0), "")

	A	B	C	D	E	F
1	Loan Payment Calculator				Periods	
2					Weekly	52
3	Loan amount	$5,000			Monthly	12
4	Annual interest rate	8%			Quarterly	4
5	Term (in years)	3			Semi-annual	2
6	Periods	Monthly	12		Annual	1
7	Payments are due	End of period	0		Payments are due	
8					End of period	0
9					Beginning of period	1

C6: `=IFERROR(VLOOKUP(B6,E2:F6,2,0),"")`
C7: `=IFERROR(VLOOKUP(B7,E8:F9,2,0),"")`

4. Write a PMT formula to calculate the periodic payment based on your cells. In our case, the formula goes as follows:

`=IFERROR(-PMT(B4/C6, B5*C6, B3, 0, C7), "")`

Please notice the following things:

- The fv argument (0) is hardcoded in the formula because we always want zero balance after the last payment. If you wish to allow your users to enter any future value, allocate a separate input cell for the fv argument.
- The PMT function preceded the minus sign to display the result as a positive number.
- The PMT function is wrapped into IFERROR to hide errors when some input values are not defined.

The above formula goes in B9. And in the neighboring cell (A9), we display a label corresponding to the selected period (B6). For this, concatenate the value in B6 and the desired text:

`=B6&" Payment"`

	A	B	C	D	E	F
1	Loan Payment Calculator				Periods	
2					Weekly	52
3	Loan amount	$50,000			Monthly	12
4	Annual interest rate	8%			Quarterly	4
5	Term (in years)	3			Semi-annual	2
6	Periods	Monthly	12		Annual	1
7	Payments are due	End of period	0		Payments are due	
8					End of period	0
9	Monthly Payment	$1,566.82			Beginning of period	1

A9: `=B6&" Payment"`
B9: `=IFERROR(-PMT(B4/C6, B5*C6,B3,0,C7),"")`

5. Finally, you can hide the lookup tables from view, add a few finishing formatting touches, and your Excel PMT calculator is good to go:

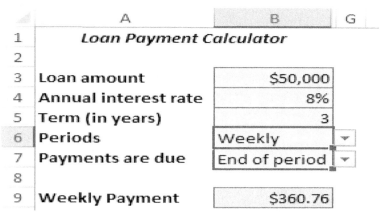

Excel PMT Function Is Not Working

If your Excel PMT formula is not working or produces wrong results, it's likely to be because of the following reasons:

- A #NUM! error may occur if the rate argument is a negative number or nper is equal to 0.
- A #VALUE! error occurs if one or more arguments are text values.
- If the result of a PMT formula is much higher or lower than expected, make sure you are consistent with the units supplied for the rate and nper arguments, meaning you have correctly converted the annual interest rate to the period's rate and the number of years to weeks, months, or quarters as shown in this example.

Here Are A Few Things To Remember About The PMT Function:

1. #NUM! error – occurs when:

- The given rate value is less than or equal to -1.
- The given nper value is equal to 0.

2. #VALUE! Error – Occurs when any of the arguments provided are non-numeric.

3. When calculating monthly or quarterly payments, we need to convert annual interest rates or the number of periods to months or quarters.

4. If we wish to find out the total amount paid for the duration of the loan, we need to multiply the PMT as calculated by nper.

Excel Functions For Finance

The topmost essential functions and formulas you need to know are plain and simple. Follow this guide, and you'll be ready to tackle any financial problems in Excel.

It should be noted that while each of these formulas and functions is useful independently, who can also use them in combinations that make them even more powerful. We will point out these combinations wherever possible.

Building Statistic Functions

1. Future Value (FV): Financial Function in Excel

If you want to find out the future value of a particular investment that has a constant interest rate and periodic payment, use the following formula:

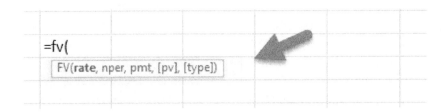

Future Value - Financial Functions In Excel

FV (Rate, Nper, [Pmt], PV, [Type])

- Rate = It is the interest rate/period
- Nper = Number of periods
- [Pmt] = Payment/period
- PV = Present Value
- [Type] = When the payment is made (if nothing is mentioned, it's assumed that the payment has been made at the end of the period)

FV Example: A has invested US $100 in 2016. The payment has been made yearly. The interest rate is 10% p.a. What would be the FV in 2019?

Solution: In excel, we will put the equation as follows:

	A	B	C
1			
2			
3		Rate	10%
4		nper	3
5		pmt	1
6		pv	-100
7		type	0
8			
9		=FV(C3,C4,C5,C6,C7)	
10			

= FV (10%, 3, 1, – 100)

= US $129.79

2. FVSCHEDULE: Financial Function In Excel

This financial function is essential when calculating the future value with the variable interest rate. Have a look at the function below:

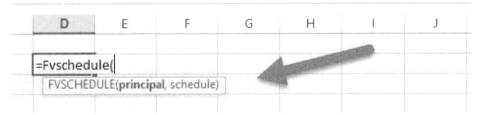

FVSCHEDULE = (Principal, Schedule)

- Principal = Principal is the present value of a particular investment
- Schedule = A series of interest rates put together (in the case of excel, we will use different boxes and select the range)

FVSCHEDULE Example: M has invested US $100 at the end of 2016. It is expected that the interest rate will change every year. In 2017, 2018 & 2019, the interest rates would be 4%, 6% & 5% respectively. What would be the FV in 2019?

Solution: In excel, we will do the following:

	A	B	C	D	E
1		Principal	100		
2		2017	4%		
3		2018	6%		
4		2019	5%		
5					
6		=FVSCHEDULE(C1,C2:C4)			
7					
8					

= FVSCHEDULE (C1, C2: C4)
= US $115.752

3. Present Value (PV): Financial Function In Excel

If you know how to calculate FV, it's easier to find out PV. Here's how:

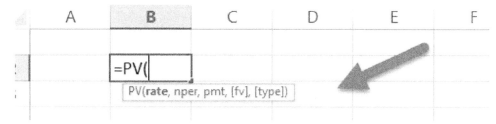

PV = (Rate, Nper, [Pmt], FV, [Type])

- Rate = It is the interest rate/period
- Nper = Number of periods
- [Pmt] = Payment/period
- FV = Future Value
- [Type] = When the payment is made (if nothing is mentioned, it's assumed that the payment has been made at the end of the period)

PV Example: The future value of an investment in the US is $100 in 2019. The payment has been made yearly. The interest rate is 10% p.a. What would be the PV as of now?

Solution: In excel, we will put the equation as follows:

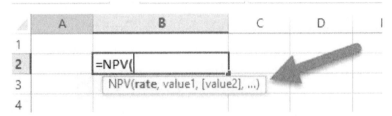

= PV (10%, 3, 1, – 100)

= US $72.64

4. Net Present Value (NPV): Financial Function In Excel

Net Present Value is the total positive, and negative cash flows over the years. Here's how we will represent it in excel:

NPV = (Rate, Value 1, [Value 2], [Value 3]...)

- Rate = Discount rate for a period
- Value 1, [Value 2], [Value 3]... = Positive or negative cash flows
- Here, negative values would be considered payments, and positive values would be treated as inflows.

NPV Example

Here is a series of data from which we need to find NPV:

Details	In US $
Rate of Discount	5%
Initial Investment	-1000
Return from 1st year	300
Return from 2nd year	400
Return from 3rd year	400

Return from 4th year	300

Find out the NPV.

Solution: In Excel, we will do the following:

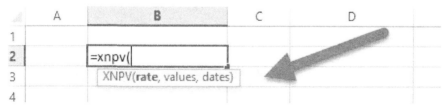

=NPV (5%, B4:B7) + B3

= US $240.87

5. XNPV: Financial Function In Excel

This financial function is similar to the NPV with a twist. Here the payment and income are not periodic. Rather specific dates are mentioned for each payment and income. Here's how we will calculate it:

XNPV = (Rate, Values, Dates)

- Rate = Discount rate for a period
- Values = Positive or negative cash flows (an array of values)
- Dates = Specific dates (a variety of dates)

XNPV Example: Here is a series of data from which we need to find NPV:

Details	In US $	Dates
Rate of Discount	5%	
Initial Investment	-1000	1st December 2011
Return from 1st year	300	1st January 2012
Return from 2nd year	400	1st February 2013

| Return from 3rd year | 400 | 1st March 2014 |
| Return from 4th year | 300 | 1st April 2015 |

Solution: In excel, we will do as follows:

	A	B	C	D	E
1					
2		Details	In US $		
3		Rate of Discount	5%		
4		Initial Investment	-1000	1-Dec-11	
5		Return from 1st year	300	1-Jan-12	
6		Return from 2nd year	400	1-Feb-13	
7		Return from 3rd year	400	1-Mar-14	
8		Return from 4th year	300	1-Apr-15	
9					
10		=XNPV(C3,C4:C8,D4:D8)			
11					
12					

=XNPV (5%, B2:B6, C2:C6)

= US$289.90

6. PMT: Financial Function In Excel

In excel, PMT denotes the periodical payment required to pay off for a particular period with a constant interest rate. Let's have a look at how to calculate it in excel:

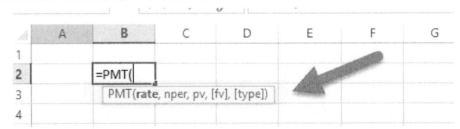

PMT = (Rate, Nper, PV, [FV], [Type])

- Rate = It is the interest rate/period
- Nper = Number of periods
- PV = Present Value
- [FV] = An optional argument that is about the future value of a loan (if nothing is mentioned, FV is considered as "0")
- [Type] = When the payment is made (if nothing is mentioned, it's assumed that the payment has been made at the end of the period)

PMT Example

The US $1000 needs to be paid in full in 3 years. The interest rate is 10% p.a., who must make the payment yearly. Find out the PMT.

Solution: In excel, we will calculate it in the following manner:

	A	B	C	D	E	
1						
2		Rate	10%			
3		nper	3			
4		PV	1000			
5		fv				
6		type				
7						
8		=PMT(C2,C3,C4,C5,C6)				

= PMT (10%, 3, 1000)

= − 402.11

7. PPMT: Financial Function In Excel

It is another version of PMT. The only difference is this – PPMT calculates payment on Principal with a constant interest rate and regular periodic payments. Here's how to figure PPMT:

PPMT = (Rate, Per, Nper, PV, [FV], [Type])

- Rate = It is the interest rate/period.
- Per = The period for which the Principal is to be calculated
- Nper = number of periods
- PV = Present Value
- [FV] = An optional argument that is about the future value of a loan (if nothing is mentioned, FV is considered as "0")
- [Type] = When the payment is made (if nothing is mentioned, it's assumed that the payment has been made at the end of the period)

PPMT Example

The US $1000 needs to be paid in full in 3 years. The interest rate is 10% p.a., who must make the payment yearly. Find out the PPMT in the first year and second year.

Solution: In excel, we will calculate it in the following manner:

1st year,

	A	B	C	D
1				
2		Rate	10%	
3		nper	3	
4		PV	1000	
5		fv		
6		type		
7				
8		=PPMT(C2,1,C3,C4)		

=PPMT (10%, 1, 3, 1000)

= US $-302.11

2nd year,

	A	B	C	D
1				
2		Rate	10%	
3		nper	3	
4		PV	1000	
5		fv		
6		type		
7				
8		=PPMT(C2,2,C3,C4)		
9				
10				

=PPMT (10%, 2, 3, 1000)

= US $-332.33

8. Internal Rate Of Return (IRR): Financial Function In Excel

To understand whether any new project or investment is profitable or not, the firm uses IRR. If IRR is more than the hurdle rate (acceptable rate/ average cost of capital), then it's profitable for the firm and vice-versa. Let's have a look at how we find out IRR in excel:

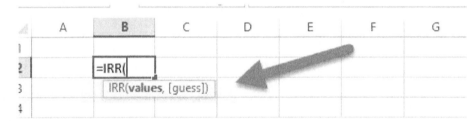

IRR = (Values, [Guess])

- Values = Positive or negative cash flows (an array of values)
- [Guess] = An assumption of what you think IRR should be

IRR Example

Here is a series of data from which we need to find IRR:

Details	In US $
Initial Investment	-1000
Return from 1st year	300
Return from 2nd year	400
Return from 3rd year	400
Return from 4th year	300

Find out IRR.

Solution: Here's how we will calculate IRR in Excel:

	A	B	C	D	E
1					
2		Details	In US $		
3		Initial Investment	-1000		
4		Return from 1st year	300		
5		Return from 2nd year	400		
6		Return from 3rd year	400		
7		Return from 4th year	300		
8					
9		=IRR(C3:C7,0.1)			
10					

= IRR (A2:A6, 0.1)

= 15%

9. Modified Internal Rate Of Return (MIRR): Financial Function In Excel

The Modified Internal Rate of Return is one step ahead of the Internal Rate of Return. MIRR signifies that the investment is profitable and is used in business. MIRR is calculated by assuming NPV as zero. Here's how to calculate MIRR in excel:

MIRR = (Values, Finance rate, Reinvestment rate)

- Values = Positive or negative cash flows (an array of values)
- Finance rate = Interest rate paid for the money used in cash flows
- Reinvestment rate = Interest rate paid for reinvestment of cash flows

MIRR Example

Here is a series of data from which we need to find MIRR:

Details	US $
Initial Investment	-1000
Return from 1st year	300
Return from 2nd year	400
Return from 3rd year	400
Return from 4th year	300

Finance rate = 12%; Reinvestment rate = 10%. Find out IRR.

Solution: Let's look at the calculation of MIRR:

= MIRR (B2:B6, 12%, 10%)

= 13%

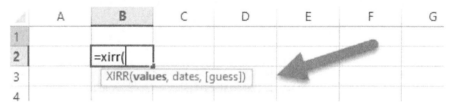

10. XIRR: Financial Function In Excel

Here we need to find out IRR, which has specific cash flow dates. That's the only difference between IRR and XIRR. Have a look at how to calculate XIRR in excel financial function:

XIRR = (Values, Dates, [Guess])

- Values = Positive or negative cash flows (an array of values)
- Dates = Specific dates (a variety of dates)
- [Guess] = An assumption of what you think IRR should be

XIRR Example

Here is a series of data from which we need to find XIRR:

Details	In US $	Dates
Initial Investment	-1000	1st December 2011
Return from 1st year	300	1st January 2012
Return from 2nd year	400	1st February 2013
Return from 3rd year	400	1st March 2014
Return from 4th year	300	1st April 2015

Solution: Let's have a look at the answer:

	A	B	C	D	E
1					
2		Details	In US $		
3		Rate of Discount	5%		
4		Initial Investment	-1000	1-Dec-11	
5		Return from 1st year	300	1-Jan-12	
6		Return from 2nd year	400	1-Feb-13	
7		Return from 3rd year	400	1-Mar-14	
8		Return from 4th year	300	1-Apr-15	
9					
10		=XIRR(C4:C8,D4:D8)			
11					

= XIRR (B2:B6, C2:C6, 0.1)

= 24%

11. NPER: Financial Function In Excel

The number of periods one requires to pay off the loan is simply the number of periods one needs. Let's see how we can calculate NPER in excel.

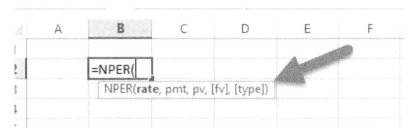

NPER = (Rate, PMT, PV, [FV], [Type])

- Rate = It is the interest rate/period
- PMT = Amount paid per period
- PV = Present Value
- [FV] = An optional argument that is about the future value of a loan (if nothing is mentioned, FV is considered as "0")
- [Type] = When the payment is made (if nothing is mentioned, it's assumed that the payment has been made at the end of the period)

NPER Example

US $200 is paid per year for a loan of US $1000. The interest rate is 10% p.a., who must make the payment yearly. Find out the NPER.

Solution: We need to calculate NPER in the following manner:

	A	B	C	D	E	F
1						
2		Rate	10%			
3		PMT	-200			
4		Loan	1000			
5						
6		=NPER(C2,C3,C4)				
7						

= NPER (10%, -200, 1000)

= 7.27 years

12. RATE: Financial Function In Excel

We can calculate the interest rate needed to pay off the loan in total for a given period. Let's have a look at how to calculate RATE financial function in excel:

	A	B	C	D	E	F
1						
2		=rate(				
3		RATE(nper, pmt, pv, [fv], [type], [guess])				
4						

RATE = (NPER, PMT, PV, [FV], [Type], [Guess])

- Nper = number of periods
- PMT = Amount paid per period
- PV = Present Value
- [FV] = An optional argument that is about the future value of a loan (if nothing is mentioned, FV is considered as "0")
- [Type] = When the payment is made (if nothing is mentioned, it's assumed that the payment has been made at the end of the period)
- [Guess] = An assumption of what you think RATE should be

RATE Example

US $200 is paid per year for a loan of US $1000 for six years, and the payment needs to be done yearly. Find out the RATE.

Solution:

	A	B	C	D	E	F
1						
2		Years	6.00			
3		PMT	-200			
4		Loan	1000			
5						
6		=RATE(C2,C3,C4,0,0,0.1)				
7						

= RATE (6, -200, 1000, 0.1)

= 5%

13. EFFECT: Financial Function In Excel

Through the EFFECT function, we can understand the effective annual interest rate. When we have the nominal interest rate and the number of compounding per year, it becomes easy to find the effective rate. Let's have a look at how to calculate EFFECT financial function in excel:

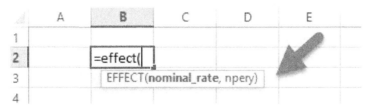

EFFECT = (Nominal_Rate, NPERY)

- Nominal_Rate = Nominal Interest Rate
- NPERY = number of compounding per year

EFFECT Example

Payment needs to be paid with a nominal interest rate of 12% when the number of compounding per year is 12.

Solution:

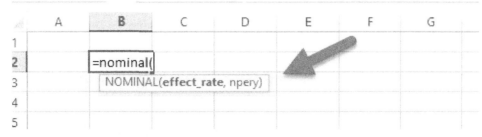

= EFFECT (12%, 12)

= 12.68%

14. NOMINAL: Financial Function In Excel

When we have an effective annual rate and the number of compounding periods per year, we can calculate the NOMINAL rate for the year. Let's have a look at how to do it in excel:

NOMINAL = (Effect_Rate, NPERY)

- Effect_Rate = Effective annual interest rate
- NPERY = number of compounding per year

NOMINAL Example

173 | Page

Payment needs to be paid with an effective interest rate or annual equivalent rate of 12% when the number of compounding per year is 12.

Solution:

	A	B	C	D
1				
2		Effective Interest Rate	12%	
3		Compounding per year	12	
4				
5		=NOMINAL(C2,C3)		
6				

= NOMINAL (12%, 12)

= 11.39%

15. SLN: Financial Function In Excel

Through the SLN function, we can calculate depreciation via a straight-line method. In excel, we will look at SLN's financial function as follows:

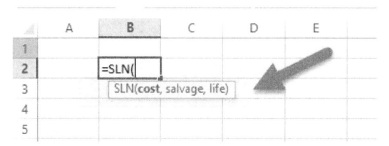

SLN = (Cost, Salvage, Life)

- Cost = cost of an asset when bought (initial amount)
- Salvage = Value of asset after depreciation
- Life = number of periods over which the asset is being depreciated

SLN Example

The initial cost of machinery is the US $5000. It has been depreciated in the Straight Line Method. Who used the machinery for ten years, and now the salvage value of the machinery is the US $300. Find depreciation charged per year.

Solution:

	A	B	C	D	E
1					
2		Cost of Machinery	5000		
3		Salvage Value	300		
4		Years	10		
5					
6		=SLN(C2,C3,C4)			
7					

= SLN (5000, 300, 10)

= the US $470 per year

CHAPTER 10: EXCEL CHARTING BASICS

What Are Graphs And Charts In Excel?

Charts and graphs elevate your data by providing an easy-to-understand visualization of numeric values. While the terms are often used interchangeably, they are slightly different. Graphs are the most basic way to represent data visually and typically display data point values over a duration of time. Charts are a bit more complex, as they allow you to compare pieces of a data set relative to the other data in that set. Charts are also considered more visual than graphs since they often take a different shape than a generic x- and y-axis.

People often use charts and graphs in presentations to give management, client, or team members a quick snapshot into progress or results. You can create a chart or graph to represent nearly any kind of quantitative data, doing so will save you the time and frustration of poring through spreadsheets to find relationships and trends.

It's easy to create charts and graphs in Excel, especially since you can also store your data directly in an Excel Workbook, rather than importing data from another program. Excel also has a variety of preset chart and graph types so you can select one that best represents the data relationship(s) you want to highlight.

Explanation Of Charts

A chart is a tool you can use in Excel to communicate data graphically. Charts allow your audience to see the meaning behind the numbers, and they make showing comparisons and trends much easier.

In this book, you will learn how to insert charts and modify them so they communicate information effectively. Each of Excel's 12 chart types has different features that make them better suited for specific tasks. Pairing a chart with its correct data-style will make the information easier to understand, enhancing the communication within your small business.

Graphs or charts help people understand data quickly. Whether you want to make a comparison, show a relationship, or highlight a trend, they help your audience "see" what you are talking about.

Among its many features, Microsoft Excel, enables you to incorporate charts, providing a way to add visual appeal to your business reports.

The Importance Of Charts

- Allows you to visualize data graphically
- It's easier to analyze trends and patterns using charts in MS Excel
- Accessible to interpret compared to data in cells

When To Use Each Chart And Graph Type In Excel

Excel offers a large library of chart and graph types to help visually present your data. While multiple chart types might "work" for a given data set, it's important to select a chart type that best fits with the story you want the data to tell. Of course, you can also add graphical elements to enhance and customize a chart or graph. In Excel 2016, there are five main categories of charts or graphs:

- Excel provides you with different types of charts that suit your purpose. Based on the type of data, you can create a chart. You can also change the chart type later.

Excel Offers The Following Major Chart Types:

- Column Chart
- Line Chart
- Pie Chart
- Doughnut Chart

- Bar Chart
- Area Chart
- XY (Scatter) Chart
- Bubble Chart
- Stock Chart
- Surface Chart
- Radar Chart
- Combo Chart

Each of these chart types has sub-types. In this book, you will have an overview of the different chart types and get to know the sub-types for each chart type.

1. Column Chart

A Column Chart typically displays the categories along with the horizontal (category) axis and values along with the vertical (value) axis. To create a column chart, arrange the data in columns or rows on the worksheet. A column chart has the following sub-types:

- Clustered Column.
- Stacked Column.
- 100% Stacked Column.
- 3-D Clustered Column.
- 3-D Stacked Column.
- 3-D 100% Stacked Column.
- 3-D Column.

2. Line Chart

Line charts can show continuous data over time on an evenly scaled axis. Therefore, they are ideal for showing trends in data at equal intervals, such as months, quarters, or years. In a Line chart:

- Category data is distributed evenly along the horizontal axis.
- Value data is distributed evenly along the vertical axis.
- To create a Line chart, arrange the data in columns or rows on the worksheet.

A-Line Chart Has The Following Sub-Types:

- Line
- Stacked Line
- 100% Stacked Line
- Line with Markers
- Stacked Line with Markers
- 100% Stacked Line with Markers
- 3-D Line

3. Pie Chart

Pie charts show the size of items in one data series, proportional to the sum of the items. The data points in a pie chart are shown as a percentage of the whole pie. To create a Pie Chart, arrange the data in one column or row on the worksheet. A Pie Chart has the following sub-types:

- Pie
- 3-D Pie
- Pie of Pie
- Bar of Pie

4. Doughnut Chart

A Doughnut chart shows the relationship of parts to a whole. It is similar to a Pie Chart with the only difference that a Doughnut Chart can contain more than one data series, whereas, a Pie Chart can contain only one data series.

A Doughnut Chart contains rings and each ring represents one data series. To create a Doughnut Chart, arrange the data in columns or rows on a worksheet.

5. Bar Chart

Bar Charts illustrate comparisons among individual items. In a Bar Chart, the categories are organized along the vertical axis and the values are organized along the horizontal axis. To create a Bar Chart, arrange the data in columns or rows on the worksheet. A Bar Chart has the following sub-types:

- Clustered Bar
- Stacked Bar
- 100% Stacked Bar
- 3-D Clustered Bar
- 3-D Stacked Bar
- 3-D 100% Stacked Bar

6. Area Chart

Area Charts can be used to plot the change over time and draw attention to the total value across a trend. By showing the sum of the plotted values, an area chart also shows the relationship of parts to a whole. To create an Area Chart, arrange the data in columns or rows on the worksheet. An Area Chart has the following sub-types:

- Area
- Stacked Area
- 100% Stacked Area
- 3-D Area
- 3-D Stacked Area
- 3-D 100% Stacked Area

7. XY (Scatter) Chart

XY (Scatter) charts are typically used for showing and comparing numeric values, like scientific, statistical, and engineering data.

A Scatter Chart Has Two Value Axes:

- Horizontal (x) Value Axis
- Vertical (y) Value Axis

It combines x and y values into single data points and displays them in irregular intervals, or clusters. To create a Scatter chart, arrange the data in columns and rows on the worksheet.

Place the x values in one row or column, and then enter the corresponding y values in the adjacent rows or columns.

Consider Using A Scatter Chart When:

- You wants to change the scale of the horizontal axis.
- You want to make that axis a logarithmic scale.
- Values for the horizontal axis are not evenly spaced.
- There are many data points on the horizontal axis.
- You wants to adjust the independent axis scales of a scatter chart to reveal more information about data that includes pairs or grouped sets of values.

- You want to show similarities between large sets of data instead of differences between data points.
- You want to compare many data points regardless of the time.
- The more data that you include in a scatter chart, the better the comparisons you can make.

A Scatter Chart Has The Following Sub-Types:

- Scatter
- Scatter with Smooth Lines and Markers
- Scatter with Smooth Lines
- Scatter with Straight Lines and Markers
- Scatter with Straight Lines

8. Bubble Chart

A Bubble chart is like a Scatter chart with an additional third column to specify the size of the bubbles it shows to represent the data points in the data series. A Bubble chart has the following sub-types:

- Bubble
- Bubble with 3-D effect

9. Stock Chart

As the name implies, stock charts can show fluctuations in stock prices. However, a Stock chart can also be used to show fluctuations in other data, such as daily rainfall or annual temperatures. To create a Stock chart, arrange the data in columns or rows in a specific order on the worksheet. For example, to create a simple high-low-close Stock chart, arrange your data with High, Low, and Close entered as column headings, in that order. A Stock chart has the following sub-types:

- High-Low-Close
- Open-High-Low-Close
- Volume-High-Low-Close
- Volume-Open-High-Low-Close

10. Surface Chart

A Surface chart is useful when you want to find the optimum combinations between two sets of data. As in a topographic map, colors and patterns indicate areas that are in the same range of values. To create a Surface chart:

- Ensure that both the categories and the data series are numeric values.
- Arrange the data in columns or rows on the worksheet.

A Surface Chart Has The Following Sub-Types:

- 3-D Surface
- Wireframe 3-D Surface
- Contour
- Wireframe Contour

11. Radar Chart

Radar charts compare the aggregate values of several data series. To create a Radar chart, arrange the data in columns or rows on the worksheet. A Radar chart has the following sub-types:

- Radar
- Radar with Markers
- Filled Radar

12. Combo Chart

Combo charts combine two or more chart types to make the data easy to understand, especially when the data is widely varied. It is shown with a secondary axis and is even easier to read. To create a Combo chart, arrange the data in columns and rows on the worksheet. A Combo chart has the following sub-types:

- Clustered Column – Line
- Clustered Column – Line on Secondary Axis
- Stacked Area – Clustered Column
- Custom Combination

Types Of Graphs In Excel

We have seen multiple uses of excel in our professional lives; it helps us analyze, sort, and extract insights from data. There are one feature of excel that helps us put insights gained from our data into a visual form: this feature helps us display data in an easy-to-understand pictorial format. We are talking about graphs in excel. Excel supports most of the commonly used graphs in statistics.

Creating different types of graphs in excel according to our data is very easy and convenient when it comes to analysis, comparing datasets, presentations, etc. In this article, we will discuss the six most commonly used types of graphs in excel. We will also discuss how to select the correct graph type for some kinds of data.

Common Types Of Graphs In Excel

The most common types of graphs used in Excel are:

- Pie Graph
- Column Graph
- Line Graph
- Area Graph
- Scatter Graph

Let's understand what the different types of graphs in Excel are and how to create them. We will start with a few examples of types of graphs in Excel.

1. The Pie Graph

As the name suggests, the pie graph is a display of data in the form of a pie or circle. This graph type is used for showing the proportions of a whole. For example, if we want to compare who did how much work in a team, we would use a pie graph to display it in an easy way to understand.

2. The Column Or Bar Graph

The next one in the list is a column graph, also called a bar graph in statistics. We use these different types of graphs where we need to see and compare values across a range. The same data that we used in the pie graph example would look like this:

There are different types of bar graphs available in Excel, such as stacked columns, 100% stacked columns, 3D columns, etc. These types of graphs can be used for expanded datasets. For example, we have been working with only two columns in the last two examples, now; if we want to include the hours worked as a third column and compare the hours worked with the number of datasets visually, we can either use a stacked column or a 100% stacked column which would look like this:

The difference between these is that while a stacked column represents actual values, a 100% stacked column represents the values as percentages. There are 3D versions as well as horizontal versions of these graphs in excel.

3. The Line Graph

The next type of graph we are going to discuss is called a line graph. This type of graph is used when we need to visualize data like an increasing or decreasing series over a period. This is an excellent graph in Excel to use for representing trends and comparing performance. For example, if we wanted to see how the current rise compares to the last raise for different people in the earlier examples, we would get something like this:

4. The Area Graph

The area graph is was available within the line graph menu. This is used for the same purpose as the line graph, which visualizes trends and compares data. In this example, we represent the relationship between the number of datasets worked on by an analyst and the number of hours they worked. The stacked area graph on the right is used for drawing attention to the difference in magnitude of two categories and displays the values as percentages.

5. The Scatter Graph

The Scatter graph is a simple representation of data points in excel. It is used when we need to compare at least two sets of data with a limited number of data points.

There are many more types of graphs available in Excel, such as Hierarchy graph, Radar graph, Waterfall graph, and Combo graphs which are combinations of two or more graphs. All these are used based on specific conditions fulfilled by the data, such as the type of data, the number of data points, etc.

How To Create Graphs In Excel?

Now that we have gone through a few examples of types of graphs in excel, we will learn how to make these graphs. The same procedure is used to make all the graphs. They are enumerated sequentially below:

1. First, choose the data you want to represent in the graph. In this case, we will select Analyst and Datasets from the practice table:

2. Click on Insert on the toolbar and navigate to the Charts menu.

3. Select the required graph from the different types of graphs; in this case, we are making a bar graph which is a horizontal column graph, but you can select any graph that suits the data you are working on:

4. A graph would appear over your data, move the graph to the required position by clicking on it and dragging it across the screen, or cut/copy the graph and paste it elsewhere where you need it:

By following the above steps and varying the type of graph you select, you can make all types of graphs available in excel. You can modify this different types of graphs like modifying a table, by specifying the data which would go into the x-axis and y-axis by right-clicking on the graph and clicking on select data, then specifying the data in the pop up that appears:

Things To Remember About Types Of Graphs In Excel

Know your data before making a graph. A type of graph that may suit a time series may, not be suitable for a set of unpatterned data.

- Sort the data before making graphs.
- Do not use unnecessary styling while making the graph.

How To Chart Data In Excel

To generate a chart or graph in Excel, you must first provide Excel with data to pull from. In this section, we'll show you how to chart data in Excel 2016.

Step 1: Enter Data Into A Worksheet

- Open Excel and select New Workbook.

- Enter the data you want to use to create a graph or chart. In this example, we're comparing the profit of five different products from 2013 to 2017. Be sure to include labels for your columns and rows. Doing so enables you to translate the data into a chart or graph with clear axis labels.
-

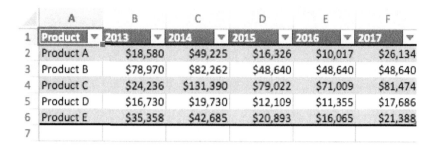

Step 2: Select Range To Create Chart Or Graph From Workbook Data
- Highlight the cells that contain the data you want to use in your graph by clicking and dragging your mouse across the cells.
- Your cell range will now be highlighted in gray and you can select a chart type.
-

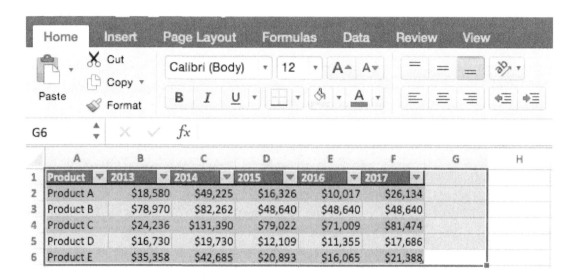

How To Make A Chart In Excel

Once you input your data and select the cell range, you're ready to choose your chart type to display your data. In this example, we'll create a clustered column chart from the data we used in the previous section.

Step 1: Select Chart Type

Once your data is highlighted in the Workbook, click the Insert tab on the top banner. About halfway across the toolbar is a section with several chart options. Excel provides Recommended Charts based on popularity, but you can click any of the dropdown menus to select a different template.

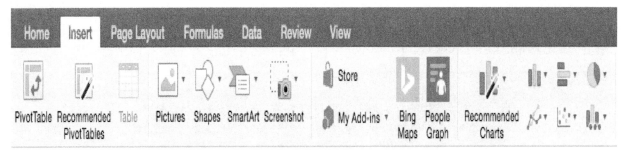

Step 2: Create Your Chart

- From the Insert tab, click the column chart icon and select Clustered Column.
-

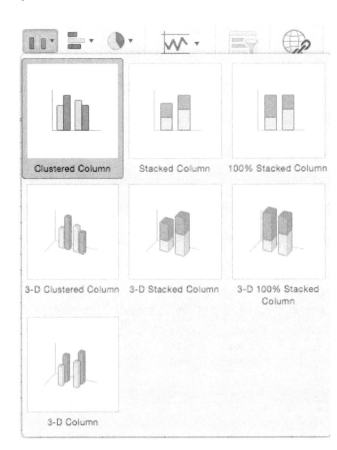

- Excel will automatically create a clustered chart column from your selected data. The chart will appear in the center of your workbook.
- To name your chart, double click the Chart Title text in the chart and type a title. We'll call this chart "Product Profit 2013 - 2017."

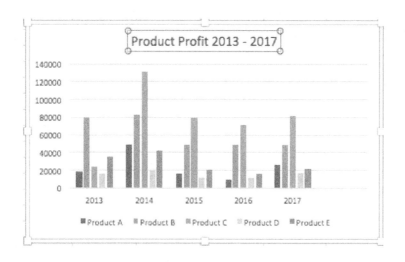

COLUMN CHART TEMPLATE

PRODUCT	2013	2014	2015	2016	2017
Product A	$18,580	$49,225	$16,326	$10,017	$26,134
Product B	$78,970	$82,262	$48,640	$48,640	$48,640
Product C	$24,236	$131,390	$79,022	$71,009	$81,474
Product D	$16,730	$19,730	$12,109	$11,355	$17,686
Product E	$35,358	$42,685	$20,893	$16,065	$21,388

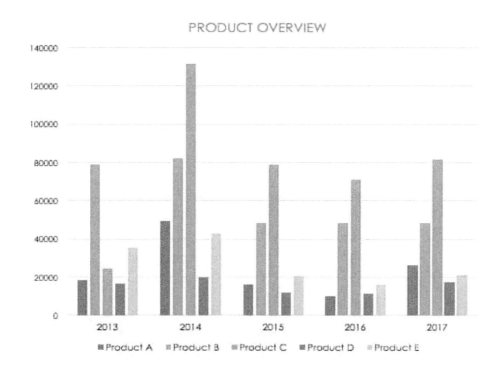

There are two tabs on the toolbar that you will use to make adjustments to your chart: Chart Design and Format. Excel automatically applies design, layout, and format presets to charts and graphs, but you can add customization by exploring the tabs. Next, we'll walk you through all the available adjustments in Chart Design.

Step 3: Add Chart Elements

Adding chart elements to your chart or graph will enhance it by clarifying data or providing additional context. You can select a chart element by clicking on the Add Chart Element dropdown menu in the top left-hand corner (beneath the Home tab).

To Display Or Hide Axes:
- Select Axes. Excel will automatically pull the column and row headers from your selected cell range to display both horizontal and vertical axes on your chart (Under Axes, there is a checkmark next to Primary Horizontal and Primary Vertical.)
-

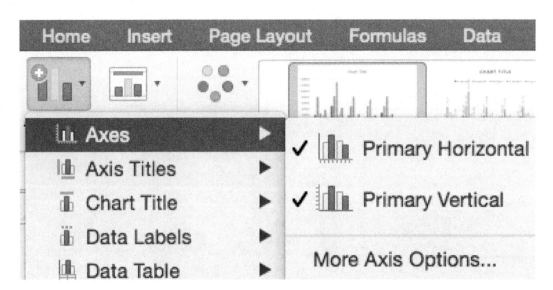

- Uncheck these options to remove the display axis on your chart. In this example, clicking Primary Horizontal will remove the year labels on the horizontal axis of your chart.

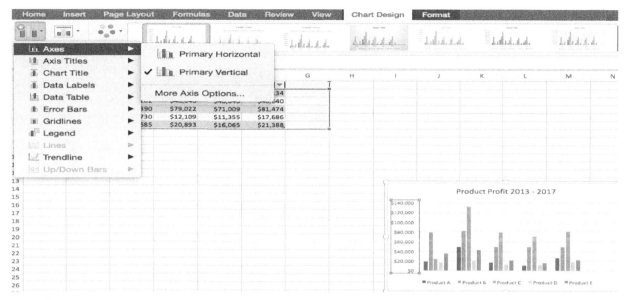

- Click More Axis Options… from the Axes dropdown menu to open a window with additional formatting and text options such as adding tick marks, labels, or numbers, or to change text color and size.

To Add Axis Titles:
- Click Add Chart Element and click Axis Titles from the dropdown menu. Excel will not automatically add axis titles to your chart; therefore, both Primary Horizontal and Primary Vertical will be unchecked.

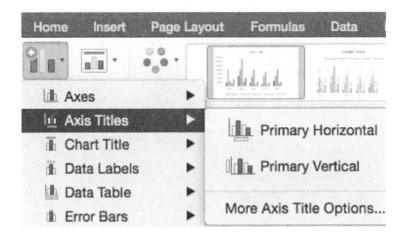

- To create axis titles, click Primary Horizontal or Primary Vertical and a text box will appear on the chart. We clicked both in this example. Type your axis titles. In this example, we added the titles "Year" (horizontal) and "Profit" (vertical).

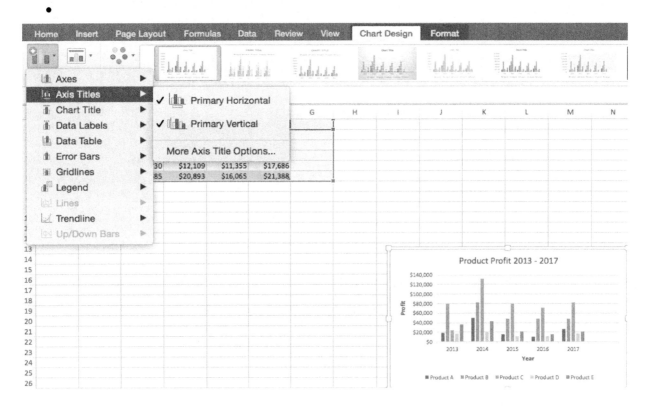

To Remove Or Move Chart Title:

- Click Add Chart Element and click Chart Title. You will see four options: None, Above Chart, Centered Overlay, and More Title Options.

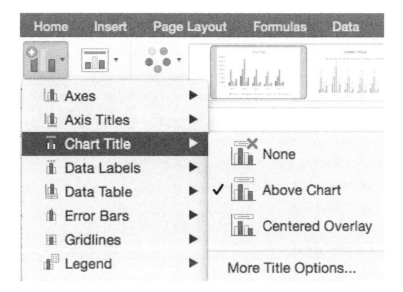

- Click None to remove the chart title.
- Click the Above Chart to place the title above the chart. If you create a chart title, Excel will automatically place it above the chart.
- Click Centered Overlay to place the title within the gridlines of the chart. Be careful with this option: you don't want the title to cover any of your data or clutter your graph.
-

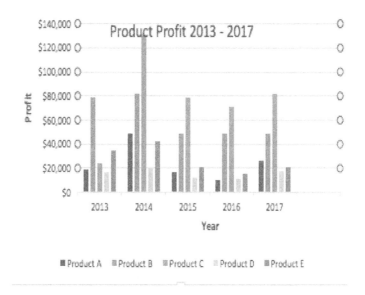

To Add Data Labels:
- Click Add Chart Element and click Data Labels. There are six options for data labels: None (default), Center, Inside End, Inside Base, Outside End, and More Data Label Title Options.

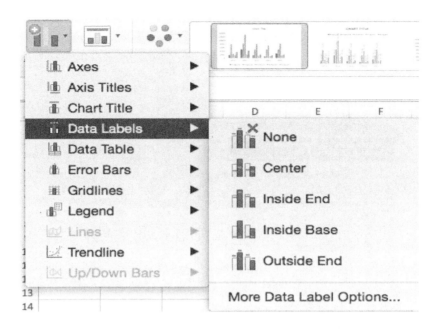

- The four placement options will add specific labels to each data point measured in your chart. Click the option you want. This customization can be helpful if you have a small amount of precise data, or if you have a lot of extra space in your chart. For a clustered column chart, however, adding data labels will likely look too cluttered.

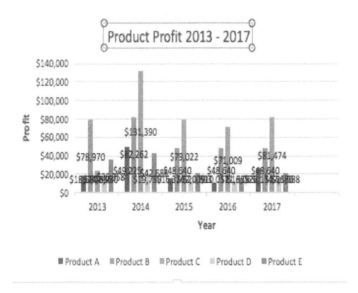

To Add A Data Table:
- Click Add Chart Element and click Data Table. There are three pre-formatted options along with an extended menu that can be found by clicking More Data Table Options:

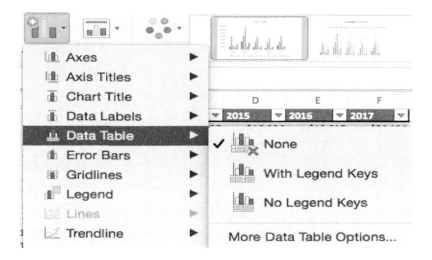

- None is the default setting, where the data table is not duplicated within the chart.
- With Legend Keys displays the data table beneath the chart to show the data range. The color-coded legend will also be included.

- No Legend Keys also displays the data table beneath the chart, but without the legend.

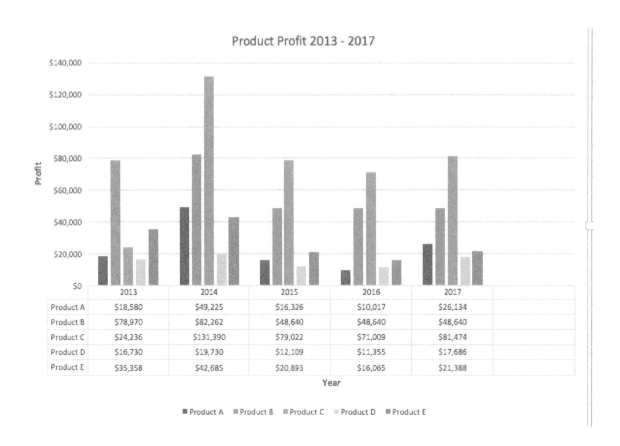

Note: If you choose to include a data table, you'll probably want to make your chart larger to accommodate the table. Simply click the corner of your chart and use drag-and-drop to resize your chart.

To Add Error Bars:

- Click Add Chart Element and click Error Bars. In addition to More Error Bars Options, there are four options: None (default), Standard Error, 5% (Percentage), and Standard Deviation. Adding error bars provide a visual representation of the potential error in the shown data, based on different standard equations for isolating error.

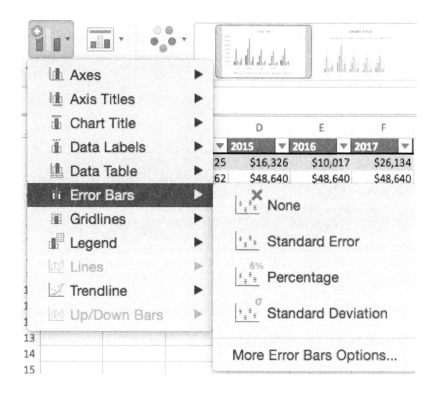

For example, when we click Standard Error from the options we get a chart

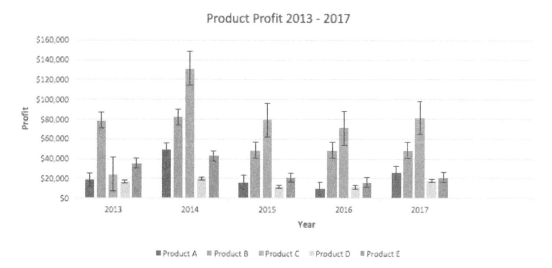

To Add Gridlines:
- Click Add Chart Element and click Gridlines. In addition to More Grid Line Options, there are four options: Primary Major Horizontal, Primary Major Vertical, Primary Minor Horizontal, and Primary Minor Vertical. For a column chart, Excel will add Primary Major Horizontal gridlines by default.

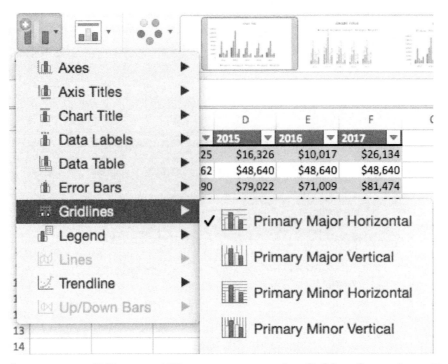

- You can select as many different gridlines as you want by clicking the options. For example, here is what our chart looks like when we click all four gridline options.

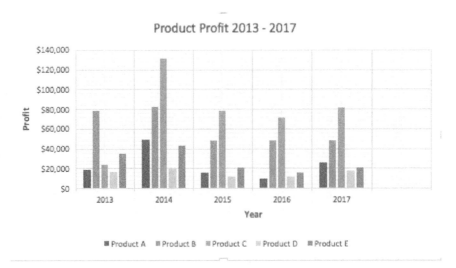

To Add A Legend:
- Click Add Chart Element and click Legend. In addition to More Legend Options, there are five options for legend placement: None, Right, Top, Left, and Bottom.

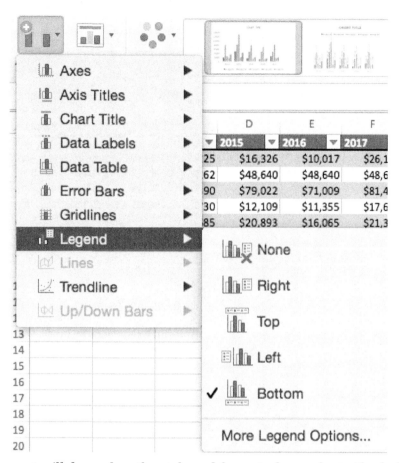

- Legend placement will depend on the style and format of your chart. Check the option that looks best on your chart.

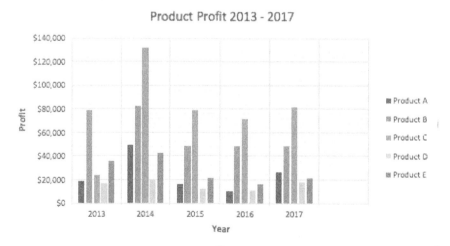

To Add Lines: Lines are not available for clustered column charts. However, in other chart types where you only compare two variables, you can add lines (e.g. target, average, reference, etc.) to your chart by checking the appropriate option.

To Add A Trendline:
- Click Add Chart Element and click Trendline. In addition to More Trendline Options, there are five options: None (default), Linear, Exponential, Linear Forecast, and Moving Average. Check the appropriate option for your data set. In this example, we will click Linear.

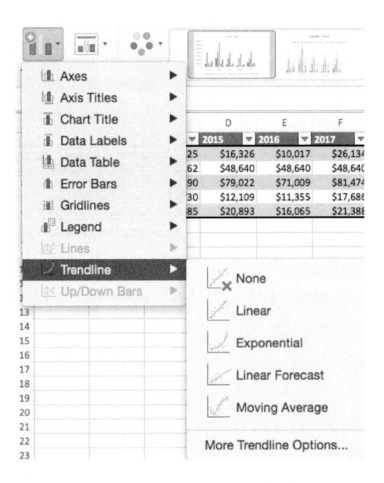

- Because we are comparing five different products over time, Excel creates a trendline for each product. To create a linear trendline for Product A, click Product A and click the blue OK button.

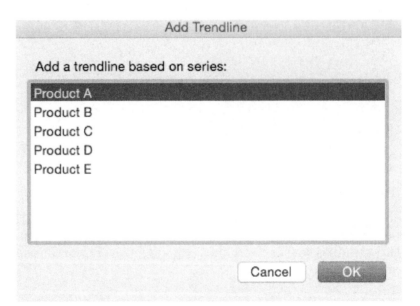

- The chart will now display a dotted trendline to represent the linear progression of Product A. Note that Excel has also added Linear (Product A) to the legend.

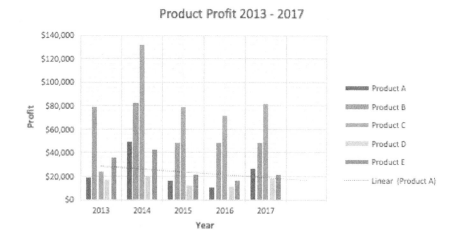

- To display the trendline equation on your chart, double click the trendline. A Format Trendline window will open on the right side of your screen. Click the box next to the Display equation on the chart at the bottom of the window. The equation now appears on your chart.

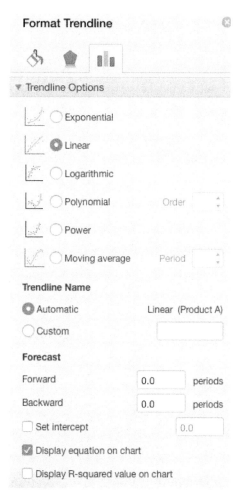

Note: You can create separate trendlines for as many variables in your chart as you like. For example, here is our chart with trendlines for Product A and Product C.

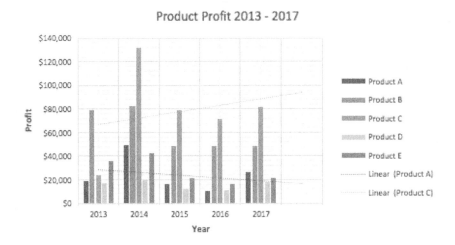

To Add Up/Down Bars: Up/Down Bars are not available for a column chart, but you can use them in a line chart to show increases and decreases among data points.

Step 4: Adjust Quick Layout

The second dropdown menu on the toolbar is Quick Layout, which allows you to quickly change the layout of elements in your chart (titles, legend, clusters, etc.).

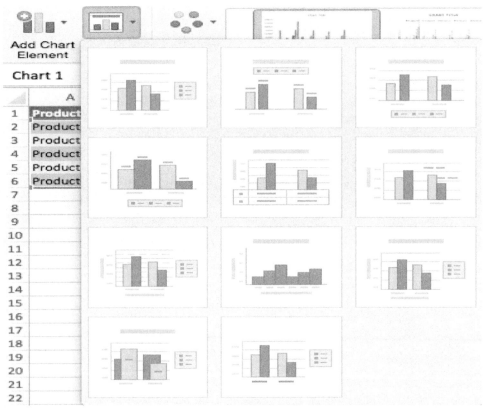

There are 11 quick layout options. Hover your cursor over the different options for an explanation and click the one you want to apply.

196 | P a g e

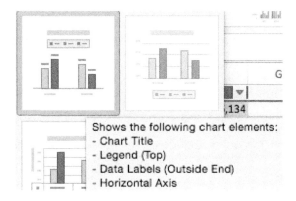

Step 5: Change Colors

The next dropdown menu in the toolbar is Change Colors. Click the icon and choose the color palette that fits your needs (these needs could be aesthetic, or match your brand's colors and style).

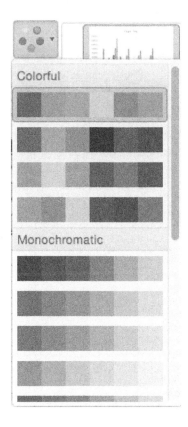

Step 6: Change Style

For cluster column charts, there are 14 chart styles available. Excel will default to Style 1, but you can select any of the other styles to change the chart appearance. Use the arrow on the right of the image bar to view other options.

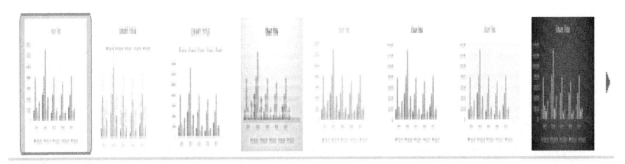

Step 7: Switch Row/Column

- Click the Switch Row/Column on the toolbar to flip the axes. Note: It is not always intuitive to flip axes for every chart, for example, if you have more than two variables.

- In this example, switching the row and column swaps the product and year (profit remains on the y-axis). The chart is now clustered by-product (not year), and the color-coded legend refers to the year (not product). To avoid confusion here, click on the legend and change the titles from Series to Years.

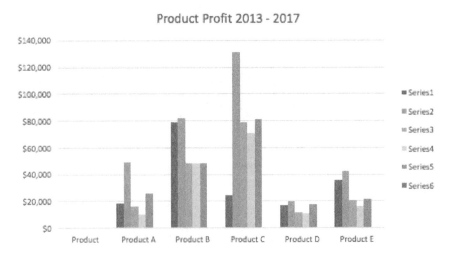

Step 8: Select Data

- Click the Select Data icon on the toolbar to change the range of your data.

- A window will open. Type the cell range you want and click the OK button. The chart will automatically update to reflect this new data range.

Step 9: Change Chart Type

- Click the Change Chart Type dropdown menu.

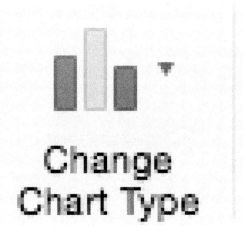

- Here you can change your chart type to any of the nine chart categories that Excel offers. Of course, make sure that your data is appropriate for the chart type you choose.
-

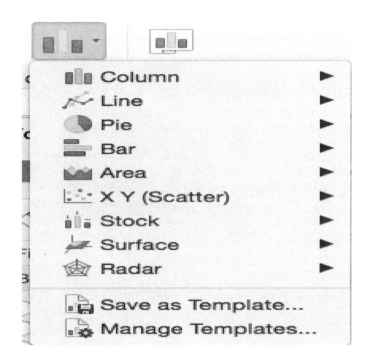

- You can also save your chart as a template by clicking Save as Template…
- A dialogue box will open where you can name your template. Excel will automatically create a folder for your templates for easy organization. Click the blue Save button.

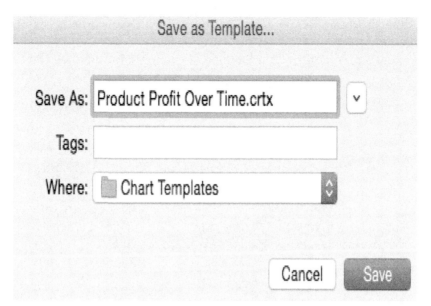

Step 10: Move Chart
- Click the Move Chart icon on the far right of the toolbar.
-

- A dialogue box appears where you can choose where to place your chart. You can either create a new sheet with this chart (New sheet) or place this chart as an object in another sheet (Object in). Click the blue OK button.

Step 11: Change Formatting
- The Format tab allows you to change the formatting of all elements and text in the chart, including colors, size, shape, fill, and alignment, and the ability to insert shapes. Click the Format

tab and use the shortcuts available to create a chart that reflects your organization's brand (colors, images, etc.).
- Click the dropdown menu on the top left side of the toolbar and click the chart element you are editing.

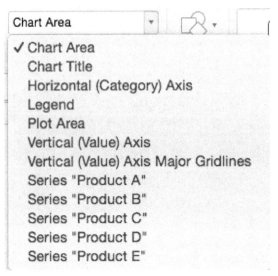

Step 12: Delete A Chart
- To delete a chart, simply click on it and click the Delete key on your keyboard.

How To Make A Graph In Excel
- Although graphs and charts are distinct, Excel groups all graphs under the chart's categories listed in the previous sections. To create a graph or another chart type, follow the steps below and select the appropriate graph type.

Select Range To Create A Graph From Workbook Data
- Highlight the cells that contain the data you want to use in your graph by clicking and dragging your mouse across the cells.
- Your cell range will now be highlighted in gray

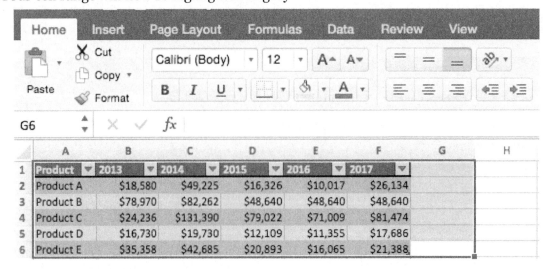

- Once the text is highlighted you can select a graph (which Excel refers to as a chart). Click the Insert tab and click Recommended Charts on the toolbar. Then click the type of graph you wish to use.

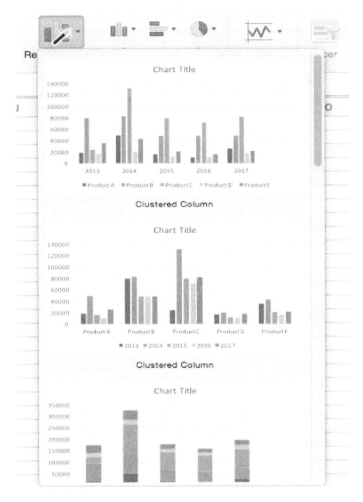

Now you have a graph. To customize your graph, you can follow the same steps explained in the previous section. All functionality for creating a chart remains the same when creating a graph.

How To Create A Table In Excel

If you don't need to make data visualization, you can also create a table in Excel using preexisting data. There are two ways to format a data set as a table:

1. Manually: In this example, we manually added data and formatted it as a table by including column and row names (products and years).

2. Use Excel's Format As Table Preset: You can also input raw data (numbers without any column and row names).

- To format data as a table, click and drag your mouse across the cells with the data range, click the Home tab, and click the Format as Table drop-down menu on the toolbar.
- Click New Table Style… (You will also see an option to use PivotTables. This feature is outside the scope of this how-to, but the concept is explained in the following section).

- A dialogue box opens and you can choose which aspects of the selected range to include in your formatted table. Click the blue OK button.

Top 5 Excel Chart And Graph Best Practices

Although Excel provides several layout and formatting presets to enhance the look and readability of your chart, using them won't ensure that you maximize the effectiveness of your chart. Below are the top five best practices to make your chart or graph as clear and useful as possible:

1. Make It Clean: Cluttered graphs with excessive colors or texts can be difficult to read and aren't eye-catching. Remove any unnecessary information so your audience can focus on the point you're trying to get across.

2. Choose Appropriate Themes: Consider your audience, the topic, and the main point of your chart when selecting a theme. While it can be fun to experiment with different styles, choose the theme that best fits your purpose.

3. Use Text Wisely: While charts and graphs are primarily visual tools, you will likely include some text (such as titles or axis labels). Be concise but use descriptive language, and be intentional about the orientation of any text (for example, it's irritating to turn your head to read text written sideways on the x-axis).

4. Place Elements Intelligently: Pay attention to where you place titles, legends, symbols, and any other graphical elements. They should enhance your chart, not detract from it.

5. Sort Data Before Creating The Chart: People often forget to sort data or remove duplicates before creating the chart, which makes the visual unintuitive and can result in errors.

Data Visualization Tips

Now you know how to create graphs and charts in Excel. However, it is not the end of the story. Data visualization is not simply stacking several graphs together but is concerned with the ability to convey the correct message from the data to the reader in a compelling way. Here are some tips that will allow you to take your data visualization skills to a new level:

1. Keep It Simple: "Keep it simple" remains the golden rule in data visualization. Always tries to make your graphs or charts as simple as possible. Remember that a reader should be able to understand the message that your chart intends to convey quickly.

2. Choose The Right Chart: Know the key differences between various types of charts such as bar, line, pie charts, etc. Learn about the advantages and disadvantages of each type of chart. This fundamental knowledge will ensure that you choose the most appropriate type of graph in your situation.

3. Pick The Right Colors: A color is a powerful tool in data visualization. Selecting the appropriate colors for a chart or graph may help your readers to grasp the key pieces of information quickly. When you use the right colors for a chart, remember that too similar colors cannot convey the differences between data points while extremely contrasting colors, as well as too many colors, can be distracting for a reader.

4. Properly Label Data: Data labeling is crucial to powerful data visualization. For example, it is always a good idea to label the axes of your chart and main data categories. Nevertheless, be aware that excessive labeling on your chart can be distracting to your readers.

5. Don't Use Special Effects: Don't use special effects (e.g., 3D) unless necessary. For example, a 3D feature on a bar chart is not necessary since a bar chart considers only two dimensions. Special effects may only distort dimensions on a chart, and a reader can be easily confused.

Related Excel Functionality

Excel is one of the most widely-used tools across any industry or type of organization. Charts and graphs are a great way to get started adding visualizations to your work, but there are several other ways to elevate your data in Excel. Below is a list of common features to create more "bang" with your data.

1. Pivot Tables: A pivot table allows you to extract certain columns or rows from a data set and reorganize or summarize that subset in a report. This is a useful tool if you only want to view a particular segment of a large data set, or if you want to view data from a new perspective.

2. Conditional Formatting: A powerful feature that allows you to apply specific formatting to specific cells in your spreadsheet. You can use conditional formatting to highlight key pieces of information, track changes, see deadlines, and perform many other data organization functions.

3. Dashboards: A powerful, visual reporting feature that pulls data from one or several datasets to display key performance indicators (KPIs), project or task status, and several other metrics. This gives the audience (team members, executives, clients, etc.) a snapshot view into project progress without surfacing private information.

4. Collaborative Charts: To avoid version control issues and allow multiple team members to edit a chart simultaneously, you'll want to use a collaborative chart tool. The desktop versions of Excel do not support this, but you can use Excel for Office 365, Microsoft's cloud-based web application, or several other online chart tools.

5. Data Series: A data series is any row or column stored in your workbook that you've slotted into a chart or graph. Once you've created your chart, you can add additional data series to it: Simply highlight the additional data you want to add and the chart will automatically update.

CHAPTER 11: PIVOT TABLE IN MS EXCEL

What Is A Pivot Table?

A pivot table summarizes your data, packaged in a chart that lets you report on and explore trends based on your information. Pivot tables are handy if you have long rows or columns that hold values you need to track the sums and easily compare to one another.

In other words, pivot tables extract meaning from that seemingly endless jumble of numbers on your screen. And more specifically, it lets you group your data in different ways so you can draw helpful conclusions more quickly.

The "pivot" part of a pivot table stems from the fact that you can rotate (or pivot) the data in the table to view it from a different perspective. You're not adding to, subtracting from, or otherwise changing your data when you make a pivot. Instead, you're simply reorganizing the data so you can reveal helpful information from it.

Key Pivot Table benefits

Simplicity: Basic pivot tables are straightforward to set up and customize. There is no need to learn complicated formulas.

Speed: You can create a good-looking, helpful report with a pivot table in minutes. Even if you are very good with formulas, pivot tables are faster to set up and require less effort.

Flexibility: Unlike formulas, pivot tables don't lock you into a particular view of your data. You can quickly rearrange the pivot table to suit your needs. You can even clone a pivot table and build a separate view.

Accuracy: As long as a pivot table is set up correctly, you can rest assured results are accurate. A pivot table will often highlight problems in the data faster than any other tool.

Formatting: A Pivot table can automatically apply consistent number and style formatting, even as data changes.

Updates: Pivot tables are designed for ongoing updates. If you base a pivot table on an Excel Table, the table resizes as needed with new data. All you need to do is click Refresh, and your pivot table will show you the latest.

Filtering: Pivot tables contain several tools for filtering data. Need to look at North America and Asia, but exclude Europe? A pivot table makes it simple.

Charts: Once you have a pivot table, you can easily create a chart.

What Are Pivot Tables Used For?

Don't worry if you're still feeling confused about what pivot tables do, don't worry. This is one of those technologies that are much easier to understand once you've seen it in action.

The purpose of pivot tables is to offer user-friendly ways to summarize large amounts of data quickly. Who can use them to understand better, display, and analyze numerical data in detail and help identify and answer random questions surrounding it?

Here Are Seven Hypothetical Scenarios Where A Pivot Table Could Be A Solution:

1. Comparing Sales Totals Of Different Products.

Say you have a worksheet containing monthly sales data for three products — product 1, product 2, and product 3 and you want to figure out which has brought in the most bucks. You could, of course, look through the worksheet and manually add the corresponding sales figure to a running total every time product 1 appears. You could then do the same for product 2 and product 3 until you have accommodations for all of them. Piece of cake, right?

Now, imagine your monthly sales worksheet has thousands and thousands of rows. Manually sorting through them all could take a lifetime. Using a pivot table, you can automatically aggregate all of the sales figures for product 1, product 2, and product 3 and calculate their respective sums in less than a minute.

2. Showing Product Sales As Percentages Of Total Sales.

Pivot tables naturally show the totals of each row or column when you create them. But that's not the only figure you can automatically produce.

Let's say you entered quarterly sales numbers for three different products into an Excel sheet and turned this data into a pivot table. The table would automatically give you three totals at the bottom of each column, adding up each product's quarterly sales. But what if you wanted to find the percentage of these product sales contributed to all company sales, rather than just those products' total sales?

You can configure each column with a pivot table to give you the column's percentage of all three column totals instead of just the column total. If three product sales totalled $200,000 in sales, for example, and the first product made $45,000, you can edit a pivot table to say this product contributed 22.5% of all company sales.

To show product sales as percentages of total sales in a pivot table, simply right-click the cell carrying a sales total and select Show Values As > % of Grand Total.

3. Combining Duplicate Data.

In this scenario, you've just completed a blog redesign and had to update many URLs. Unfortunately, your blog reporting software didn't handle it very well and split the "view" metrics for single posts between two different URLs. So in your spreadsheet, you have two separate instances of each blog post. To get accurate data, you need to combine the view totals for each of these duplicates.

That's where the pivot table comes into play. Instead of manually searching for and combining all the metrics from the duplicates, you can summarize your data (via pivot table) in my blog post title, and voilà: the view metrics from those duplicate posts will be aggregated automatically.

4. Getting An Employee Headcount For Separate Departments.

Pivot tables are helpful for automatically calculating things that you can't easily find in a basic Excel table. One of those things is counting rows that all have something in common.

If you have a list of employees in an Excel sheet, for instance, and next to the employees' names are the respective departments they belong to, you can create a pivot table from this data that shows you each department's name and the number of employees that belong to those departments. The pivot table effectively eliminates your task of sorting the Excel sheet by department name and counting each row manually.

5. Adding Default Values To Empty Cells.

Not every dataset you enter into Excel will populate every cell. If you're waiting for new data to come in before entering it into Excel, you might have many empty cells that look confusing or need a further explanation when showing this data to your manager. That's where pivot tables come in.

You can easily customize a pivot table to fill empty cells with a default value, such as $0 or TBD (for "to be determined"). For large tables of data, being able to tag these cells quickly is a valuable feature when many people are reviewing the same sheet.

To automatically format the empty cells of your pivot table, right-click your table and click PivotTable Options. Check the Empty Cells As box in the window and enter what you'd like displayed when a cell has no other value.

How To Create A Pivot Table

- Enter your data into a range of rows and columns.
- Sort your data by a specific attribute.
- Highlight your cells to create your pivot table.
- Drag and drop a field into the "Row Labels" area.
- Drag and drop a field into the "Values" area.
- Fine-tune your calculations.

Now that you have a better sense of what pivot can use for tables let's get into the nitty-gritty of how to create one.

Step 1. Enter Your Data Into A Range Of Rows And Columns.

Every pivot table in Excel starts with a basic Excel table, where all your data is housed. Simply enter your values into specific rows and columns to create this table. Use the topmost row or the top column to categorize your values by what they represent.

For example, to create an Excel table of blog post performance data, you might have a column listing each "Top Pages," a column listing each URL's "Clicks," and a column listing each post's "Impressions," and so on. (We'll be using that example in the steps that follow.)

	A	B	C	D	E
1	Top pages	Clicks	Impressions	CTR	Position
2	https://blog.hubspot.com/sales/famous-quotes	1026357	29679820	3.46%	5.45
3	https://blog.hubspot.com/sales/small-business-ideas	685091	12847519	5.33%	8.91
4	https://blog.hubspot.com/marketing/instagram-best-time-post	330548	6119298	5.40%	4.06
5	https://blog.hubspot.com/sales/business-name-ideas	291512	4693144	6.21%	9.53
6	https://blog.hubspot.com/marketing/post-to-instagram-from-comp	290584	3181539	9.13%	5.35
7	https://blog.hubspot.com/marketing/instagram-captions	287172	15258895	1.88%	7.91
8	https://blog.hubspot.com/sales/please-find-attached	272861	3563986	7.66%	12.36
9	https://blog.hubspot.com/marketing/professional-bio-examples	242311	2758974	8.78%	5.78
10	https://blog.hubspot.com/marketing/inspiring-company-mission-st	199199	3202086	6.22%	7.08
11	https://blog.hubspot.com/marketing/free-email-accounts	187233	4459481	4.20%	11.74
12	https://blog.hubspot.com/marketing/what-is-your-greatest-weakne	180857	2754893	6.56%	7.41
13	https://blog.hubspot.com/marketing/teamwork-quotes	177810	2087848	8.52%	6.92
14	https://blog.hubspot.com/marketing/how-to-repost-on-instagram	159573	2278343	7.00%	7.52
15	https://blog.hubspot.com/marketing/company-profile	156022	1516735	10.29%	5.72
16	https://blog.hubspot.com/marketing/ice-breaker-games	154548	1833468	8.43%	9.73

Step 2. Sort Your Data By A Specific Attribute.

When you have all the data you want to be entered into your Excel sheet, you'll want to sort it somehow so it's easier to manage once you turn it into a pivot table.

To sort your data, click the Data tab in the top navigation bar and select the Sort icon underneath it. In the window that appears, you can opt to sort your data by any column you want and in any order.

For example, to sort your Excel sheet by "Views to Date," select this column title under the column and select whether you want to order your posts from smallest to largest or from largest to smallest.

Select OK on the bottom-right of the Sort window, and you'll successfully reorder each row of your Excel sheet by the number of views each blog post has received.

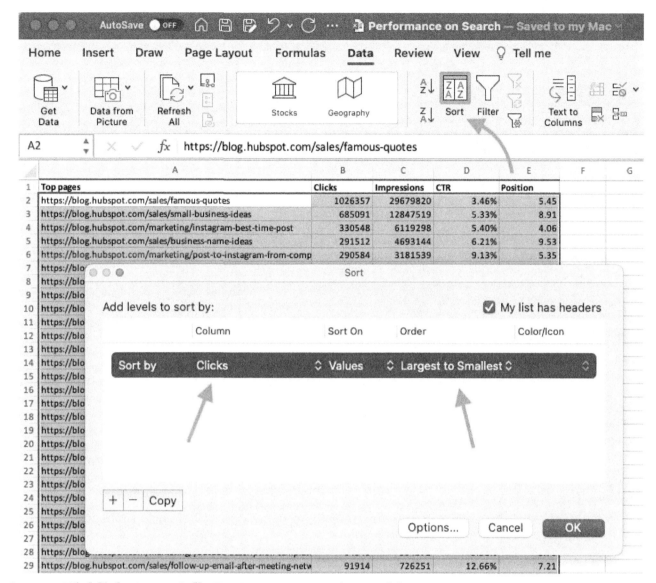

Step 3. Highlight Your Cells To Create Your Pivot Table.

Once you've entered data into your Excel worksheet and sorted it to your liking, highlight the cells you'd like to summarize in a pivot table. Click Insert along with the top navigation, and select the PivotTable icon. You can also click anywhere in your worksheet, select "PivotTable," and manually enter the range of cells you'd like included in the PivotTable.

This will open an option box where, in addition to setting your cell range, you can select whether or not to launch this pivot table in a new worksheet or keep it in the existing worksheet. If you open a new sheet, you can navigate to and away from it at the bottom of your Excel workbook. Once you've chosen, click OK.

Alternatively, you can highlight your cells, select Recommended PivotTables to the right of the PivotTable icon, and open a pivot table with pre-set suggestions for how to organize each row and column.

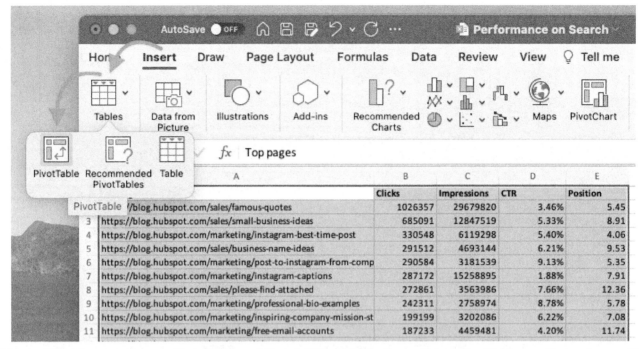

Note: If you're using an earlier version of Excel, "PivotTables" may be under Tables or Data along with the top navigation, rather than "Insert." In Google Sheets, you can create pivot tables from the Data drop-down and the entire navigation.

Step 4. Drag And Drop A Field Into The "Row Labels" Area.

After completing step 3, Excel will create a blank pivot table. Your next step is to drag and drop a field labelled according to the names of the columns in your spreadsheet into the Row Labels area. This will determine what unique identifier blog post title, product name, and so on the pivot table will organize your data by.

For example, let's say you want to organize many blogging data by post title. You'd simply click and drag the "Top pages" field to the "Row Labels" area.

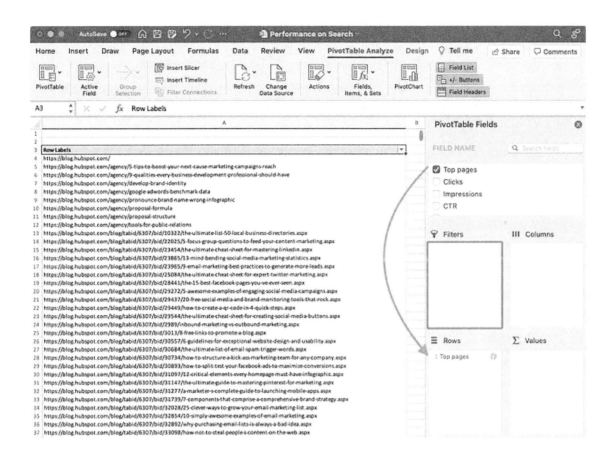

Note: Your pivot table may look different depending on which version of Excel you're working with. However, the general principles remain the same.

Step 5. Drag And Drop A Field Into The "Values" Area.

Once you've established how you're going to organize your data, your next step is to add in some values by dragging a field into the Values area.

Sticking with the blogging data example, let's say you want to summarize blog post views by title. You'd simply drag the "Views" field into the Values area.

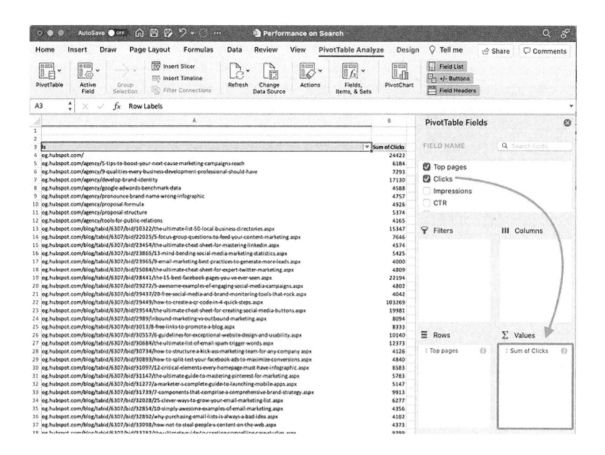

Step 6. Fine-Tune Your Calculations.

The sum of a particular value will be calculated by default. Still, you can easily change this to something like average, maximum, or minimum, depending on what you want to calculate.

On a Mac, you can do this by clicking on the small I next to a value in the "Values" area, selecting the option you want, and clicking "OK." Once you've made your selection, who will update your pivot table accordingly.

If you're using a P.C., you'll need to click on the small upside-down triangle next to your value and select Value Field Settings to access the menu.

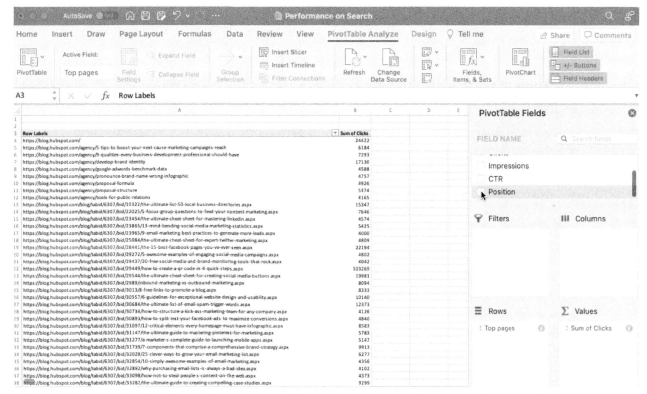

When you've categorized your data to your liking, save your work and use it as you please.

An Introduction To Pivot Table In Excel

Pivot tables are among the most useful and powerful features in Excel. We use them in summarizing the data stored in a table. They organize and rearrange statistics (or "pivot") to draw attention to the valuable facts. You can take an extremely large data set and see the relevant information you need in a clean, concise, manageable way.

Insert A Pivot Table

To insert a pivot table, execute the following steps.

1. Click any single cell inside the data set.
2. On the Insert tab, in the Tables group, click PivotTable.

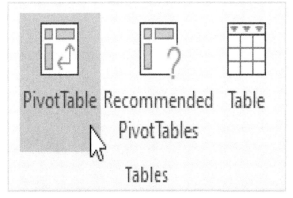

The following dialogue box appears. Excel automatically selects the data for you. The default location for a new pivot table is New Worksheet.

3. Click OK.

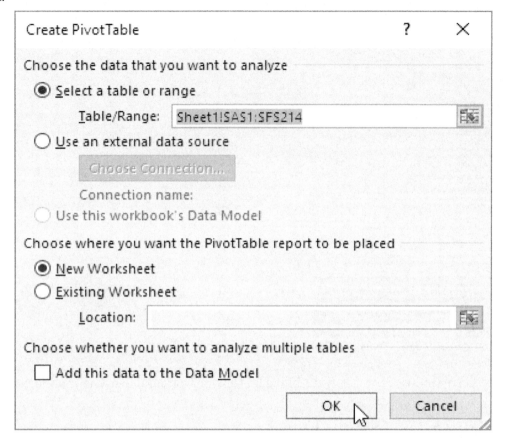

Drag Fields

The PivotTable Fields pane appears. To get the total amount exported of each product, drag the following fields to the different areas.

1. Product field to the Rows area.

2. Amount field to the Values area.

3. Country field to the Filters area.

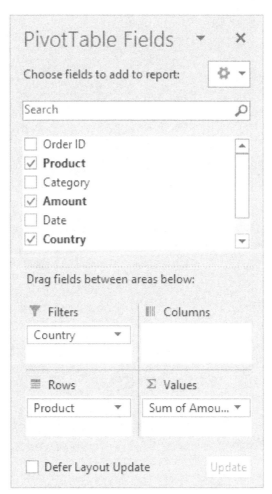

Below you can find the pivot table. Bananas are our main export product. That's how easily pivot tables can be!

	A	B	C
1	Country	(All)	
2			
3	Row Labels	Sum of Amount	
4	Apple	191257	
5	Banana	340295	
6	Beans	57281	
7	Broccoli	142439	
8	Carrots	136945	
9	Mango	57079	
10	Orange	104438	
11	Grand Total	1029734	
12			

Sort

To get Banana at the top of the list, sort the pivot table.

1. Click any cell inside the Sum of Amount column.

2. Right-click and click on Sort, Sort Largest to Smallest.

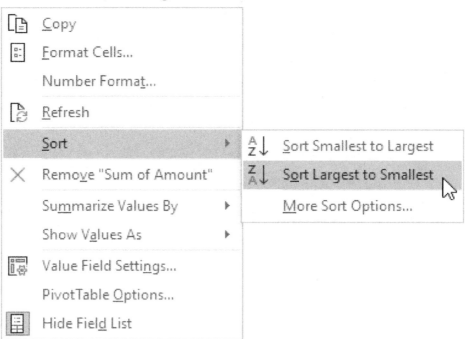

Result.

	A	B	C
1	Country	(All)	
2			
3	Row Labels	Sum of Amount	
4	Banana	340295	
5	Apple	191257	
6	Broccoli	142439	
7	Carrots	136945	
8	Orange	104438	
9	Beans	57281	
10	Mango	57079	
11	Grand Total	1029734	
12			

Filter

Because we added the Country field to the Filters area, we can filter this pivot table by country. For example, which products do we export the most to France?

1. Click the filter drop-down and select France.

Result. Apples are our main export product to France.

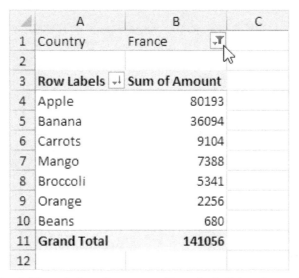

Note: you can use the standard filter (triangle next to Row Labels) only to show the amounts of specific products.

Change Summary Calculation

By default, Excel summarizes your data by either summing or counting the items. To change the type of calculation you want to use, execute the following steps.

1. Click any cell inside the Sum of Amount column.

2. Right-click and click on Value Field Settings.

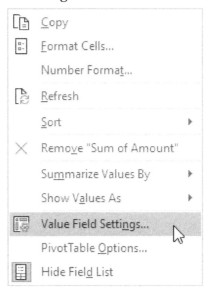

3. Choose the type of calculation you want to use. For example, click count.

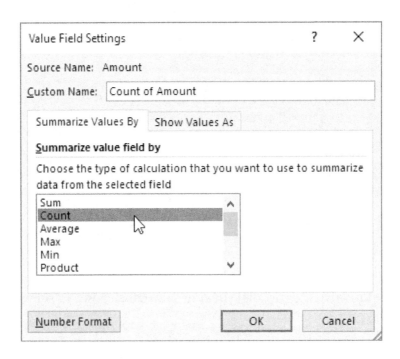

4. Click OK.

Result. 16 out of the 28 orders to France were 'Apple' orders.

	A	B	C
1	Country	France	
2			
3	Row Labels	Count of Amount	
4	Apple	16	
5	Banana	7	
6	Carrots	1	
7	Mango	1	
8	Orange	1	
9	Beans	1	
10	Broccoli	1	
11	Grand Total	28	
12			

Two-Dimensional Pivot Table

You can create a two-dimensional pivot table by dragging a field to the Rows and Columns areas. First, insert a pivot table. Next, pull the following fields to the different regions to get the total amount exported to each product country.

1. Country field to the Rows area.

2. Product field to the Columns area.

3. Amount field to the Values area.

4. Category field to the Filters area.

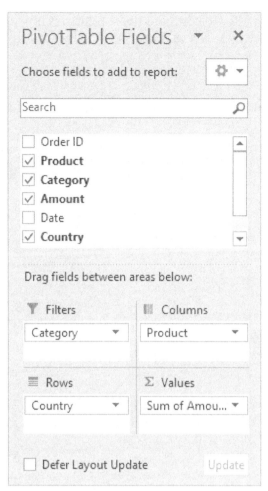

Below you can find the two-dimensional pivot table.

	Apple	Banana	Beans	Broccoli	Carrots	Mango	Orange	Grand Total
Category	(All)							
Sum of Amount	Column							
Row Labels	Apple	Banana	Beans	Broccoli	Carrots	Mango	Orange	Grand Total
Australia	20634	52721	14433	17953	8106	9186	8680	131713
Canada	24867	33775		12407		3767	19929	94745
France	80193	36094	680	5341	9104	7388	2256	141056
Germany	9082	39686	29905	37197	21636	8775	8887	155168
New Zealand	10332	40050		4390			12010	66782
United Kingdom	17534	42908	5100	38436	41815	5600	21744	173137
United States	28615	95061	7163	26715	56284	22363	30932	267133
Grand Total	191257	340295	57281	142439	136945	57079	104438	1029734

Create a pivot chart and apply a filter to compare these numbers quickly. Maybe this is one step too far for you, but it shows you one of Excel's many robust pivot tables features.

Value Field Settings

By default, Excel gives the summation of the values put into the Values section. You can change that from the Value Field Settings.

1. Click on the Sum of Sales in the Values field.

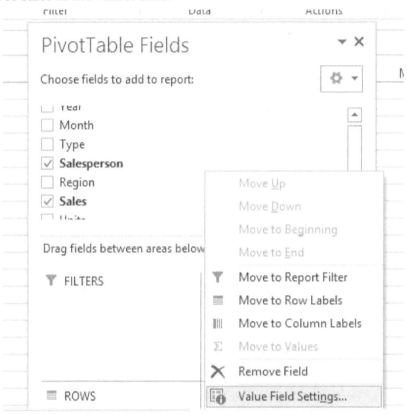

2. Choose the type of calculation you want to use.

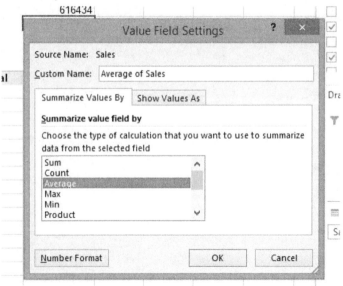

3. Click OK.

Row Labels	Average of Sales
Bishop	6849.266667
Lee	7899.25
Parker	7933.029412
Pullen	6441.75
Watson	9597.5
Grand Total	7693.824324

Percentage Contribution In A Pivot Table

There are various ways to display the values in a table. One way is to show the value as a percentage of the total.

1. Add the sales field again to the values section.
2. Right-click on the second instance and select % of Grand Total.

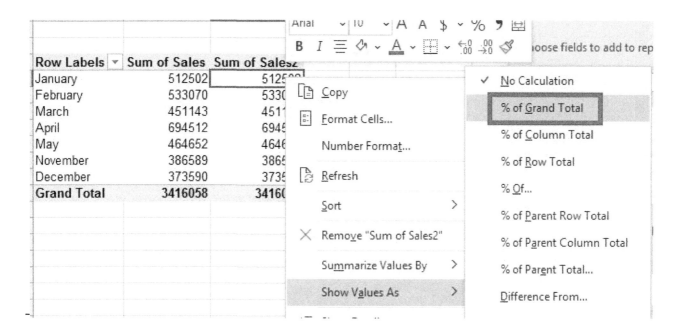

221 | P a g e

Practical Examples Of A Pivot Table
1. Pivot Table Count With Percentage

	A	B	C	D	E	F	G	H	I
1									
2		Pivot table count with percentage							
3									
4		First	Last	Department		Department	Count	%	
5		Janet	McFadden	Fulfillment		Engineering	8	12.5%	
6		Steven	Batista	Sales		Fulfillment	24	37.5%	
7		Evelyn	Monet	Fulfillment		Marketing	10	15.6%	
8		Marilyn	Stephens	Fulfillment		Sales	16	25.0%	
9		Jon	Addington	Marketing		Support	6	9.4%	
10		Adrian	Birt	Engineering		**Grand Total**	64	100.0%	
11		Julie	Irons	Marketing					
12		Erica	Baisley	Fulfillment					
13		Harold	Clayton	Fulfillment					
14		Sharyn	Corriveau	Support					
15		Leslee	Mosley	Sales					
16		Wanda	Menard	Engineering					

You can use a pivot table to display data in categories with a count and percentage breakdown. In the example shown, the field "Last" has been added as a value field twice – once to show count, once to show percentage. The pivot table shows the count of employees in each department and a percentage breakdown.

Fields

The pivot table shown is based on two fields: Department and Last. The Department field is configured as a Row field, and the Last field is a Value field, added twice:

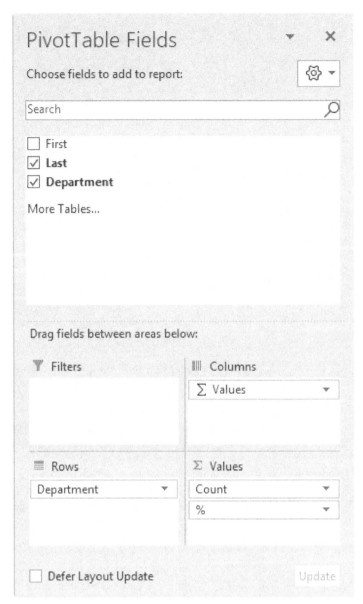

The Last field has been added twice as a value field. The first instance has been renamed "Count" and set summarize by count:

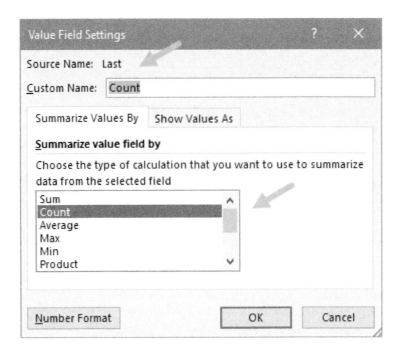

The second instance has been renamed to "%". The summarize value setting is also Count, Show Values As is set to a percentage of the total:

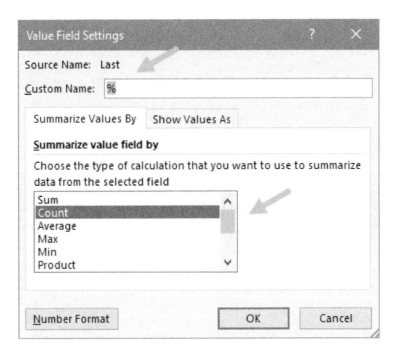

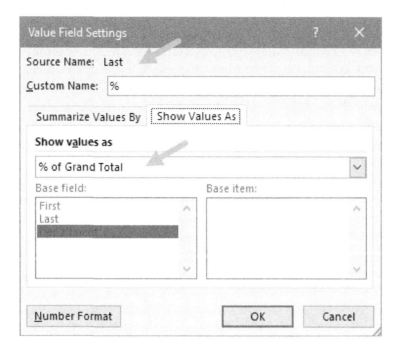

Steps

- Create a pivot table
- Add department as a Row field
- Add Last as a Value field
    - Rename to "Count"
    - Summarize by Count
- Add Last as a Value field
    - Rename to "%."
    - Summarize by Count
    - Display Percent of Grand Total
    - Change number formatting to percentage

2. Pivot Table Count Blanks

A pivot table is an easy way to count blank values in a data set. In the example shown, the source data is a list of 50 employees, and some employees are not assigned to a department. The Pivot Table is configured to group data by department and automatically creates a category called "(blank)" for employees without a department value.

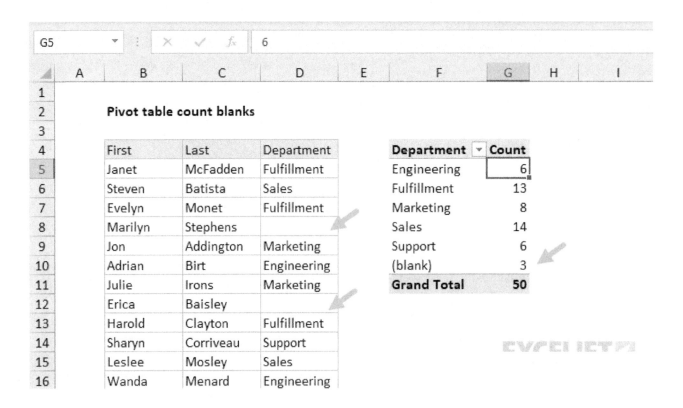

Fields

The pivot table shown is based on three fields: First, Last, and Department. The Department field is configured as a Row field, and Last is configured as a Value field, renamed "Count".

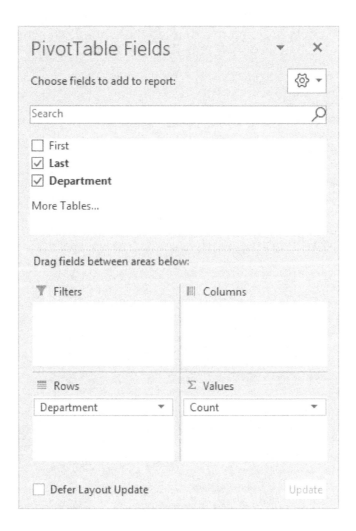

The Last field is renamed "Count" and configured to summarize by count:

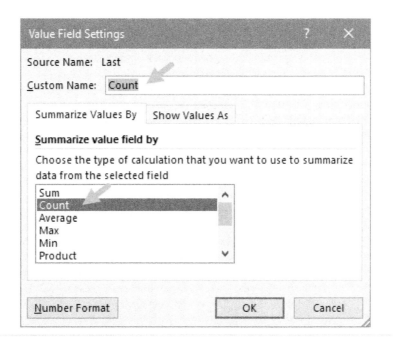

The pivot table uses the Last field to generate a count in the example shown. Any text field in the data that is guaranteed to have data can be used to calculate the count.

Steps

- Create a pivot table
- Add the Department field to the rows area
- Add Last field Values area

Notes

- who can use any non-blank field in the data in the Values area to get a count?
- When a text field is added as a Value field, Excel will display a count automatically.

3. Pivot Table Conditional Formatting

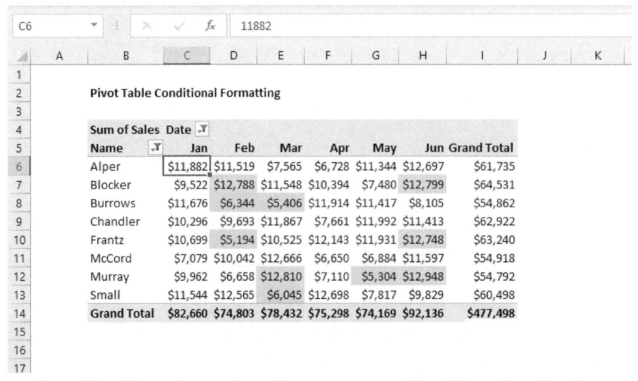

To apply conditional formatting to a pivot table, create a new conditional formatting rule and pay particular attention to the "apply the rule to" settings described below. In the example shown, there are two rules applied. The green shows the top 5 values using power like this:

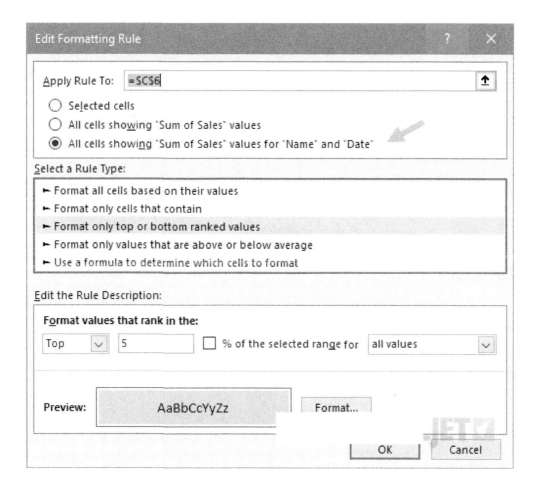

Details

Pivot tables are dynamic and frequently change when data is updated. Suppose you created conditional formatting rules based on "selected cells" only. You might find that the conditional formatting is lost or not applied to all data when the pivot table is changed or when data is refreshed.

The best option is to set up the rule correctly from the start. Select any cell in the data you wish to format and then choose "New rule" from the conditional formatting menu on the Home tab of the ribbon. At the top of the window, you will see the setting for which cells to apply conditional formatting to. For the example shown, we want:

"All cells showing the sum of "sales values" for name and "date."

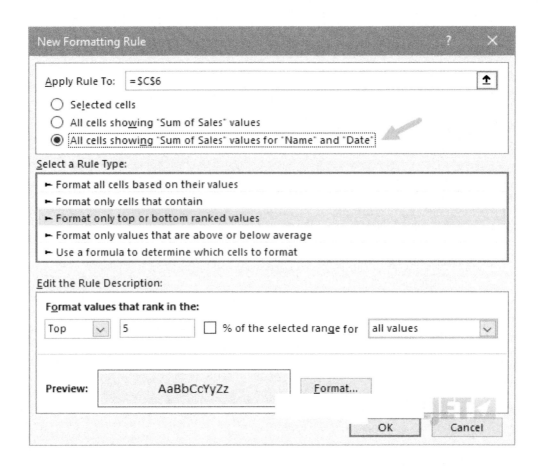

Note: Selecting "All cells showing the sum of "sales values" will include total rows and columns, which you ordinarily don't want.

Editing Existing Rules To Fix Broken Formatting

If you already have a rule set up that is not correctly formatting all values as needed, edit the rule and change the cell selection option if required. You can access existing laws at Home > Conditional Formatting > Manage Rules.

In the example shown, the rule manager displays two rules like this:

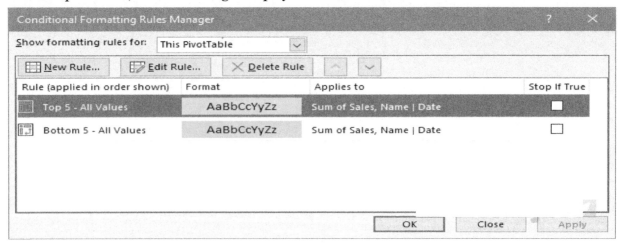

230 | P a g e

Select the rule and click the "Edit Rule" button to edit a rule. Then adjust settings in the "Apply rule to" section.

Note: conditional formatting is lost when removing the target field from a pivot table.

4. Pivot Table Calculated Field Example

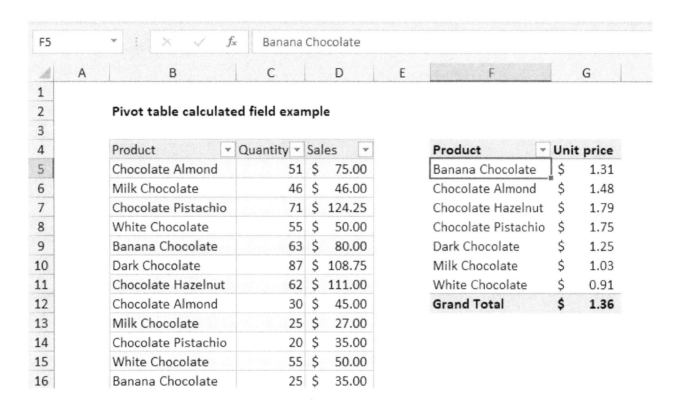

Standard Pivot Tables have a simple feature for creating calculated fields. You can think of a calculated field as a virtual column in the source data. A computed area will appear in the field list window but will not take up space in the source data. In the example shown, a calculated field called "Unit Price" has been created with a formula that divides Sales by Quantity. The pivot table displays the computed unit price for each product in the source data.

Note: data ends on row 18, so the calculation is as follows: $1,006.75 / 739 = $1.36

Fields

The source data contains three fields, Product, Quantity, and Sales. A fourth field called "Unit Price" is a calculated field.

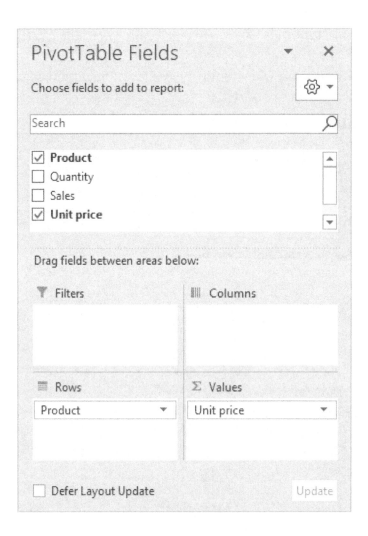

The calculated field was created by selecting "Insert Calculated Field" in the "Fields, Items, and Sets" menu on the ribbon:

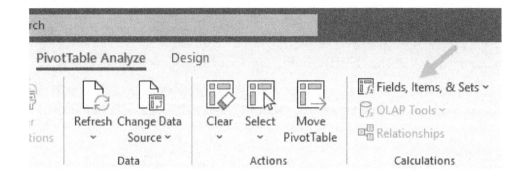

The calculated field is named "Unit Price" and defined with the formula "=Sales/Quantity", as seen below:

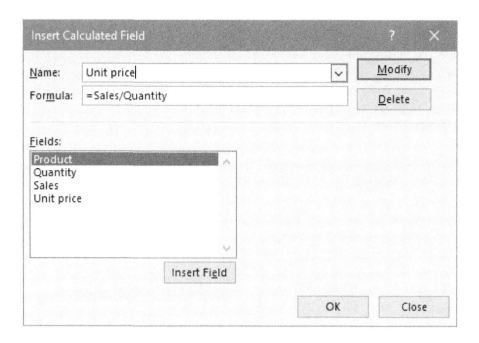

Note: who must wrap field names with spaces in single quotes ('). Excel will add these automatically when you click the Insert Field button or double-click a field in the list.

The Unit Price field is renamed "Unit Price " (note the extra space) after it has been added to the Values area:

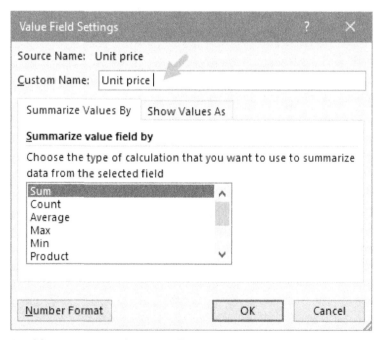

The extra space is required because Excel won't allow you to use precisely the same field name that appears in the data in a pivot table.

Steps
- Create a pivot table
- Create the Calculated field "Unit Price."

- Add Unit Price to the field to the Values area
    - Rename field "Unit Price."
    - Set number format as desired

5. Pivot Table Basic Sum

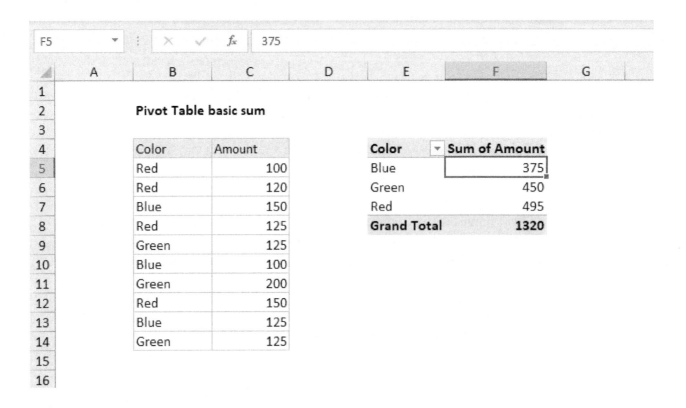

Pivot tables make it easy to sum values in various ways quickly. A pivot table calculates amounts by colour in the example shown.

Fields

The pivot table shown is based on two fields: Color and Amount. The Color field is configured as a row field, and the Amount field is a value field, as seen below:

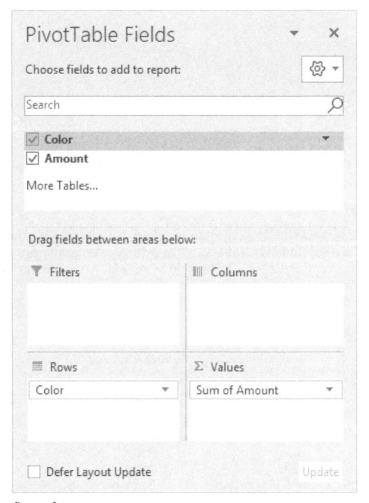

The Amount field is configured to sum:

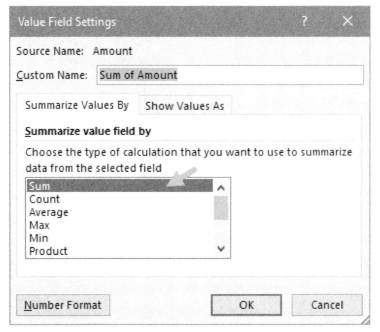

You are free to rename "Sum of Name" as you like.

Steps
- Create a pivot table
- Add a category field the rows area (optional)
- Add field to count to the Values area
- Change value field settings to show some if needed

Notes
- When the numeric field is added as a Value field, Excel automatically displays a sum.
- Without a Row field, the sum will be the total of all Amounts.

6. Pivot Table Latest Values

To build a pivot table that shows the latest n values by date, you can add the date as a value field set to show maximum value, then (optionally) add an area as a row-column and filter by value to show n values. In the example shown, the date is a value field set to Max, and Sales is a Row field filtered by value to show the top 1 items.

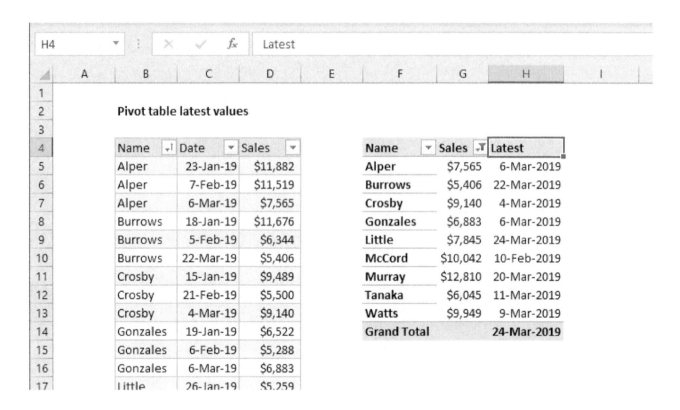

Pivot Table Fields

In the pivot table shown, there are three fields, Name, Date, and Sales. Name is a Row field, Sales is a Row field filtered by value, and date is a Value field set to Max.

236 | P a g e

The Date field settings are set as shown below. Note the field has been renamed to "Latest" and set to Max:

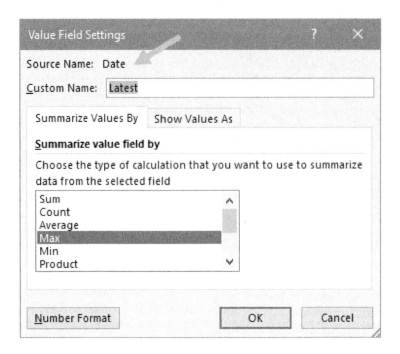

The Sales field has a Value filter applied to show the top 1 item by Latest (Date):

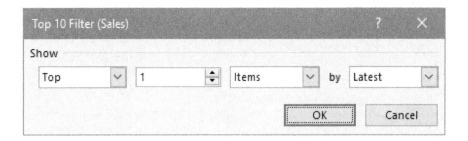

Steps

- Create a pivot table
- Add Row field(s) as needed
- Add the Date field as a Value field and set it to Max (rename if desired)
- Apply a Value filter to show the Top 10 items and customize as needed

7. Pivot Table Count By Year

Pivot tables have a built-in feature to group dates by year, month, and quarter. A pivot table counts colours per year in the example shown. This is the number of records for each colour in a given year.

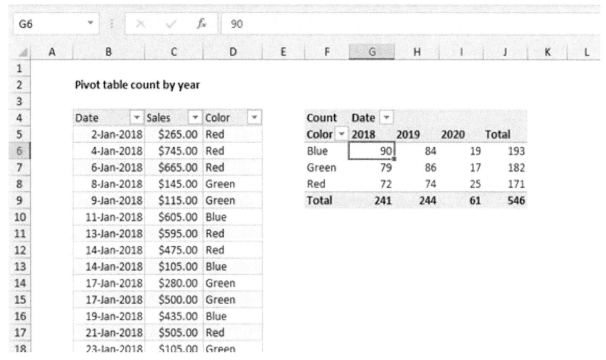

Fields

The source data contains three fields: Date, Sales, and Color. Only two fields are used to create the pivot table: Date and Color.

The Color field has been added as a Row field to group data by colour. The Color field has also been added as a Value field and renamed "Count":

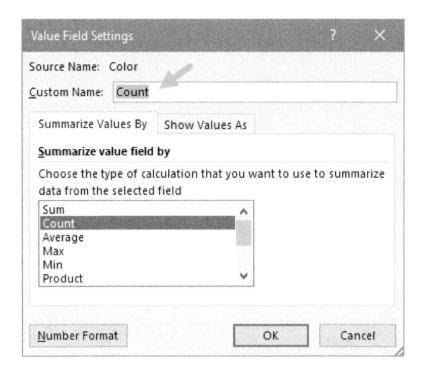

The Date field has been added as a Column field and grouped by year:

Steps

- Create a pivot table
- Add Color field to Rows area
- Add Color field Values area, rename to "Count."
- Add a Date field to the Columns area, group by year.
- Change value field settings to show count if needed

Notes

- who can use any non-blank field in the data in the Values area to get a count.

- When a text field is added as a Value field, Excel will display a count automatically.
- Without a Row field, the count represents all data records.

8. Pivot Table Count Birthdays By Month

Pivot tables can group dates by year, month, and quarter. This comes in handy if you want to count birthdays that occur each month while ignoring the year. There are 100 names and birthdays in the source data in the example shown. A pivot table is used to count the birthdays that occur each month of the year.

Fields

The source data contains two fields: Name and Birthdate. Both fields are used to create the pivot table:

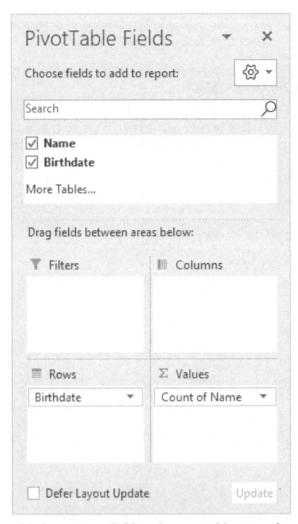

The Birthdate field has been added as a Row field and grouped by Months only:

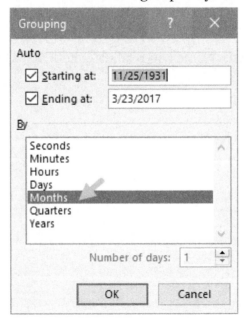

The Name field has been added as a Value field. Because the name is a text field, the field is summarized by count automatically:

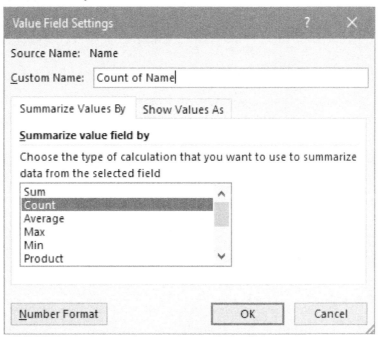

Helper Column Alternative

As an alternative to automatic date grouping, you can add a helper column to the source data and use a formula to extract the month. Then add the Month field to the pivot table directly.

Steps

- Create a pivot table
- Add Birthdate field to Rows area
- Group by Months only
- Add the Name field to the Values area

Notes

- Who can use any non-empty field in the data in the Values area to get a count.
- When a text field is added as a Value field, Excel will display a count automatically.

9. Pivot Table Filter By Weekday

To create a pivot table with a filter for a day of the week (i.e. filter on Mondays, Tuesdays, Wednesdays, etc.), you can add a helper column to the source data with a formula to count the weekday name, then use the helper column to filter the data in the pivot table. The pivot table is configured to show data for Mondays only in the example shown.

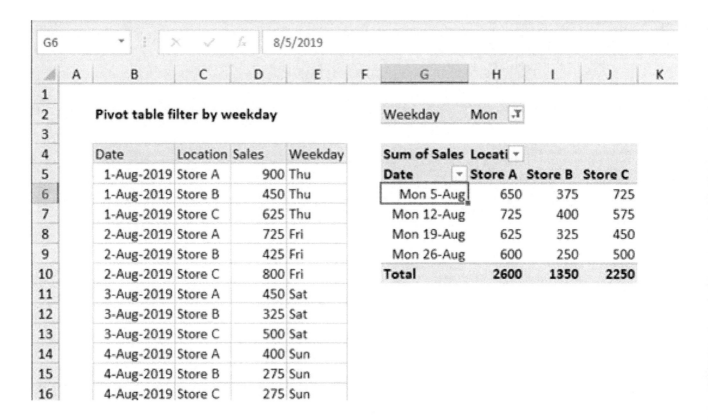

Pivot Table Fields

In the pivot table shown, there are four fields: Date, Location, Sales, and Weekday. The date is a Row field, Location is a Column field, Sales is a Value field, and weekday (the helper column) is a Filter field, as seen below. The filter is set to include Mondays only.

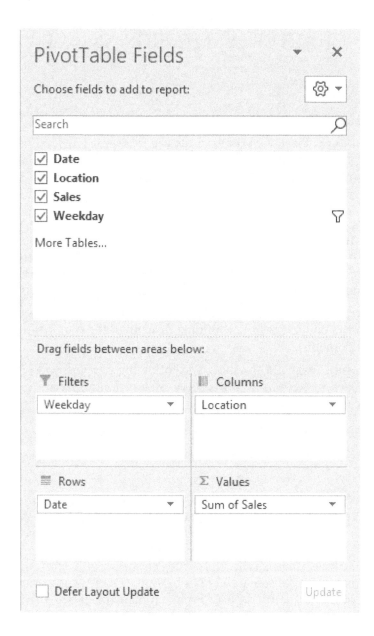

Steps

- Add helper column with a formula to data as shown
- Create a pivot table
- Add fields to Row, Column, and Value areas
- Add helper column as a Filter
- Set filter to include weekday (s) as needed

Notes

- You can use the helper column to group by weekday as well.

CHAPTER 12: MACROS AND VBA

Explanation Of Macros

What Is An Excel Macro?

Excel Macro is a record and playback tool that simply records your Excel steps, and the macro will play it back as many times as you want. VBA Macros save time as they automate repetitive tasks. It is a programming code that runs in an Excel environment, but you don't need to be a coder to program macros. Though, you need basic knowledge of VBA to make advanced modifications in the macro.

Why Is Excel Macros Used In Excel?

As humans, we are creatures of habit. There are certain things that we do daily, every working day. Wouldn't it be better if there were some magical way of pressing a single button and who did all of our routine tasks? I can hear you say yes. Macro in Excel helps you to achieve that. A macro is defined as recording your regular steps in Excel that you can replay using a single button in a layman's language.

For example, you are working as a cashier for a water utility company. Some of the customers pay through the bank, and at the end of the day, you must download the data from the bank and format it to meet your business requirements.

You can import the data into Excel and format. The following day you will be required to perform the same ritual. It will soon become tedious. Macros solve such problems by automating such routine tasks. You can use a macro to record the steps of:

- Importing the data
- Formatting it to meet your business reporting requirements.

Why Use Excel Macros?

Learning how to automate Excel is one of the easiest ways to speed up your work--mainly because Excel is used in many work processes. Say every week you export analytics data from your content management system (CMS) to create a report about your site. The only problem is that those data exports aren't always in an Excel-friendly format. They're messy and often include far more data than your report requires. This means you have to clean up empty rows, copy and paste data into the right place, and create your charts to visualize data and make it print-friendly. All of these steps may take you hours to complete.

If there only was a way to press one button and let Excel do it for you in an instant... Well, can you guess what I'm about to say next?

There is!

All it requires is a little bit of time to set up a macro, and then that code can do the work for you automatically every time. It's not even as difficult as it sounds.

How To Record A Macro In Excel

Excel macros reside on the Developer tab, hidden by default, like other VBA tools. So, the first thing you need to do is add the Developer tab to your Excel ribbon.

To Record A Macro In Excel, Carry Out These Steps:

1. On the Developer tab, in the Code group, click the Record Macro button.

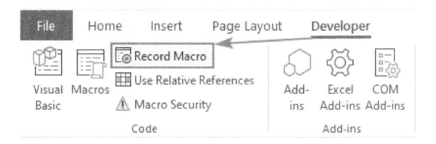

Alternatively, click the Record Macro button on the left side of the Status bar:

- If you prefer working with the keyboard rather than the mouse, press the following key sequences Alt, L, R (one by one, not all the keys at a time).

2. In the Record Macro dialogue box that appears, configure the main parameters of your macro:
   - In the Macro name box, enter the name for your macro. Try to make it meaningful and descriptive so that you can find the macro in the list quickly later on.
   - You can use letters, numbers, and underscores; the first character must be a letter. Spaces are not allowed, so you should either keep a name single-worded, starting each part with a capital letter (e.g. MyFirstMacro) or separate words with underscores (e.g. My_First_Macro).

Type any letter in the Shortcut key box to assign a keyboard shortcut to the macro (optional).

Both uppercase or lowercase letters are allowed, but you'd be wise to use uppercase key combinations (Ctrl + Shift + letter) because macro shortcuts override any default Excel shortcuts. In contrast, the workbook containing the macro is open. For example, if you assign Ctrl + S to a macro, you will lose the ability to save your Excel files with a shortcut. Assigning Ctrl + Shift + S will keep the standard saving shortcut.

From the Store macro in the drop-down list, choose where you want to store your macro:
- **Personal Macro Workbook:** Stores the macro to a particular workbook called Personal. xlsb. All the macros stored in this workbook are available whenever you use Excel.
- **This workbook (default):** The macro will be stored in the current workbook and available when you reopen it or share it with other users.
- **New Workbook:** Creates a new workbook and records the macro to that workbook.
- In the Description box, type a short description of what your macro does (optional).

Though this field is optional, I'd recommend you always provide a brief description. When you create a lot of different macros, it will help you quickly understand what each macro does.
- Click OK to start recording the macro.

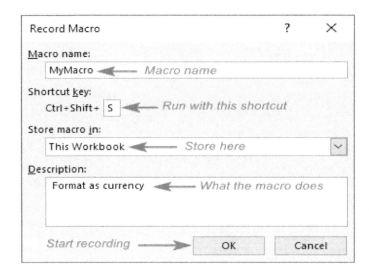

3. Perform the actions you want to automate.
4. When finished, click the Stop Recording button on the Developer tab:

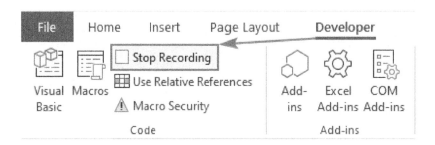

- Or the similar button on the Status bar:

Example Of Recording A Macro In Excel

Let's record a macro that applies some formatting to the selected cells to see how it works in practice. For this, do the following:

1. Select one or more cells that you want to format.
2. On the Developer tab or Status bar, click Record Macro.
3. In the Record Macro dialogue box, configure the following settings:
    - Name the macro Header_Formatting (because we will format column headers).
    - Place the cursor in the Shortcut key box and press the Shift + F keys simultaneously. This will assign the Ctrl + Shift + F shortcut to the macro.
    - Choose to store the macro in this workbook.
    - For description, use the following text explaining what the macro does: Makes text bold, adds fill colour, and centres.

- Click OK to start recording.

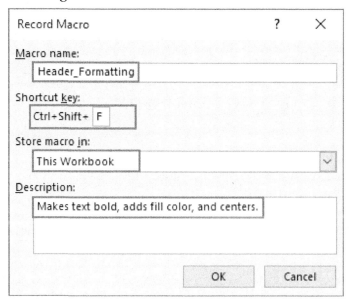

Example Of Recording A Macro

4. Format the pre-selected cells the way you want. We use bold text formatting, light blue fill colour, and centre alignment for this example.

- Tip. Do not select any cells after you've started recording the macro. This will ensure that all the formatting applies to the selection, not a specific range.

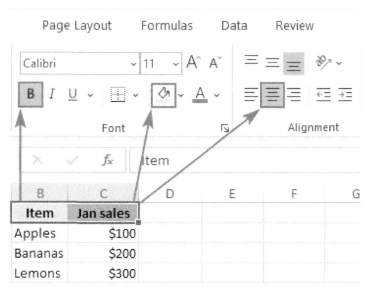

5. Click Stop Recording on either the Developer tab or the Status bar.

That's it! Your macro has been recorded. Now, you can select any range of cells in any sheet, press the assigned shortcut (Ctrl+ Shift + F), and your custom formatting will be immediately applied to the selected cells.

Item	Feb sales	Tax
Apples	$150	$15
Bananas	$220	$22
Lemons	$330	$33

[Ctrl + Shift + F] →

Item	Feb sales	Tax
Apples	$150	$15
Bananas	$220	$22
Lemons	$330	$33

How To Work With Recorded Macros In Excel

who can access excel's main options for macros via the Macro dialogue box. To open it, click the Macros button on the Developer tab or press the Alt+ F8 shortcut.

In the dialogue box that opens, you can view a list of macros available in all open workbooks or associated with a particular workbook and make use of the following options:

- **Run - Executes** the selected macro.
- **Step Into:** Allows you to debug and test the macro in the Visual Basic Editor.
- **Edit:** Opens the selected macro in the VBA Editor, where you can view and edit the code.
- **Delete:** Permanently deletes the selected macro.
- **Options:** Allows changing the macro's properties, such as the associated Shortcut key and description.

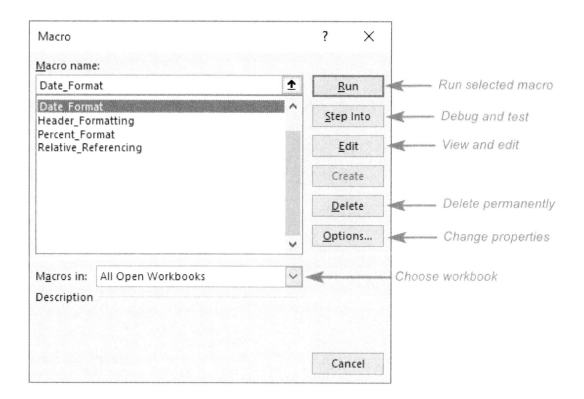

How To View Macros In Excel

The code of an Excel macro can be viewed and modified in the Visual Basic Editor. To open the Editor, press Alt + F11 or click the Visual Basic button on the Developer tab.

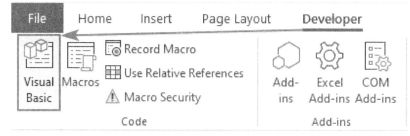

If you see the V.B. Editor for the first time, please do not feel discouraged or intimidated. We will not talk about the structure or syntax of the VBA language. This section will give you a basic understanding of how Excel macros work and what recording a macro does.

The VBA Editor has several windows, but we'll focus on the two main ones:
- Project Explorer: Displays a list of all open workbooks and their sheets. Additionally, it shows modules, user forms and class modules.
- Code Window: This is where you can view, edit and write VBA code for each object displayed in the Project Explorer.

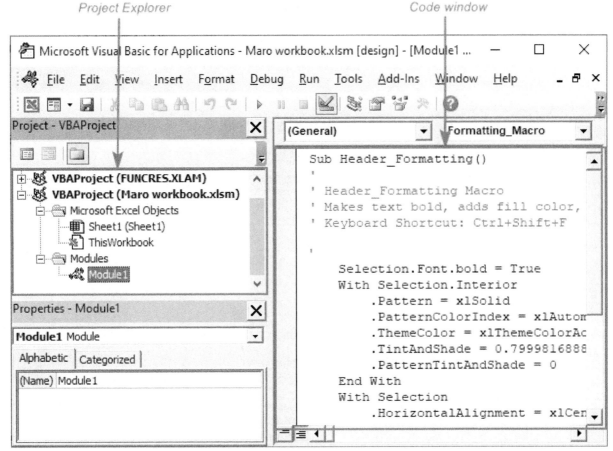

When we recorded the sample macro, the following things occurred in the backend:

- Who wrote the VBA code of the macro in the Code window.
- To see the code of a specific module, double-click the module (Module1 in our case) in the Project Explorer window. Normally, a macro code has these parts:

Macro Name

In VBA, any macro starts with Sub followed by the macro name and ends with End Sub, where "Sub" is short for Subroutine (also called Procedure). Our sample macro is named Header_Formatting(), so the code starts with this line:

Sub Header_Formatting()

If you wish to rename the macro, simply delete the current name and type a new one directly in the Code window.

Comments

Lines prefixed with an apostrophe (') and displayed in green by default are not executed. These are comments added for information purposes. Who can safely remove the comment lines without affecting the code's functionality.

Usually, a recorded macro has 1 - 3 comment lines: macro name (obligatory), description and shortcut (if specified before recording).

Executable code

After comments, there comes the code that executes the actions you've recorded. Sometimes, a recorded macro may have a lot of redundant code, which may still help figure out how things work with VBA :)

The below image shows what each part of our macro's code does:

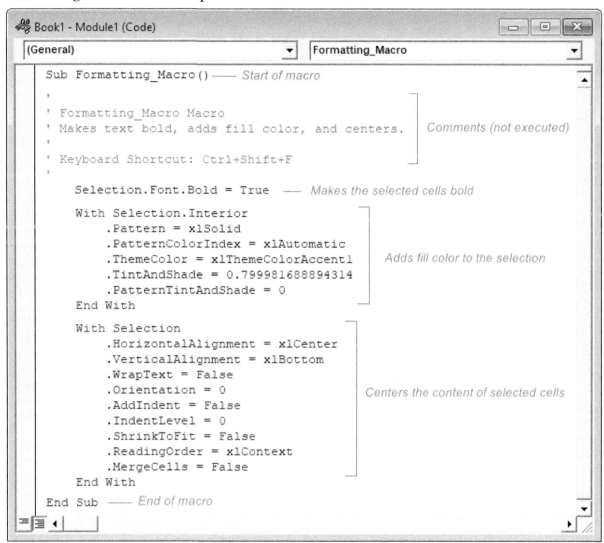

How To Run A Recorded Macro

By running a macro, you tell Excel to go back to the recorded VBA code and execute the same steps. There are a few ways to run a recorded macro in Excel, and here are the fastest ones:

- Press that shortcut if you've assigned a keyboard shortcut to the macro.
- Press Alt + 8 or click the Macros button on the Developer tab. In the Macro dialogue box, select the desired macro and click Run.

- It is also possible to run a recorded macro by clicking your button. Here are the steps to make one: How to create a macro button in Excel.

How To Save Macros In Excel

You need to keep the workbook as macro-enabled (.xlms extension) to save the macro, whether you recorded a macro or wrote VBA code manually. Here's how:

- Click the Save button or press Ctrl + S in the workbook containing the macro.
- In the Save As dialogue box, choose Excel Macro-Enabled Workbook (*.xlsm) from the Save as type drop-down list, and then click Save:

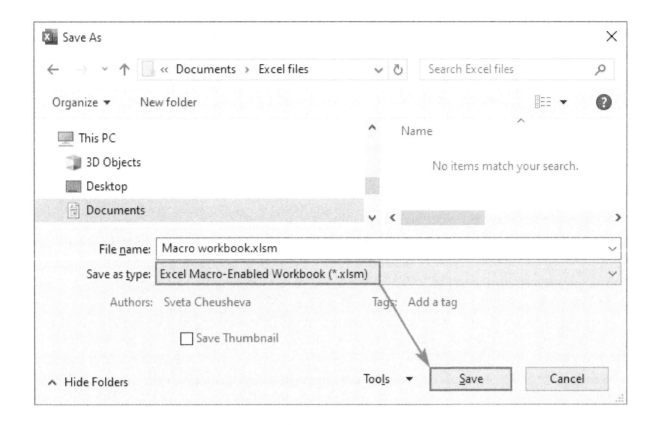

Excel Macros: What Is And What Isn't Recorded

As you have just seen, it's pretty easy to record a macro in Excel. But to create effective macros, you need to understand what's going on behind the scenes.

What Is Recorded

Excel's Macro Recorder captures quite many things - almost all mouse clicks and keypresses. So, you should think over your steps carefully to avoid excess code that may result in unexpected behaviour of your macro. Below are a few examples of what Excel records:

- You are selecting cells with the mouse or keyboard. Only the last selection before the action gets recorded. For instance, if you choose the range A1:A10 and then click cell A11, it will register only the section of A11.
- Cell formatting includes fill and font colour, alignment, borders, etc.
- Number formatting such as percentage, currency, etc.
- Editing formulas and values. Changes are recorded after you press Enter.
- Scrolling, moving Excel windows, switching to other worksheets and workbooks.
- Adding, naming, moving and deleting worksheets.
- Creating, opening and saving workbooks.
- Running other macros.

What Cannot Be Recorded

Despite many different things that Excel can record, certain features are beyond the capabilities of the Macro Recorder:

Customizations Of The Excel Ribbon And Quick Access Toolbar.

Actions inside Excel dialogues such as Conditional Formatting or Find and Replace (only the result gets recorded).

Interactions with other programs. For example, you cannot record copy/pasting from an Excel workbook into a Word document.

Anything that involves the VBA Editor. This imposes the most significant limitations - many things that who can do at the programming level cannot be recorded:

Creating custom functions

Displaying custom dialogue boxes

Making loops such as For Next, For Each, Do While, etc.

You are evaluating conditions. In VBA, you can use the IF Then Else statement to test a condition and run some code if the state is actual or another code if the condition is false.

Executing code based on events. With VBA, you can use many occasions to run a code associated with that event (such as opening a workbook, recalculating a worksheet, changing selection, and so on).

I am using arguments. When writing a macro in the VBA Editor, you can supply input arguments for a macro to perform a particular task. A recorded macro cannot have any arguments because it's independent and is not connected to other macros.

Understanding logic. For example, if you record a macro that copies specific cells, say in the Total row, Excel will only record the addresses of the copied cells. With VBA, you can code the logic, i.e. copy the values in the Total row.

Although the above limitations set many boundaries for recorded macros, they are still a good starting point. Even if you have no idea of the VBA language, you can quickly register a macro and analyze its code.

Valuable Tips For Recording Macros In Excel

Below you will find a few tips and notes that can potentially save you a lot of time and nerves making your learning curve smoother and macros more efficient.

Use Relative References For Macro Recording.

By default, Excel uses absolute referencing to record a macro. That means your VBA code would always refer to precisely the same cells that you selected, no matter where you are in the worksheet when running the macro.

However, it is possible to change the default behaviour to relative referencing. In this case, VBA won't hardcode cell addresses but will work relative to the active (currently selected) cell.

Click the Use Relative References button on the Developer tab to record a macro with relative referencing. To return to absolute referencing, click again to toggle it off.

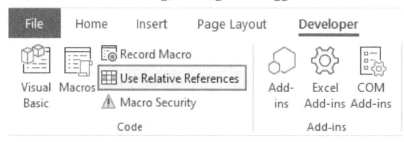

For example, if you record setting up a table with the default absolute referencing, your macro will always recreate the table in the same place (in this case, Header in A1, Item1 in A2, Item2 in A3).

```
Sub Absolute_Referencing()
 Range("A1").Select
    ActiveCell.FormulaR1C1 = "Header"
    Range("A2").Select
    ActiveCell.FormulaR1C1 = "Item1"
    Range("A3").Select
    ActiveCell.FormulaR1C1 = "Item2"
End Sub
```

If you record the same macro with relative referencing, the table will be created wherever you put the cursor before running the macro (Header in the active cell, Item1 in the below cell, and so on).

```
Sub Relative_Referencing()
    ActiveCell.FormulaR1C1 = "Header"
    ActiveCell.Offset(1, 0).Range("A1").Select
    ActiveCell.FormulaR1C1 = "Item1"
    ActiveCell.Offset(1, 0).Range("A1").Select
    ActiveCell.FormulaR1C1 = "Item2"
    ActiveCell.Offset(1, 0).Range("A1").Select
End Sub
```

Notes:
- When using relative references, select the initial cell before you start recording a macro.
- Relative referencing does not work for everything. Some Excel features, e.g. converting a range to a table, require absolute references.
- Select ranges by using keyboard shortcuts

- Excel writes the cell addresses when you select a cell or a range of cells using the mouse or arrow keys. Consequently, whenever you run a macro, who will perform the recorded operations precisely on the same cells. If this is not what you want, use shortcuts for selecting cells and ranges.

As an example, let's record a macro that sets a specific format (d-mmm-yy) for the dates in the table below:

	A	B
1	Order date	Delivery date
2	1-Jan-20	10-Jan-20
3	1-Jan-20	11-Jan-20
4	2-Jan-20	12-Jan-20

You record the following operations: press Ctrl + 1 to open the Format Cells dialogue> Date > choose format > OK. If your recording includes selecting the range with the mouse or arrow keys, Excel will produce the following VBA code:

```
Sub Date_Format()
    Range("A2:B4").Select
    Selection.NumberFormat = "d-mmm-yy"
End Sub
```

Running the above macro would select the range A2:B4 every time. If you add some more rows to your table, they won't be processed by the macro.

Now, let's see what happens when you select the table using a shortcut.

Put the cursor in the top-left cell of the target range (A2 in this example), start recording and press Ctrl + Shift + End. As a result, the first line of the code will look like this:

```
Range(Selection, ActiveCell.SpecialCells(xlLastCell)).Select
```

This code automatically selects all cells from the active cell to the last used cell, meaning that all new data will be automatically included in the selection.

Alternatively, you can use Ctrl + Shift + Arrows combinations:
- Ctrl + Shift + Right arrow to select all used cells to the right, followed by
- Ctrl + Shift + Down arrow to select all used cells down.

This will generate two code lines instead of one, but the result will be the same - who will select all cells with data down and to the right of the active cell:

```
Range(Selection, Selection.End(xlToRight)).Select
Range(Selection, Selection.End(xlDown)).Select
```

Record A Macro For Selection Rather Than Specific Cells

The above method (i.e. selecting all used cells beginning with the active cell) works great for performing the same operations on the entire table. However, you may want the macro to process a specific range rather than the whole table in some situations.

VBA provides the Selection object that refers to the currently selected cell(s). who can also do most things with a range of the selection? What advantage does it give to you? In many cases, you don't need to select anything while recording - just write a macro for the active cell. And then, choose any range you want, run the macro, and it will manipulate the entire selection.

For example, this one-line macro can format any number of selected cells as percentages:

```
Sub Percent_Format()
    Selection.NumberFormat = "0.00%"
End Sub
```

Plan Carefully What You Record

The Microsoft Excel Macro Recorder captures almost all your activity, including the mistakes you make and correct. For example, if you press Ctrl + Z to undo something, that will also be recorded. Eventually, you might end up with a lot of unnecessary code. To avoid this, either edit the code in the V.B. Editor or stop recording, delete a short macro and start recording anew.

Back Up Or Save The Workbook Before Running A Macro

who cannot undo the result of Excel macros? So, before the first run of a macro, it makes sense to create a copy of the workbook or save your current work to prevent unexpected changes. If the macro does something wrong, simply close the workbook without saving.

Keep Recorded Macros Short.

When automating a sequence of different tasks, you may be tempted to record them all in a single macro. There are two main reasons not to do this. Firstly, it's hard to record a long macro smoothly without mistakes. Secondly, large macros are difficult to comprehend, test and debug. Therefore, splitting a large macro into several parts is a good idea. For example, when creating a summary table from multiple sources, you can use one macro to import information, another to consolidate data, and a third one to format the table.

How To Code Your Own Excel Macros

Macros are just bits of code in Excel that do your bidding. Once you write the code in the VBA Editor, you can run it and let the code work its magic on your spreadsheet. But what's even better is to build your macro into your spreadsheet, and the best tool for that is buttons.

So first, before we start coding, let's add a button to run our macro.

Add A Button To Run Your Macro

You can use various Excel objects like buttons for running macros, but I prefer to use a shape from the "Insert" tab. When inserting your shape, right-click it and select "Assign Macro...." Then select the macro you want to run when the shape is clicked, perhaps the one you just made with a recording; save it by clicking "OK".

Now, when you click the shape that we just turned into a button, Excel will run the macro without opening the code each time.

One other thing to note before we get started: saving your spreadsheet with Macros. Excel spreadsheet files with a .xlsx extension cannot include macros by default. Instead, when you reserve your spreadsheet, select the "Excel Macro-Enabled Workbook (*.xlsm)" format, and add your file name as usual.

Go ahead and do that to save your spreadsheet before we start coding.

Now, let's get started with actual coding!

Copying and pasting is the simplest way to move data around, but it's still tedious. What if your spreadsheet could do that for you? With a macro, it could. Let's see how to code a macro that will copy data and move it around in a spreadsheet.

Open the project file you downloaded earlier and make sure the "Copy, cut, and paste" sheet is selected. This is a sample employee database with the names, departments, and salaries of some employees.

Let's copy all the data in columns A through C into D through F using VBA. First, let's look at the code we need:

Copying Cells With VBA

Copying in VBA is relatively easy. Just insert this code into the VBA Editor: Range("Insert range here"). Copy. Here are some examples:

- Range("A:C").Copy ← copies of columns A through C
- Range("A1:C100").Copy ← copies the range A1:C100

Remember when you recorded a macro before? The macro had Sub Nameofmacro() and End sub at the top and bottom line of the code. Who must always include these lines? Excel makes that easy, too: When you type in "Sub" followed by the macro name at the beginning of the code, the End sub is automatically inserted at the bottom line.

Tip: Remember to enter these lines manually when not using the macro recorder.

Pasting Cells With VBA

Who can do pasting differently depending on what you want to paste? 99% of the time, you'll need one of these two lines of code:

- Range("The cell/area where you want to paste").Paste special ← pastes as usual (formulas and formatting)
- Range("The cell/area where you want to paste").Paste special xlPasteValues ← only pastes values.

Cutting Cells With VBA

If you want to relocate your data instead of copying it, you need to cut it. Cutting is relatively easy and follows the same logic as copying.

Here's the code: **Range("Insert range here"). Cut**

When cutting, you can't use the 'PasteSpecial' command. That means that you can't paste values only or formatting only. Therefore, you need these lines to paste your cells with VBA: Range("Insert where you want to paste"). Select ActiveSheet.Paste

For example, here's the code you'd need to cut the range A: C and paste it into D1:

- Range("A:C").Cut
- Range("D1").Select
- ActiveSheet.Paste

Copying, cutting, and pasting are simple actions that can do manually without breaking a sweat. But when you copy and paste the same cells several times a day, a button that does it for you can save a bunch of time. Additionally, you can automatically combine copying and pasting in VBA with some other relaxed code to do even more in your spreadsheet.

Adding Loops To VBA

I just showed you how to take a simple action (copying and pasting) and attach it to a button so that you can do it with a mouse click. That's just one automated action. When you have the code to repeat itself, it can do more extended and more complex automation tasks in seconds.

Take a look at the "Loops" sheet in the project file. It's the same data as in the previous sheet, but every third row of the data is now moved to one column to the right. This faulty data structure is not unusual when exporting data from older programs.

This can take a lot of time to fix manually, mainly if the spreadsheet includes thousands of rows instead of the small sample data in this project file.

Let's make a loop that fixes it for you. Enter this code in a module, then look at the explanations below the picture:

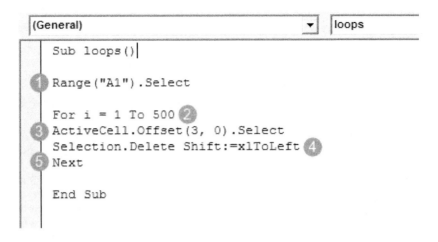

1. This line makes sure the loop starts at the top-left cell in the sheet and does not accidentally mess the data up by creating it somewhere else.

2. The For i = 1 To 500 line means that the number of times the loop has run (represented by i) is an increasing number that starts with 1 and ends with 500. This means that the loop will run 500 times. The number of times the loop should run depends on the actions you want it to do. Use your good sense here. Five hundred times is way too many for our sample dataset but would fit perfectly if the database had 1500 rows of data.

3. This line recognizes the active cell and tells Excel to move 3 rows down and select that cell, which becomes the new active cell. If every fourth row was misplaced in our data, instead of every third, we could just replace the 3 with a 4 in this line.

4. This line tells Excel what to do with this newly selected cell. In this case, we want to delete the partition so that the cells to the right of the cell are moved left. That is achieved with this line. If we wanted to do something else with the misplaced rows, this is the place to do it. If we wanted to delete every third row entirely, then the line should've been: Selection. Entire row. Delete.

5. This line tells Excel that there are no more actions within the loop. In this case, 2 and 5 are the frame of the circle and 3 and 4 is the actions within the loop.

When we run this macro, it will result in a neat dataset without any misplaced rows.

Adding Logic To VBA

Logic is what brings a piece of code to life by making it more than just a machine that can do simple actions and repeat itself. The reason is what makes an Excel sheet almost human, it lets it make intelligent decisions on its own. Let's use that to automate things!

This section is about IF statements that enable the "if-this-then-that" logic, just like the IF function in Excel.

The export from our website CMS was even more erroneous than expected. Every third row is still misplaced, but now, some of the misplaced rows are placed 2 columns to the right instead of 1 column to the right. Take a look at the sheet "IF-statement" in the project file to see what it looks like.

How do we take this into account in our macro? We add an IF-statement to the loop!

Let's Formulate What We Want Excel To Do:

We start in cell A1. Then we go three rows down (to cell A4, A7, A10, etc.) until there are no more data. Every time we go three rows down, we check this row to see if the data has been misplaced by 1 or 2 columns. Then move the data in the row either 1 or 2 columns to the left.

Now, let's translate this into VBA code. We'll start with a simple loop, as before:

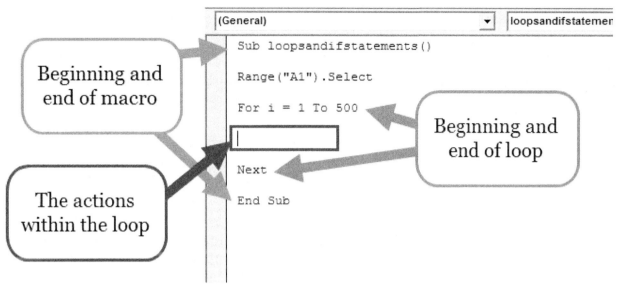

The only need now to write what should happen within the loop. This is the "go three rows down" part that we developed back in the section about circles. We're adding an IF statement that checks how much the data is misplaced and corrects it.

This is the final code to copy into your module editor, with each step explained below:

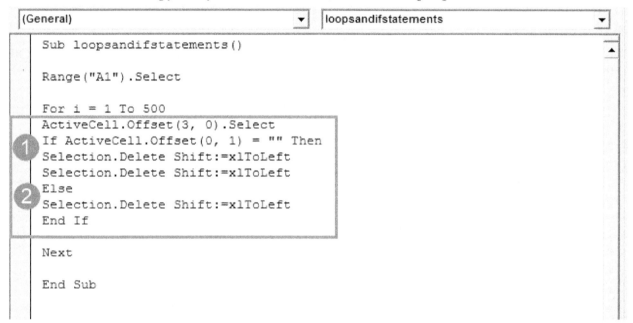

1. This is the first part of the IF statement. It says that if the cell right of the active cell (or Activecell.Offset(0,1) in VBA code) is blank (represented by =" "), then do something. This something is the same action as we did when we created the loop in the first place: deleting the active cell and moving the active row one cell to the left (accomplished with the Selection. Delete Shift:=xlToLeft code). This time, we do it two times instead of one because there are two blank cells on the left side of the row.

2. If the above is not valid, and the cell right of the active cell is not blank, then the active cell is empty. Therefore, we only need to delete the active partition and move the active row one cell to the left one time.

The IF-statement must always end with an End If to tell Excel it's finished running. After the IF statement, the loop can repeatedly run, repeating the IF statement each time.

Excel Macro Basics

Macros are one of the developer's features. By default, the tab for developers is not displayed in Excel. You will need to declare it via the customized report.

Who can use Excel Macros to compromise your system by attackers? By default, they are disabled in Excel. If you need to run macros, you will need to enable running macros and only run macros that you know come from a trusted source.

If you want to save Excel macros, then you must protect your workbook in a macro-enabled format *.xlsm. The macro name should not contain any spaces.

Always fill in the description of the macro when creating one. This will help you and others to understand what the macro is doing.

What Is VBA In A Layman's Language?

VBA is the acronym for Visual Basic for Applications. Excel's programming language is used to record your steps as you perform routine tasks. You do not need to be a programmer or a very technical person to enjoy the benefits of macros in Excel. Excel has features that automatically generate the source code for you.

What Is VBA?

Visual Basic for Application is a human-readable and editable programming code generated when you record a macro. It is widely used with other Microsoft Office applications such as MS-Word, MS-Excel, and MS-Access.

What is Excel VBA?

VBA, short for Visual Basic for Application, is a programming language used in Microsoft Office applications such as Excel. Who created VBA in the 1990s to unify macro languages across individual applications. Using VBA in Excel is an excellent way to automate workflows and generate practical tools to manage projects and accounts. VBA programming allows for exchanging data, tables, and diagrams across individual Microsoft 365 applications.

How Does VBA Work?

The VBA programming language has been available in Excel since version 95. Thanks to many VBA tutorials available online, it is relatively easy to learn, even for non-programmers. Much like any Office application, Excel comprises multiple objects, including spreadsheets, cells, and tables. Methods and features can be manipulated and adjusted manually or using VBA programming. If you find yourself executing the same activities repeatedly, Excel Visual Basic programming could save you lots of time. Using Excel VBA, you can create, select, or delete objects on the command.

But how does that work? Excel integrates a VBA Editor, which can use to generate automatic operations. It's not as complicated as it sounds because the individual coding blocks are fixed. This means that there's already a completed chunk of code for every standard operation. You'll only need to arrange the respective code blocks to personalize the solution you're looking for.

These solutions are called Excel macros, and they make it easy to organize format or import data. But before you get started, it's best to familiarize yourself with the VBA codes to put them together correctly.

Getting Set Up To Write VBA In Excel

Developer Tab

To write VBA, you'll need to add the Developer tab to the ribbon to see the ribbon like this.

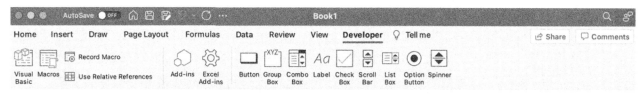

To add the Developer tab to the ribbon:
- On the File tab, go to Options > Customize ribbon.
- Under Customize the Ribbon and under Main Tabs, select the Developer check box.

After you show the tab, the Developer tab stays visible unless you clear the check box or have to reinstall Excel. For more information, see Microsoft help documentation.

VBA Editor

Navigate to the Developer tab, and click the Visual Basic button. A new window will pop up - this is the Visual Basic Editor. You need to be familiar with the Project Explorer pane and the Property Properties pane.

Excel VBA Tutorial: Learn The Foundations

It's a good idea to start with the foundations of Visual Basic before you get into arranging the individual coding blocks in Excel. Our short, step by step VBA tutorial demonstrates how to create a simple Excel macro.

Launch the VBA Editor from the Developer tab and insert a new module. If the Developer tab is not shown, click on Excel -> Preferences -> Ribbon & Toolbar. In the Macros dialogue, select the Developer checkbox and click Save.

Excel VBA: Menu Options To Add Macros

- Choose "Developer" from the menu options.
- Once the Developer tab has been added to the Excel dashboard (next to the View tab), click on Visual Basic to launch the editor window and Insert -> module.
- Select the "Developer" tab in the VBA Editor to insert a new module.
- A pop-up window will open. Enter "Option Explicit" and then "Option Base 1." This will allow you to work with Subs and Functions. Subs are programs made of only commands. There are no return values. Return values are used when entering functions, so they're suitable for mathematical calculations.

Excel VBA Main Window

Enter "Option Explicit" and "Option Base 1" by writing the commands into the pop-up window.

Adding variables

In Excel Visual Basic, variables are used similarly to mathematic equations. They're not just placeholders for values but also character strings or objects. Using variables is a good idea if certain elements are activated more than once. You need to declare a variable as a data type in the VBA code. Use the following DIM command: Dim [Variable] As [Data type].

For example, Dim datStart As Date tells VBA that a variable with the name of "Start" of data type "Date" should be created.

Depending on the content of your variable, you'll need to choose the correct type of data in Excel VBA. The most-used data types and declaration symbols are:
- **Variant:** Can contain arbitrary data, for example, numerical values, character strings, time and date values. A variant is automatically shown where the data type is not explicitly declared. Symbol: not defined.
- **Integer:** Used for whole numbers of values between -32,768 to 32,767. Symbol: **%()

- **Long:** Used for whole numbers between values of -2,147,483.648 to 2,147,483.647. Symbol: (&)
- **Double:** Encompasses all floating-point numbers from plus/minus 1.79 * 10^308. Symbol:(#)
- **Boolean:** These are true or false variables displayed as "True" or "False" or #TRUE# or #FALSE#
- **String:** Strings are character arrangements of variable or fixed length. Symbol: (**$**)
- **Date:** Used for date and time designations. Times from 00:00:00 (midnight) to 23:59:59.9999999 can be entered. The date format is M/T/JJJ or JJJJ-MM-TT.

The most common VBA commands

- Do...Loop Command
- Do
- [statement]
- Loop [While/Until] Print

The "Do loop" allows you to define repeated commands until the loop matches a predefined condition. Using "while" repeats the loop until the condition becomes "False". Using "Until", the circle is repeated until "True".

- For...Next Command
- For [start value] To [value] Step [value]
- [Do1]
- Next [Variable]

The "For loop" repeats commands as specified. The loop starts as soon as the specified variable is reached and increases by the value specified in "Step" until the final deal.

- If...Then...Else Command
- If [statement1] Then
- [Do1]
- Elseif [statement2] Then
- [Do2]
- Else
- [Do3]

End if

The "If-Then" command executes a series of orders depending on whether the statement is matched. If statement 1 is correct in the example above, the command "Do1" is automatically executed. If it's not right, statement 2 is checked. If statement 2 is correct, command "Do2" is completed. If neither of the statements is accurate, command Do3 is performed.

Tip: Besides VBA programming, Excel shortcuts are a great way to make working in Excel more efficient.

Excel VBA Code Examples

The macro code examples in this list have been split into categories to make it easier to find those that you are interested in using.

Common Excel tasks

- AutoFit column widths
- Copy and paste
- Clear all hyperlinks on a sheet
- Format cells with formulas
- Convert formulas to values

Worksheet codes
- Unhide all columns
- Protect a worksheet
- Loop through all the worksheets of a workbook

Workbook codes
- Unhide all worksheets
- Protect a workbook
- Opening and closing a workbook
- Email the active workbook with Outlook

Files and folders
- Export each worksheet as a single PDF
- Export the active sheet as a PDF
- Export multiple sheets to a single PDF
- Loop through all the files in a folder
- Selecting a file with a FileDialog

Useful Excel features
- Sorting columns
- Filter your data
- Create a chart

Events
- Go to a specific worksheet on Open
- Perform action on Cell Change

How Is VBA Used?

1. For Most of Us

Within MS Office applications, Visual Basic for Applications allows users to perform myriad functions beyond simple word processing and spreadsheet operations. For the typical user, VBA helps to make frequent everyday tasks less repetitive via macros.

Macros can automate just about any task, like generating customized charts and reports and performing word- and data-processing functions. For example, you can write a macro that, with a single click, will make Excel create an entire balance sheet from a series of accounting entries in a spreadsheet.

2. For Computer Professionals

Programmers, however, use macros in more complex ways, like replicating large pieces of code, merging existing program functions, and designing specific languages.

3. For Companies And Organizations

VBA can also work in external, that is, non-Microsoft settings using a COM interface technology, which allows commands to interact across computer boundaries. Many firms have implemented VBA within their proprietary and commercial applications, including AutoCAD, ArcGIS, CATIA, Corel, raw, and SolidWorks.

Any firm may use VBA to customize Excel for a unique purpose, such as discerning how long it would take to earn $1 million in an investment portfolio based on a specific interest rate and other factors, like the number of years until retirement.

CHAPTER 13: TIPS AND SHORTCUT FOR MS EXCEL

Microsoft Excel Shortcut Keys

Microsoft Excel is extensively used across the globe to store and analyze data. Despite various new data analytics tools in the market, Excel remains the go-to product for working with data. It has numerous in-built features, making it easier for you to organize your data.

The shortcut keys in Excel help you work on your data instantly. In this book, we'll be discussing the various Excel shortcuts. These keyboard shortcuts are used to perform tasks faster and more effectively.

Need For Excel Shortcuts

Excel supports many keyboard shortcuts that help you work efficiently and increase productivity. Instead of accessing the toolbar with a mouse, two or three keystrokes are used to perform significant functions. Isn't that easier and time-saving? Using Excel shortcuts drastically increases the speed and thus reduces work time.

Now the question is, if you have to memorize these shortcuts, the answer is no. However, it would be an advantage if you could remember a few of them. With regular practice, you will be able to remember most of the standard Excel shortcuts.

Microsoft Excel Shortcut keys

Shortcut Description

1. Ctrl + N: To create a new workbook.
2. Ctrl + O: To open a saved workbook.
3. Ctrl + S: To save a workbook.
4. Ctrl + A: To select all the contents in a workbook.
5. Ctrl + B: To turn highlighted cells bold.
6. Ctrl + C: To copy cells that are highlighted.
7. Ctrl + D: To fill the selected cell with the cell's content right above.
8. Ctrl + F: To search for anything in a workbook.
9. Ctrl + G: To jump to a specific area with a single command.
10. Ctrl + H: To find and replace cell contents.
11. Ctrl + I: To italicize cell contents.
12. Ctrl + K: To insert a hyperlink in a cell.
13. Ctrl + L: To open the create table dialogue box.
14. Ctrl + P: To print a workbook.
15. Ctrl + R: To fill the selected cell with the cell's content on the left.
16. Ctrl + U: To underline highlighted cells.
17. Ctrl + V: To paste anything that who copied.
18. Ctrl + W: To close your current workbook.
19. Ctrl + Z: To undo the last action.

20. Ctrl + 1: To format the cell contents.
21. Ctrl + 5: To put a strikethrough in a cell.
22. Ctrl + 8: To show the outline symbols.
23. Ctrl + 9: To hide a row.
24. Ctrl + 0: To hide a column.
25. Ctrl + Shift + ::: To enter the current time in a cell.
26. Ctrl +: To enter the current date.
27. Ctrl + `: To change the view from displaying cell values to formulas.
28. Ctrl + ': To copy the formula from the cell above.
29. Ctrl + -: To delete columns or rows.
30. Ctrl + Shift + =: To insert columns and rows.
31. Ctrl + Shift + ~: To switch between displaying Excel formulas or their values in the cell.
32. Ctrl + Shift + @: To apply time formatting.
33. Ctrl + Shift + !: To apply comma formatting.
34. Ctrl + Shift + $: To apply currency formatting.
35. Ctrl + Shift + #: To apply date formatting.
36. Ctrl + Shift + %: To apply percentage formatting.
37. Ctrl + Shift + &: To place borders around the selected cells.
38. Ctrl + Shift + _: To remove a border.
39. Ctrl + -: To delete a selected row or column.
40. Ctrl + Spacebar: To select an entire column.
41. Ctrl + Shift + Spacebar: To select an entire workbook.
42. Ctrl + Home: To redirect to cell A1.
43. Ctrl + Shift + Tab: To switch to the previous workbook.
44. Ctrl + Shift + F: Open the fonts menu under format cells.
45. Ctrl + Shift + O: To select the cells containing comments.
46. Ctrl + Drag: To drag and copy a cell or the same worksheet.
47. Ctrl + Shift + Drag: To drag and insert copy.
48. Ctrl + Up arrow: Go to the top cell in a current column.
49. Ctrl + Down arrow: To jump to the last cell in a current column.
50. Ctrl + Right arrow: Go to the last cell in a selected row.
51. Ctrl + Left arrow: To jump back to the first cell in a selected row.
52. Ctrl + End: Go to the last cell in a workbook.
53. Alt + Page down: Move the screen towards the right.
54. Alt + Page Up: Move the screen towards the left.
55. Ctrl + F2: To open the print preview window.
56. Ctrl + F1: To expand or collapse the ribbon.

57. Alt: To open the access keys.
58. Tab: Move to the next cell.
59. Alt + F + T: To open the options.
60. Alt + Down arrow: To activate filters for cells.
61. F2: To edit a cell.
62. F3: To paste a cell name if the cells have been named.
63. Shift + F2: To add or edit a cell comment.
64. Alt + H + H: To select a fill colour.
65. Alt + H + B: To add a border.
66. Ctrl + 9: To hide the selected rows.
67. Ctrl + 0: To hide the selected columns.
68. Esc: To cancel an entry.
69. Enter: Complete the entry in a cell and move to the next one.
70. Shift + Right arrow: To extend the cell selection to the right.
71. Shift + Left arrow: To extend the cell selection to the left.
72. Shift + Space: To select the entire row.
73. Page up/ down: Move the screen up or down.
74. Alt + H: Go to the Home tab in the ribbon.
75. Alt + N: Go to the Insert tab in the ribbon.
76. Alt + P: Go to the Page Layout tab in the ribbon.
77. Alt + M: Go to the Formulas tab in the ribbon.
78. Alt + A: Go to the Data tab in the ribbon.
79. Alt + R: Go to the Review tab in the ribbon.
80. Alt + W: Go to the View tab in the ribbon.
81. Alt + Y: To open the Help tab in the ribbon.
82. Alt + Q: To quickly jump to search.
83. Alt + Enter: To start a new line in a current cell.
84. Shift + F3: To open the Insert function dialogue box.
85. F9: To calculate workbooks.
86. Shift + F9: To calculate an active workbook.
87. Ctrl + Alt + F9: To force calculate all workbooks.
88. Ctrl + F3: To open the name manager.
89. Ctrl + Shift + F3: To create names from values in rows and columns.
90. Ctrl + Alt + +: To zoom in inside a workbook.
91. Ctrl + Alt +: To zoom out inside a workbook.
92. Alt + 1: To turn on Autosave.
93. Alt + 2: To save a workbook.

94. Alt + F + E: To export your workbook.
95. Alt + F + Z: To share your workbook.
96. Alt + F + C: To close and save your workbook.
97. Alt or F11: To turn critical tips on or off.
98. Alt + Y + W: To know what's new in Microsoft Excel.
99. F1: To open Microsoft Excel help.
100. Ctrl + F4: To close Microsoft Excel.

Useful Microsoft Excel Tips

1. Conditional Formatting
2. PivotTables
3. Paste Special
4. Add Multiple Rows
5. Absolute References
6. Print Optimization
7. Extend Formula Across/Down
8. Flash Fill
9. INDEX-MATCH
10. Filters

Ways To Improve Your Excel Skills

MS Excel is the most commonly used spreadsheet program in the world. Microsoft developed Excel, and it has been in production since 1987. Currently, it is available for Windows, macOS, Android, and iOS operating systems. M.S. Excel is spread across various disciplines of education, research, analytics, business, and administration. An MS Excel expert can earn an average salary of $39,000 in the U.S. But one should undergo Excel 2016 Intermediate training before going from basic to advanced level.

You Can Also Use The Following Tips To Improve Your Excel Skills:

1. Master The Shortcuts: Using the mouse and keyboard to explore all the menus and different options seems convenient, but it's often time-consuming. If you know the correct shortcut for the task, you can complete it within seconds instead of minutes. This will increase your productivity and accuracy in the long term.

2. Import Data From A Website: You often need to pick data from websites for use in your project. Doing this task manually can be time-consuming, especially if the data is enormous. Excel gives you the option of directly converting the data from a website into a worksheet. You have to go to File > Import External Data and click on New Web Query. Paste the link of the web page you want to use in the address bar of the window opening, click OK, and import your data.

3. Result Filtering: MS Excel allows you to filter the enormous amount of data you need to process according to your requirements. For example, you can filter the data according to a person's age. To access the auto filtering featuring M.S. Excel, go to data> Filter > AutoFilter and click on one of the small boxes to filter the results according to your requirements.

4. Autocorrect And Autofill: To increase your productivity, M.S. Excel provides features like AutoCorrect and AutoFill so that you can type less and do more. AutoCorrect corrects your mistakes like misspelt words and other typos automatically. You can enable this feature by selecting AutoCorrect in the Tools tab.

5. Excel Intermediate Training: MS Excel is software used in almost every organization in one way or the other. So, having it in your skillset increases your chances of getting the job you want. Excel certifications can help improve Excel skills and increase your chances of success.

TO GET YOUR BONUSES GO TO

https://excel2022.wixsite.com/tutorial

Printed in Great Britain
by Amazon